Contemporary Critical Perspectives
Series Editors: Jeannette Baxter, Sebastian Groes and Sean Matthews
Consultant Editor: Dominic Head

Guides in the *Contemporary Critical Perspectives* series provide companions to reading and studying major contemporary authors. They include new critical essays combining textual readings, cultural analysis and discussion of key critical and theoretical issues in a clear, accessible style. Each guide also includes a preface by a major contemporary writer, a new interview with the author, discussion of film and TV adaptation and guidance on further reading.

Titles in the series include:

J. G. Ballard edited by Jeannette Baxter
Kazuo Ishiguro edited by Sean Matthews and Sebastian Groes

IAN McEWAN

Contemporary Critical Perspectives

Edited by
Sebastian Groes

continuum

Continuum International Publishing Group

The Tower Building   80 Maiden Lane
11 York Road   Suite 704
London SE1 7NX   New York NY 10038

www.continuumbooks.com

British Library Cataloguing-in-Publication Data
A catalogue record for this book is available from the British Library.

ISBN: 978-0-8264-9721-5 (hardback)
      978-0-8264-9722-2 (paperback)

Library of Congress Cataloging-in-Publication Data
A catalog record for this book is available from the Library of Congress.

Typeset by Newgen Imaging Systems Pvt Ltd, Chennai, India
Printed and bound in Great Britain by MPG Books Ltd, Bodmin, Cornwall

Contents

Foreword

Ian McEwan and the Rational Mind

Matt Ridley

The novelist's privilege, according to Ian McEwan, is to step inside the consciousness of others, and to lead the reader there like a psychological Virgil. Again and again in McEwan's books, it is the interior monologue of the characters, and that monologue's encounter with the 'truth' in the outside world, that grips us. Whether paralysed, obsessed, filled with guilt or operated on, the brains of McEwan's protagonists construct their mental world as we, the readers, watch and empathize.

It is this ability to replicate consciousness in text that distinguishes a literary novelist from a writer of potboilers. Dan Brown's plots are ingenious, but his characters never feel like rounded people. For McEwan that is what a novelist does, at least since Samuel Richardson wrote *Clarissa*, or perhaps since Shakespeare wrote *Hamlet*: he gives you a full sense of what it is to be someone else. What he is in effect doing, is milking the human instinct for what psychologists call a theory of mind, which explores our innate tendency to construct an understanding of what others are thinking. In a good novel not only does the reader know what the character is thinking; the reader knows what the character thinks that another character is thinking.

The theory of mind is one of evolutionary psychology's favourite notions. People spend a large part of their waking day guessing what others are thinking. Indeed, they go so far that they anthropomorphize their pet rabbits, they impute malign intentionality to intransigent tools and thunderstorms, and they believe in gods. Human beings are not unique in having a theory of mind, but they are far more sophisticated than any other creature. Monkeys can easily handle second-order intentionality – 'I think that you are angry'. Maybe chimpanzees will prove to be capable of a third order – 'I think that you think that I am angry'. The zoologist Robin Dunbar reckons that modern humans can handle fifth-order intentionality – 'I think that you think that he thinks that she thinks I am angry'. Dunbar is cleverer than me.

In *Enduring Love*, McEwan's most 'scientific' novel, Jed thinks that Joe does not realize that he really loves Jed, and Joe thinks that he understands Jed's delusion as a medical condition, while Clarissa, the Keats scholar, is eventually exasperated by Joe's attempted rationalization of emotion. The book is explicitly about the neo-Darwinian idea that emotions evolved for adaptive purposes. Anger, for example, emphasizes your commitment to punish a wrong, even at some irrational cost to yourself, and thus has a deterrent effect; love enables somebody both to monopolize and to reward the loved one, keeping rivals at bay while keeping the object of affection interested. However, it is also a warning against hoping that reason will be able to bring closure, redemption or happiness in a world of messy relationships and contingent choices. Joe's destiny is to be disillusioned by reason's inability to resolve the horror in which he finds himself.

Ah, horror! On the few occasions when real, gut-clenching dread pervaded my mind, it felt no different in kind from the horror I remembered from reading *The Comfort of Strangers*, the disgust in *The Innocent*, the dread in *Atonement* and the shock of *Enduring Love*'s balloon scene. Somewhere in the reader's mind, when reading those books, neurons fire in such a way as to produce a conscious experience. That mental experience, presumably in the cerebral cortex, causes – probably – the activation of circuits and the release of neurochemicals in the amygdala, triggering real fear. It actually alters the heart rate, the skin conductance and even the adrenalin content of the blood through the sympathetic nervous system. The author reaches into the minds of his willing readers and alters their synapses – what a power! McEwan even switches genes on and off in his readers' genomes: as we now know, the expression or repression of genes happens throughout our lives in response to experiences, which is mainly why nature and nurture are not opposites. Research in New Zealand, for example, demonstrates that one version of a serotonin gene raises the chance of clinical depression – but only in those who suffer stressful life experiences.

Does McEwan's interest in the human mind make him a scientist? I think so. Science is, or should be, a state of mind rather than a professional elect. McEwan is motivated by curiosity and rational inquiry, not to mention a sense of wonder and hard-nosed scepticism. He uses fiction to understand the mind and to explore human nature, as well as uses words to alter readers' consciousness. Now that neuroscientists can tentatively begin to understand how thought works, McEwan argues that psychology is in a sense only catching up with fiction, that neuroscience may be about to trespass on the territory of the writer. Imagine, for example, a neurosurgeon (Henry Perowne in *Saturday*?) deliberately stimulating a patient's brain to induce a thought – he is merely doing clumsily and invasively what a novelist does from a distance. Some outrageous comparisons: Shakespeare was a better psychologist than Freud, Jane Austen has more to say about human nature than Margaret Mead, Dostoevsky than Pavlov, Proust than Piaget. (An exception: the philosopher-psychologist William James was at least the equal of his novelist brother Henry in terms of insight into the human mind.)

To many artists of the modern age other than writers, science has seemed philistine. It is unimaginatively spoilsport: explaining things that are better left unexplained, scornful of things it cannot explain. Newton unweaves Keats's rainbow and is mocked by Blake. Reason, so artists mutter under their breath, is pedestrian, mundane and profane compared to the ethereal wonders of the imagination. It must have been especially sweet for rationalist McEwan to trick so many reviewers into arguing that *Enduring Love* was a duller book because it was based on a real case study of a rare mental disorder, De Clérambault's syndrome. If the real is duller than the imaginary, then *Enduring Love* is a better book because the case study, too, was imaginary and its authors, Wenn and Camia, were an anagram of Ian McEwan. Deception, too, is a favourite topic of evolutionary psychology.

Yet for writers, the chasm that opened between the two cultures of science and art in the Romantic movement is surely now closing as more and more writers come to believe that there is, in Charles Darwin's words, 'grandeur in this view of life' – that there is more mystery and imaginative space in quantum mechanics and deep geological time than there ever was in folk tales and creation myths. Science does not destroy mysteries. It creates new and deeper ones.

Playwrights lead the way this time, not poets. Michael Frayn and Tom Stoppard are doing what Alexander Pope and Erasmus Darwin did in the eighteenth century: to philosophize and speculate, to explore ideas and discoveries through writing. Caryl Churchill and Timberlake Wertenbaker have followed suit, as have novelists from A. S. Byatt and Penelope Fitzgerald to Margaret Atwood and David Lodge. Indeed, so fashionable is it for novelists to plunder science, and biology in particular, that it caused the critic Cressida Connolly, reviewing *Enduring Love*, to call for an 'immediate, worldwide moratorium on novelists reading works of science' (Connelly 1997: 3).

McEwan is less direct than some in his scientific eavesdropping. The evolutionary psychology in *Enduring Love*, or the neurogenetics in *Saturday*, are servants rather than masters of plot and character. But there is no doubt that McEwan is a groupie of Enlightenment rationalism – so long as science subjects itself to the same rigorous scepticism that it does to myth. As he once told me, he is fascinated by the moment when Voltaire, exiled in London in 1727, attends Isaac Newton's funeral at Westminster Abbey, and professes himself amazed and thrilled that a country should so celebrate a mere man of reason. With the help of Emilie de Chatelet, Voltaire then devoted much of his *Lettres Philosophique* to exploring and explaining Newton's ideas to a French reading public, becoming, in McEwan's eyes, almost the first science writer.

Let me get personal. As an irredeemably male, technophile man (and it seems to me that McEwan is much more popular among my male than my female acquaintances), at home with British logical positivism and steeped in neo-Darwinian ultra-rationalism, as an almost Aspergerish systemizer rather than a touchy-feely empathizer, as somebody who consumes far more non-fiction than fictional writing (I get much of my fiction from the screen) – as such a creature, I am bound to find

McEwan's philosophical bent to my taste. Then as somebody slightly less stereotypically male who loves to be told stories, is fascinated by the power of words to conjure images, and is transfixed by the great mysteries of life – what is consciousness? – I salute a great image-conjuring storyteller exploring human nature.

Series Editors' Preface

The readership for contemporary fiction has never been greater. The explosion of reading groups and literary blogs, of university courses and school curricula, and even the apparent rude health of the literary marketplace, indicate an ever-growing appetite for new work, for writing which responds to the complex, changing and challenging times in which we live. At the same time, readers seem ever more eager to engage in conversations about their reading, to devour the review pages, to pack the sessions at literary festivals and author events. Reading is an increasingly social activity, as we seek to share and refine our experience of the book, to clarify and extend our understanding.

It is this tremendous enthusiasm for contemporary fiction to which the Contemporary Critical Perspectives series responds. Our ambition in these volumes is to offer readers of current fiction a comprehensive critical account of each author's work, presenting original, specially commissioned analyses of all aspects of their career, from a variety of different angles and approaches, as well as directions towards further reading and research. Our brief to the contributors was to be scholarly, to draw on the latest thinking about narrative, or philosophy, or psychology, indeed whatever seemed to them most significant in drawing out the meanings and force of the texts in question, but also to focus closely on the words on the page, the stories and scenarios and forms which all of us meet first when we open a book. We insisted that these essays be accessible to that mythical beast, the Common Reader, who might just as readily be spotted at the Lowdham Book Festival as in a college seminar. In this way, we hope to have presented critical assessments of our writers in such a way as to contribute something to both of those environments, and also to have done something to bring together the important qualities of each of them.

Jeannette Baxter,
Sebastian Groes and Sean Matthews

Acknowledgements

The editor and publishers wish to thank Ian McEwan for his generous and continued support for this book, which is partly the result of the 'Perspectives on Ian McEwan' conference held at the University of East Anglia, Norwich, on 15 November 2003. Vic Sage and Jon Cook are also thanked for giving permission to publish their conversation with Ian McEwan, which was part of UEA's International Writing Festival in conjunction with the conference. Special thanks are due to Matt Ridley, whose preface in this volume gives a unique insight into the perception of literature from a science writer's point of view. Many thanks also to my fellow Series Editors Jeannette Baxter, Dominic Head and, in particular, *il miglior fabbro*, Sean Matthews, for their careful attention and editorial help during the preparation of this book. I would like to thank Anna Fleming and Colleen Coalter at Continuum for their patience and professional assistance. I thank Liverpool Hope University for their support of the Contemporary Critical Perspectives project. Finally, I would like to thank my wife, José Lapré, without whose enduring support, encouragement and love this book would not have been possible.

S G
London, August 2008

Contributors

Natasha Alden is Lecturer in Contemporary British Fiction at Aberystwyth University. She wrote her doctorate on contemporary historical fiction, war and memory, focusing on second generation memory in the work of Ian McEwan, Pat Barker, Adam Thorpe and Graham Swift at the University of Oxford, and has published articles on McEwan and Barker. She is currently working on a monograph on postmemory in contemporary British fiction.

Jeannette Baxter is Senior Lecturer in English Literature at Anglia Ruskin University. She is the author of *J. G. Ballard's Surrealist Imagination: Spectacular Authorship* (Ashgate, 2009), and the editor of *J. G. Ballard: Contemporary Critical Perspectives* (Continuum, 2009). Recent and forthcoming publications include articles and chapters on Angela Carter, J. G. Ballard, Kazuo Ishiguro and Primo Levi. Her current project, *Surrealism and the British Novel*, is a study of the cultural and intellectual legacies of surrealism in British literature from 1936 to the present day.

Claire Colebrook is Professor of Modern Literary Theory at the University of Edinburgh. She has written books on literary theory, irony, gender and contemporary European philosophy. Her most recent book is *Milton, Evil and Literary History* (Continuum, 2008).

Jon Cook is Professor of Literature at the University of East Anglia. He has written on poetry, culture, creativity, and the links between literature and philosophy. His most recent book is *Hazlitt in Love* (Short Books, 2007).

Alistair Cormack is the author of *Yeats and Joyce: Cyclical History and the Reprobate Tradition* (Ashgate, 2008) and essays on contemporary British writers including Monica Ali and J. G. Ballard. He lives and teaches in Norfolk.

Sebastian Groes is Lecturer in English Literature at Liverpool Hope University. He specializes in modern and contemporary culture and literature, and representations of cities. Recent and forthcoming publications include essays on Modernist writers such as Stella Gibbons and Rebecca West, and post-war writers including Iris Murdoch, W. G. Sebald, Monica Ali, J. G. Ballard, Nell Dunn and Iain Sinclair. He is the author of *British Fiction in the Sixties* (Continuum, 2009) and the co-editor of *Kazuo Ishiguro: Contemporary Critical Perspectives* (Continuum, 2009).

M. Hunter Hayes is Assistant Professor of English at Texas A&M University-Commerce (USA), where he specializes in twentieth-century and contemporary British literature. He is the author of *Understanding Will Self* (University of South Carolina Press, 2007).

Dominic Head is Professor of Modern English Literature at the University of Nottingham. He has published numerous books on modern and contemporary fiction, including *The Modernist Short Story* (Cambridge, 1992), *Modern British Fiction, 1950–2000* (Cambridge, 2002) and a Blackwell Manifesto, *The State of the Novel: Britain and Beyond* (Oxford, 2008). He is the author of books on Nadine Gordimer (Cambridge, 1994), J. M. Coetzee (Cambridge, 1997) and Ian McEwan (Manchester, 2007), and has published on literary ecocriticism.

Laura Marcus is Regius Professor of Rhetoric and English Literature at the University of Edinburgh. She is author of *Auto/biographical Discourses: Theory, Criticism, Practice* (1994); *Virginia Woolf: Writers and their Work* (1997) and *The Tenth Muse: Writing about Cinema in the Modernist Period* (2007). She has edited a number of volumes, including *The Actuality of Walter Benjamin* (1993); *Sigmund Freud's* The Interpretation of Dreams: *New Interdisciplinary Essays* (1999); and *Mass-Observation as Poetics and Science* (2001). She is also one of the editors of the journal *Women: a Cultural Review*.

Matt Ridley is a science writer whose books include *The Red Queen* (1993), *The Origins of Virtue* (1996), *Nature via Nurture* (2003) and *Francis Crick* (2006). His work has been shortlisted for six literary awards and translated into 25 languages. He lives near Newcastle where he was the first chairman of the International Centre for Life. Matt Ridley is also a Visiting Professor at Cold Spring Harbour Laboratory.

Victor Sage is Emeritus Professor of Literature at the University of East Anglia. His books include *The Gothic Novel: A Casebook* (Macmillan, 1990), *Gothick Origins and Innovations* (Amsterdam: Rodopi, 1994) and *Le Fanu's Gothic: The Rhetoric of Darkness* (PalgraveMacmillan, 2004). His novels include *A Mirror for Larks* (Secker & Warburg, 1993) and *Black Shawl* (Secker & Warburg, 1995).

Chronology of Ian McEwan's Life

1948   Ian Russell McEwan born on 21 June in the garrison town of Aldershot, Hampshire, England, to the Scotsman David McEwan, a soldier and later Major in the British army, and Rose Lilian McEwan, (née Wort), whose husband had died in the Second World War and by whom she already had two children.

1951–59   McEwan grows up as an only child on military bases in the United Kingdom and at military outposts abroad (Singapore, Libya and Germany).

1959–66   Sent from Tripoli, Libya, to attend state-run boarding school Woolverstone Hall in Suffolk whilst parents continue to live abroad.

1967–70   Reads English and French at the University of Sussex. Begins writing fiction.

1970–71   Enrols for the MA in English Literature at the University of East Anglia. McEwan is the first student on the creative writing course, taught and mentored by Malcolm Bradbury and Angus Wilson. Works on a collection of short stories, *First Love, Last Rites*.

1971–72   Spends part of this post-MA year travelling the 'hippy trail' to Afghanistan, the North West Frontier Province, and Greece; consumes psychotropic drugs. First story ('Homemade') sold to *New American Review*.

1973   Finds a literary agent, Deborah Rogers, for representation.

1974   Moves from Norwich to an attic room in Stockwell, South London.

1975   Debut collection of short stories, *First Love, Last Rites* published. Writes *Conversations with a Cupboardman* for BBC Radio.

1976   Wins Somerset Maugham Award for *First Love, Last Rites*. *Jack Flea's Birthday Celebration* (Dir. Mike Newell) transmitted on television in 'Second City Firsts' series. Travels to the USA.

1978   *In Between the Sheets* (stories) and first novel *The Cement Garden* published.

1979   Production of *Solid Geometry* (Dir. Mike Newell) for TV halted by BBC over 'grotesque and bizarre sexual elements in the play'.

1980   *The Imitation Game* broadcast as a BBC 'Play for Today'.

1981   *The Comfort of Strangers* published and nominated for Booker Prize. *The Imitation Game* (television plays) published.

1982   Marries spiritual counsellor and healer Penny Allen, with whom he has two children.

1983   *Or Shall We Die?*, an oratorio with a score by Michael Berkeley, performed at the Royal Festival Hall, London, by the London Symphony Orchestra and Chorus. Included in *Granta*'s list of Best Young British Novelists. Writes script for *The Ploughman's Lunch* (Dir. Richard Eyre), wins the *Evening Standard* Award for Best Screenplay. Elected to Fellowship of the Royal Society of Literature.

1984   Adapts *Last Day of Summer* (Dir. Derek Banham) for Channel Four.

1985   *Rose Blanche*, a children's book with illustrations by Roberto Innocenti, published.

1987   *The Child in Time* published and awarded the Whitbread Novel Award and the Prix Fémina Etranger (France). Visits the Soviet Union as part of a delegation from European Nuclear Disarmament (END).

1988   Writes screenplay *Soursweet* based on Timothy Mo's 1982 novel.

1989   Awarded an honorary D.Litt. by the University of Sussex. Travels to Berlin with his wife to watch the fall of the Berlin Wall.

1990   *The Innocent* published. *The Comfort of Strangers* (Dir. Paul Schrader), adapted by Harold Pinter, released.

1992   *Black Dogs* published.

1993   *The Cement Garden* (Dir. Andrew Birkin) released, winning several nominations and prizes. *The Innocent* (Dir. John Schlesinger), adapted by McEwan himself, released. *The Good Son* (Dir. Joseph Ruben) released. McEwan refuses further involvement after original screenplay was rewritten to suit Macaulay Culkin, who was cast in starring role.

1994   Novel for children, *The Daydreamer*, published.

1995   Divorce from Penny Allen.

1997   *Enduring Love* published and shortlisted for the James Tait Black Memorial Prize. Marries Annalena McAfee, journalist and editor of *Guardian Review*. *First Love, Last Rites*, adapted by David Ryan, released, winning director Jesse Peretz the Fipresci Prize at Rotterdam International Film Festival.

1998   *Amsterdam* published, winning the Booker Prize.

1999   Awarded the Shakespeare Prize by the Alfred Toepfer Foundation (Germany). Custody battle over sons with Allen.

2000   Awarded CBE.

2001   *Atonement* published and shortlisted for the Booker Prize; shortlisted for the Whitbread Novel Award.

2002   *Solid Geometry* adapted and directed by Denis Lawson for television. WH Smith Literary Award for *Atonement*. Discovers he has a brother six years older, bricklayer David Sharpe, who had been given up for adoption during the Second World War. Sharpe was born to Rose from an affair with David McEwan whilst her husband Ernest was fighting in the war. The story becomes public knowledge in 2007.

2003   Wins National Book Critics' Circle Fiction Award and *Los Angeles Times* Prize for Fiction for *Atonement*. 'Perspectives on Ian McEwan' conference held at UEA (Norwich, UK).

2004   Associate Producer of the film *Enduring Love* (Dir. Roger Michell), adapted by Joe Penhall. Wins Santiago Prize for European Novel for *Atonement*.

2005   *Saturday* published, shortlisted for the Booker Prize. *Butterflies* adapted and directed by Max Jacoby for television, winning Prix UIP at Venice Film Festival for European Short Film. McEwan part of an expedition of artists and scientists on a ship near the North Pole discussing climate change.

2006   Wins James Tait Black Memorial Prize for *Saturday*.

2007   *On Chesil Beach* published. DVD about the novel, *Ian McEwan: On Chesil Beach*, released. Film of *Atonement* (Dir. Joe Wright) released, with seven Oscar nominations including Adapted Screenplay, winning for Score.

2008   Libretto, *For You*, set to music by Michael Berkeley, premiered at the Royal Opera House, London, 28 October.

A Cartography of the Contemporary: Mapping Newness in the Work of Ian McEwan

SEBASTIAN GROES

The literary imagination has a significant contribution to make in mapping the workings of the private life and the personal imagination, and the wider concerns of the nation and the world, and Ian McEwan is the foremost cartographer of our time. Over the past three decades, his books have been both critically – and academically – acclaimed and embraced by audiences across the world. Since his debut collection of short stories *First Love, Last Rites* (1975) was awarded the Somerset Maugham Award, McEwan has won almost every existing national and international literary award and Fellowship, including the Whitbread Novel Award for *The Child in Time* (1987), the James Tait Black Memorial Prize for *Saturday* (2005) and the Booker Prize for *Amsterdam* (1998). His popular appeal was boosted considerably by the critically and commercially successful adaptations of his fiction for the screen – Harold Pinter adapted *The Comfort of Strangers* (1990), Joe Penhall rewrote *Enduring Love* (2004) for Roger Michell, and Christopher Hampton received an Oscar nomination for his direction of Joe Wright's *Atonement* (2007).

McEwan's work has also, almost continuously, provoked cultural debates and moral outcries. The exploration of grotesque and disturbing themes (such as the breaking of social conventions, codes and taboos, incest, sado-masochism, rape, pornography and the murder of children) in the early work earned him the illustrious nickname 'Ian Macabre'. McEwan's alignment with the feminist movement in the seventies and eighties led to his being co-opted and derided as 'the male feminist' (Haffenden 1985: 176). His investigation and portrayal of science and scientists in later novels such as *Enduring Love* (1997) and *Saturday* (2005) has evoked hostile responses from the liberal, *Guardian*-reading section of his critics and readership, a fire he fed with statements in which he declares that '[g]ood science will serve us well [. . .] Leave nothing to idealism or outrage, or even good art – we know in our hearts that the very best art is entirely and splendidly useless' (McEwan 2005b). And because of his tentative support for the war in Iraq, he was deemed to be part of 'the vanguard of British literary neoconservatives [. . .] the "Blitcons"' (Sardar 2006). As his status and reputation as Britain's most successful living author has grown, so have the revelations about his private life. In 1995, there was a messy divorce from his first wife, the spiritual healer and therapist Penny Allen, which caused what McEwan described as 'mayhem – at street level' (Leith 1998: 8). In 2007, it became public knowledge that McEwan, who had grown up as an only child, had discovered in 2002 that he had a full brother, the bricklayer David Sharpe, which for McEwan provoked a 'forced and continuing reappraisal of the past' (McEwan 2008c). These controversies about his private life too have contributed to anchoring McEwan in the popular imagination.

Another unique characteristic of McEwan's output is its creative versatility: although primarily a novelist, McEwan has also successfully written short stories, a novel for children, *The Daydreamer* (1995), and several television scripts and screenplays. Amongst his collaborative outings we find two librettos with composer Michael Berkeley, *Or Shall We Die* (1983) and *For You* (2008) and an illustrated children's book, *Rose Blanche* (1985), which tells the story of a young German girl resisting the Nazis. McEwan has also delivered numerous lectures, amongst which are the prestigious Dutch *Van der Leeuw Lezing* (2002), on the relationship between science and literature in understanding human nature, and the Royal Society of Arts/New Writing Worlds lecture 2007, 'End of the World Blues', a damning statement against the perils of religious fundamentalism. John Haffenden called him a 'man for all media' (Haffenden 1985: 168). Across these many forms his work retains a distinctive character which explores questions of morality, nationhood and history, sexuality, and the nature of the imagination and human consciousness. As Matt Ridley suggests in his Foreword to this collection, McEwan is one of the few writers able 'to step inside the consciousness of others, and to lead the reader there like a psychological Virgil'.

Contemporary readers are looking to McEwan's work precisely for his continued quest for 'the contemporary', that slippery term comprising the distinctive elements that make up the elusive *Zeitgeist*, the 'spirit' of our times. Since the very beginning of his career in the mid-seventies, McEwan has been highly conscious of the state of the world. As a cultural commentator, he has written on a wide range of topical issues, including feminism, the dangerous proliferation of nuclear weapons during the Cold War, religious fundamentalism and millennialism, terrorism, and the condition of the post-9/11 world. Since the early eighties he has engaged with climate change: in *Or Shall We Die* (1983) McEwan compares man's assault on nature with rape, and indicts all governments who have not 'contemplated the redirection of its economy in the face of these problems', asserting that 'no major political party of the left or right has begun to think of breaking with the doomed fixation on endless economic growth' (McEwan 1989: 23; xxiii). In 2005, he joined a team of artists, scientists and journalists during the Cape Farewell Art/ Science Expedition to travel to Tempelfjorden to experience the Arctic environment and to debate climate change, inspiring a new novel (Soal 2008). McEwan's desire to be a witness of history has also spurred him on to chase major global events. In 1987, McEwan visited the Soviet Union as part of a delegation from European Nuclear Disarmament (END), and two years later he witnessed the collapse of the Iron Curtain in Berlin. Of the terrorist attacks on America, on 11 September 2001, he stated that 'even the best minds, the best or darkest dreamers of disaster on a gigantic scale [. . .] could not have delivered us into the nightmare available on television channels' (McEwan 2001b). In *Saturday*, he captures the anxious and uncertain post-9/11 climate while anticipating the terrorist attacks on London, 7 July 2005, that followed shortly after the novel's publication: 'London [. . .] lies wide open, impossible to defend, waiting for its bomb' (McEwan 2005a: 276). The next day he commented that we 'have been savagely woken from a pleasant dream' and that we as citizens again had to renegotiate 'that deal we must constantly make and remake with the state – how much power must we grant Leviathan, how much freedom will we be asked to trade for our security' (McEwan 2005c).

He is similarly aware of the culture and literature within which he works, and within which he is highly likely to endure as a central figure. He has commented on the death of the novel in the seventies, on the state of British television and cinema in the early eighties, and the state of the arts at the beginning of the twenty-first century. McEwan has written on fellow writers including James Joyce, George Orwell, Graham Greene, John Updike, the German novelist Peter Schneider, and Salman Rushdie, whom he calls 'the dissenting fabulist' (McEwan 1989: xvii). He has acknowledged drawing inspiration from William Golding's *Lord of the Flies* (1954) – 'the very stuff of my fantasy life' (McEwan 1986: 157) – for *The Cement Garden*. Saul Bellow's work has also been an enduring influence, and McEwan's novels too 'are not simply set in the twentieth century, they are about that century – its awesome transformations, its savagery, its new machines, the great battles of its thought systems, the resounding failure of totalitarian systems, the mixed blessings of the American way' (McEwan 2005c). He has written about the changing perception of Darwin's work and his admiration of Richard Dawkins' *The Selfish Gene* (1976), which he finds 'one extended invitation addressed to us non-scientists to enjoy science, to indulge ourselves in the feast of human ingenuity' (McEwan 2006).

McEwan's debate with the modern world and his ability to capture 'newness' only truly begin when he transforms such concerns into carefully crafted and historically acute literary works of art. The collapse of the Berlin Wall is transfigured in *Black Dogs* (1992), in which Bernard and his son-in-law, the narrator Jeremy, visit Berlin to witness the collapse of the Iron Curtain:

> It was twenty minutes to the Victory Monument, and from there, stretch-
> ing ahead of us, was the broad June 17 approach to the Gate. Someone had
> tied a piece of cardboard over the street sign and painted 'November 9th'.
> Hundreds of people were moving in the same direction. A quarter of a mile
> away the Brandenburg Gate stood illuminated, looking rather too small, too
> squat for its global importance. At its base, the darkness appeared to inten-
> sify in a wide band. Only when we reached it would we discover that this
> was the gathering crowd. (McEwan 1998b: 82)

The passage starts off in a journalistic fashion, with the factual witnessing of the historical event 'in action', as it were. The significance
of the Brandenburg Gate, a national monument rooting Germany into
European history, is transformed by the historical shift taking place.
However, Bernard and Jeremy become involved in a riot during which
neo-Nazis set upon a Turkish immigrant: the 'darkness' against which
this moment of liberation is taking place suggests that the oppression
during the Cold War will come to haunt the city in a new guise under
capitalist democracy.

It is only the novel form that is able to situate historical events
within a wider matrix of socio-political and cultural meanings and to
represent their metaphysical dimension. The trajectory of McEwan's
later work should be read as his increasing engagement with the canon
of English literature, and in particular the sublime genre within the
Western literary tradition, as McEwan acknowledges in the interview
included here: 'I want narrative authority. I want Saul Bellow, I want
John Updike, I want Chekhov, I want Nabokov and Jane Austen. I want
the authorial presence taking full responsibility for everything.' This
realignment starts with *Enduring Love* (1997) and its open attention to
the work of John Keats, and the engagement with the satirical novel in
Amsterdam (1998). *Atonement* (2001), a complex and moving historical
narrative set before, during and after the Second World War, which
continuously wrong-foots the reader, brutally punishing us for our
willingness to suspend our disbelief, continues McEwan's alignment
with English fiction. As Alistair Cormack suggests in this collection,
this novel evidences McEwan's interest in the work of English literary
critic F. R. Leavis (1895–1978), while Laura Marcus explores the influence of Virginia Woolf in McEwan's *Atonement* and his circadian novel
Saturday (2005). The latter also brings to the fore a renewed interest in
the Victorian critic and poet Matthew Arnold (1822–1888), as Sebastian
Groes argues. McEwan's virtuously composed and bold novella *On
Chesil Beach* (2007) and libretto *For You* (2008) continue this arch as meditations on the moral questions surrounding the creative and destructive powers of the imagination, and the relationship between literary
ethics and aesthetics.

McEwan's authorship emerges, however, from a profound questioning of himself, and of the possibilities of fiction. In late May 1978, while writing his second novel, *The Comfort of Strangers* (1981), McEwan stayed three nights at the cottage of Angus Wilson in Felsham Woodside, Suffolk. McEwan, who had been a regular guest at Wilson's home since embarking on his postgraduate studies at the University of East Anglia, was restlessly walking the woods during the day, contemplating his latest writing project and struggling with questions that had come up in talks with his mentor: 'Could the contemporary world be rendered in fiction at all, McEwan asked himself?' (Drabble 1995: 523).

To understand this inquiry into himself and fiction-making, we have to situate it within both McEwan's personal background and the wider historical context. McEwan was raised on army bases across the world (Tripoli in Libya, Singapore, and Germany), instilling a great sense of geographical and psychological dislocation. At the age of eleven he was sent alone to a state boarding school, Woolverstone Hall in Suffolk, continuing his cultural and linguistic displacement, the fecund ambivalence of which he traces in a short essay, 'Mother Tongue' (2002):

> Exile from a homeland, through obviously a distressing experience, can bring a writer into a fruitful, or at least usefully problematic, relationship with an adopted language. A weaker version of this [. . .] is the internal exile of social mobility, particularly when it is through the layered linguistic density of English class. (McEwan 2002: 37)

It was because of his unusual upbringing that McEwan took his cue from a set of twentieth-century, bohemian writers who embodied alienation and displacement, and who were part of a European tradition of Diasporic writing. McEwan had fallen under the spell cast by a wide range of experimental, mainly continental writers who included Modernists (Kafka and Beckett in particular); Existentialists; radical and experimental authors such as Jean Genet, Louis Ferdinand Céline and William Burroughs; writers part of the *nouveau roman* movement (Alain Robbe-Grillet); the Theatre of the Absurd; and Literature of Exhaustion. As Stephen Lewis (whose name recalls Joyce's alter ego Stephen Dedalus) notes in *The Child in Time* (1987): 'As a potential Joyce, Mann or Shakespeare he belonged without question to the European cultural tradition, the grown-up one' (McEwan 1988: 30).

McEwan's early writing – the short story collections *First Love, Last Rites* (1975) and *In Between the Sheets* (1978), the novels *The Cement Garden* (1978) and *The Comfort of Strangers* (1981) – show traces of a dissatisfaction with fiction-writing as a means of representing what seemed an unceasing military, technological and cultural crisis in modernity, but the fiction is still dominated by a multiplicity of private worries. McEwan's turn to feminism was clearly a means of addressing family problems he grew up in. In 'Mother Tongue', McEwan explains that:

> In my twenties I was often defending, or trying to defend, [my mother] Rose against [my father] David, or promote her cause somehow. The effect on my writing was fairly direct [. . .] I had read *The Female Eunuch* in 1971 and thought it was a revelation. The feminism of the 1970s spoke directly to a knot of problems at the heart of our family's life. I developed a romantic notion that if the spirit of women was liberated, the world would be healed. My female characters became the repository of all the goodness that men fell short of. In other words, pen in hand, I was going to set my mother free. (McEwan 2002b: 41–42)

Feminism enabled him to connect the private concerns to a wider social and political agenda: the 'Women's Movement had presented ways of looking at the world, both its present and its past, that were at once profoundly dislocating and infinite in possibility' (McEwan 1981: 16). However, as David Malcolm observes, McEwan posits a stringent gender, and sexual, dichotomy: 'Men will destroy the world; women will save it. Men are linear, Newtonian exploiters of the natural world; women are the source of life and healing, with a much less absolutist and controlling set of mind' (Malcolm 2002a: 186–187). In his polemical 'Venus Envy' (1990), Adam Mars-Jones would later severely criticize *The Child in Time* (1987): 'Ian McEwan may be one of the few successful examples of the New Man [. . .] but in his vision of the relationship between the sexes there is much that is atavistic, patriarchal, even patristic' (Mars-Jones 1990: 32); yet he also sensed a 'new style [. . .] of faintly synthetic introspection' that was the result of rethinking masculinity, and the emergence of the 'New Man' author.

In hindsight, such questions and uncertainties appeared to reflect an economic, political and cultural crisis in the seventies, and they gave voice to an anxiety about social, cultural and moral decline after the end of Britain's imperial power had become vividly apparent. The dark mood of the period was captured by Malcolm Bradbury: 'In Britain the mood seemed one of decline, especially once recession grew: growing conflict and terrorism in Northern Ireland, a miners' strike, and then a serious balance-of-payments deficit, weakened successive governments, and all culminated in the Winter of Discontent of 1978, which opened the way to Mrs Thatcher and Thatcherism' (Bradbury 1993: 379–80). McEwan channelled these events into a dark, Gothic world, but as a result he felt he had written himself into a corner, and he now tended to distance himself somewhat from the early work. McEwan has for instance spoken of 'a lack in me, a dwindling of the youthful fire, or perhaps it's a genuine spread of tolerance' (McEwan 2002: 35). At the time he also 'wanted to break the isolation of writing fiction', which he described as 'the essentially crackpot activity of sitting down alone several hours a day with an assortment of ghosts' (McEwan 1981: 9), and he started writing for television and film – here explored by Hunter M. Hayes and Sebastian Groes in Chapter Two – which he saw as the medium to engage with the contemporary world while giving him a new means, and audience, to express his left-wing political views.

McEwan's 'uncertainty' about the potential of fiction should, however, be called into question. The early work forms an intricate part of the entire *oeuvre*, and an important foundation without which the later work could not have emerged, and it also contains many of the thematics and obsessions that he continues to explore, in a more subtle and refined way, in the later works. This volume re-evaluates McEwan's early work which, as Lorna Sage notes in a review of *The Comfort of Strangers*, captured a new cultural energy: 'McEwan has exactly touched the obscure nerve that registers "newness" in English fiction, and it may be a measure of the oddness of the cultural climate – it ought to be the measure of something – that this is all about regression' (Sage 1981: 1145). McEwan's fear of regression is, however, countered by his exploration of its counterpart, transgression, the breaking of social and moral boundaries and taboos, as displaced desire for transcending the limitations of the self.

In Chapter One, Jeannette Baxter picks up and develops McEwan's interest in Freudian psychology by rereading the early work through the lens of the French philosopher and dissident surrealist Georges Bataille (1897–1962), whose writings have recently attracted renewed critical attention. Baxter posits that McEwan's unnerving short stories can be 'read as experiments in a form of dissident Surrealism', and she points out how McEwan's engagement with this tradition allows him to challenge received social conventions in relationship to individual identity and sexuality. Three lines of inquiry are offered to illuminate the early work: Baxter traces McEwan's use of the pornographic imagination to criticize the commodification of sexuality in *First Love, Last Rites* (1975), his exploration of base materialism as socio-historical critique in *In Between the Sheets* (1978), and the creation of a sense of vertigo in McEwan's first novel, *The Cement Garden* (1978), as a troubling resource 'for breaking through the limits of consciousness'. Baxter shows that the early work defamiliarizes socially constructed conventions and disorientates the reader, while confronting readers with dark corners of their own selves, making them complicit in the crimes and the cruelty.

Hunter M. Hayes and Sebastian Groes continue this reappraisal of the early work in Chapter Two by exploring McEwan's screenwriting not as a form of apprenticeship or as groundwork for the novels, but as works that stand in a dialogic relationship to his fiction. In the seventies, McEwan turned to television because it allowed him to shed the constraints associated with fiction writing, and to experiment with the generic conventions of another medium. We locate an important hinge moment in the transition from *The Imitation Game* (1980), in which McEwan broadens out his thinking by connecting his personal preoccupations (the troubled family life, feminism) with political events of the time by embedding these concerns within a wider historical perspective – a feature which has become central to McEwan's mature writing. His subsequent move into writing features for film has provided him with the medium to investigate his socio-political and cultural concerns in an even more overt and direct manner, leading to a powerful anti-Thatcherite triptych: *The Ploughman's Lunch* (1985); McEwan's only direct engagement with the problems of ethnic identity and the multicultural society, *Soursweet* (1988); and his unhappy Hollywood outing *The Good Son* (1993). While these films can be situated as part of a wider, and fiercely contemporary, criticism of life and culture under Reagan and Thatcher, the screenwriting also sparks a reinvigorated and confident return to the novel in the mid-1980s, and they should therefore be seen as a vital component of McEwan's *oeuvre*.

The key problem of McEwan's writing at this early stage of his career lies not in his use of fiction as a means of expression, but in his interest in psychoanalysis as a structure for understanding the self and the world. In a story such as 'Dead As They Come' (1978), in which a wealthy narcissist falls in love with a fashion dummy, McEwan taps into a Gothic vein by reworking the German Romantic E. T. A. Hoffmann's novella 'The Sandman' (1816) – which Freud uses as a key story to illustrate the uncanny in his famous essay of the same name (1919). McEwan's subversion of social conventions, however, reaffirms and locks him into the stable geometry of Freudian psychology that reinforces male-dominated and capitalist ideologies. It is the mature, historically aware McEwan emerging from his work in other genres and media who breaks free from the constraints of what he himself describes as 'the simple oppositions' (Haffenden 1985: 172), by deconstructing such familial relationships. From the orphan Jeremy and his surrogate parents in *Black Dogs* (1992) to Henry Perowne's fatherless upbringing in *Saturday* (2005), one hardly ever finds representations of the nuclear family (or its subversion) after *The Comfort of Strangers* (1981). This mode arguably reaches its extreme in *Enduring Love*, which has an astonishing lack of father figures: the one father is killed off in the opening scene. This new mode of thinking, first present in *The Child in Time* (1987) and developed in the late eighties, also allows him to renegotiate his vision of the world, yielding a more intricate and profoundly disturbing engagement with, for instance, family, the relationship between the private and public, and the historical dimension of the contemporary. McEwan acknowledges this cultural shift in the fascinating interview included in this volume: 'As the influence of Freud in literary and intellectual culture has faded, we have returned to the idea that childhood *is* a form of innocence [. . .] They come into the world not responsible for it, and they are sometimes acted upon by people with terrible intent.'

This complex process is examined by Claire Colebrook's reading of McEwan's Cold War spy novel, *The Innocent* (1990), as criticism of the cultural pornography of the child. In Chapter Three Colebrook continues, and reframes, Baxter's exploration of McEwan's pornographic imagination by arguing that McEwan is 'a profoundly anti-oedipal writer' who destroys the organic wholeness of his novels to liberate his narration from the tyranny of fixed meaning and closed interpretation. For Colebrook, *The Innocent* anticipates our society at the beginning of the twenty-first century, when the circulation of images of missing or murdered children, such as those of Madeleine McCann, evokes a collective but false fantasy about our own lost innocence. Colebrook begins by demonstrating how McEwan exploits the complex temporality involved in such fantasies, and she takes us through *The Innocent*, which represents 'sexuality as a double and conflicting tendency within those who would once again be a child, and the adult who (always remaining a child) lives adult life as a fantasy of mature mastery'. The result is a view of McEwan's novel as criticism that deconstructs 'the opposition between knowing and not-knowing, between science and art, between adult and child, between sexuality and innocence.'

His writing too has remained under continuous attack. The publication of *Atonement* (2001) was followed by accusations of plagiarism in 2006. McEwan had, it was claimed, lifted material from manuscripts by novelist Lucilla Andrews and a nurse, Mrs A. Radloff. The scholar whose doctoral research was at the heart of the row, Natasha Alden, here sets the record straight by publishing her findings in detail for the first time. In Chapter Four, Alden suggests that McEwan has used historical material in order 'to demonstrate what fiction *can* do with history that history *cannot*' rather than maliciously, or carelessly, copying from the text of Andrews and Radloff. Alden recounts and contextualizes the plagiarism affair by drawing attention to the ethical dimension of the questions and by embedding these within a revision of postmodern accounts of historiographical metafiction. Alden takes us through *Atonement* and its source material, explaining in detail the motives behind McEwan's inclusion and exclusion of information, and his alteration, highlighting or suppression of atmospheric details. Alden concludes that McEwan 'offers a passionate ethical argument against postmodern fabulism, reasserting the difference between historical and fictional forms of narrative and creating a new form of historiographical metafiction'. *Atonement* reaffirms McEwan as a novelist acutely aware of his ethical responsibilities to history, while underscoring his continued attempts at reinventing the novel form.

The ethics of fiction-making are also central to Alistair Cormack's analysis in Chapter Five of *Atonement*'s wide variety of novelistic discourses. He agrees that McEwan rejects postmodern relativism, but whereas Alden argues that McEwan is looking forward to finding a new form of historical fiction after postmodernism, Cormack finds that McEwan's later work arrives back at the Leavisite moral tradition of the realist novel, the Humanist tradition, and empiricism. Cormack starts off by taking the reader through F. R. Leavis's *The Great Tradition* (1948), then through modernism and postmodernism, after which he examines the myriad of intertexts and discourses by means of a critical examination of the novel's form. He also offers a close textual analysis of Briony and Robbie, who is 'a means by which Leavisite aesthetics may be promoted'. We arrive at an insightful comparison between McEwan and Jane Austen who, in the wake of the French Revolution, rejected liberal ideas in favour of the Humanist tradition and individualism. Cormack concludes that throughout 'McEwan's novel the imagination is portrayed as dangerous, untrustworthy and originating in self-interest'. What is more, *Atonement* forms an attack on the imagination itself: 'Fiction is presented as a lie – a lie that, if believed, comforts, distorts and finally produces unethical action.'

In Chapter Six Laura Marcus examines McEwan's interest in the modernist aesthetic by focusing on 'modernist time' – the explosion of interest in dynamic temporalities and variable time caused by scientific progress – in *Atonement* and *Saturday*. Her analysis introduces modernist time by examining *The Child in Time* (1987) and moves on to explore McEwan's narration of time via his engagement with Virginia Woolf, whose writings have been instrumental in the formation of McEwan's later work. McEwan borrows *Atonement*'s tripartite structure from Woolf's *To the Lighthouse*, but there are also clear echoes of *The Waves*. Marcus continues Colebrook's exploration of temporality by investigating the irony and pathos of *Atonement*'s 'posthumous ironies', but she also draws attention to McEwan's representation of the many different, and gendered, ways in which we experience time. Although McEwan presents Woolf's texts as evasive denials of human acts and their consequences, he brings her work back into the fold because she plays out 'the dissolution and the recreation of character in the novel, and the separation between, and interrelationship of, individual consciousness'. She concludes that 'McEwan brings to the fore a new interest amongst writers in neuroscience and the relations between mind and brain. The novel would appear to be committed to a new way of aligning narrative and mental processes, and the forms of knowledge and enquiry associated with both literature and science', underscoring both McEwan's continuous quest for newness and his role within this developing field, which includes work by Margaret Atwood, David Lodge, Martin Amis and Kazuo Ishiguro.

Attacks on McEwan have been increasingly common, as the publication of McEwan's most urgent engagement with 'newness' in the twenty-first century, *Saturday* (2005), demonstrates. The novel engages with a variety of concerns, attempts to capture the anxious and uncertain post-9/11 climate of terror, and is particularly interested in debating the war in Iraq. John Banville accused the 'connoisseur of catastrophe' of having written a New Labourite 'neoliberal polemic gone badly' (Banville 2005). In an extradorinary episode, a commissioner from the Equality and Human Rights Commission, Ziauddin Sardar, conflated Henry Perowne (a fictional character) with Ian McEwan (writer of fiction) and accused the author of producing orientalist propaganda for Western culture, literature and ideology. Sardar proceeded to lump McEwan together with the outspokenly pro-American Martin Amis and Salman Rushdie, who, together with Christopher Hitchins, had already been proclaimed George W. Bush's bed-fellows in the *New Statesman* (Lloyd 2002). McEwan did not respond to these accusations, but he did jump to the defence of his friend Martin Amis, after he was accused of being a racist by Terry Eagleton in autumn 2007 (Eagleton 2007). After an Italian journalist misrepresented McEwan's thoughts on the extreme fringes of Islam in *Corriere della Sera*, British newspapers and the Muslim Council of Great Britain portrayed McEwan as anti-Muslim (Martin 2008). This prompted McEwan to publish a statement on his website, explaining that he had spoken out against Islamism and jihadists, not against Islam: 'It is merely to invoke a common humanity which I hope would be shared by all religions as well as all non-believers' (McEwan 2008b).

McEwan wrote *Saturday* (2005) because, he suggested, he 'felt some responsibility to the present. The times have become horribly interesting' (Bragg 2005), and the novel gives us an image of ourselves at the beginning of the twenty-first century. For a literary, liberal readership, *Saturday* is a counter-intuitive novel, which makes us travel through the mind of a middle-class scientist who sympathizes with Anglo-American intervention in Iraq. McEwan's depiction of happiness, the most challenging of subjects a novelist could attempt to capture, in what are essentially dark and uncertain times, runs counter to the *Zeitgeist*. In Chapter Seven Sebastian Groes considers the ways in which *Saturday* engages with these problems through a consideration of the representation of London. Groes argues that we can use McEwan's ideas about the contemporary city to understand his complex, uncertain meditation on the state of the world at the beginning of the twenty-first century: the divorce of the private and public realms, the relationship between science and the arts, democracy, and the war in Iraq. These debates are traced through the complex but carefully orchestrated intertexts the novel contains, with a particular focus, first, on the hypercanonic modernist texts of Kafka, Joyce and Woolf, and, secondly, on the Victorian cultural critic and poet Matthew Arnold. While McEwan rejects the radical experiments of high modernism, and appears to revert to classic Arnoldian conceptions of culture, both the form and content of his novel remain ambivalent. *Saturday* attempts to reinvigorate the novel as an important imaginary space where dialogues about politics, society and morality can be held in a democratic fashion. This chapter concludes by making a claim for McEwan's reinvention of what Lorna Sage, in her analysis of Iris Murdoch's work, called 'the middle ground' (Sage 1992: 72). However, rather than inhabiting the realist territory of the nineteenth-century novel, McEwan's complex voices in the later work inhabit the intricacy and uncertainty of consciousness and experience via modernist representations, resulting in a modified form of realism.

Dominic Head's monograph on McEwan has aligned McEwan's work with that of Iris Murdoch, and with the tradition of the social novel as 'the privileged form of moral discourse in a secular world' (Head 2004: 251). In the closing chapter, Head investigates McEwan's provocative use of the novella form in *Amsterdam* (1998) and *On Chesil Beach* (2007), arguing that he stretches the genre by incorporating discussions of society and history that we normally associate with the novel. Head corrects the initial, rather superficial reception of the novella as an exploration of pre-Swinging Sixties themes and events, by pointing out the darker subtexts embedded in the work. Although it is set 'in a time when a conversation about sexual difficulties was plainly impossible' (McEwan 2007: 3), McEwan's novella sets out to provoke a debate about morality, sexuality, and taboos in contemporary society. Unlike Amis's writing, which equates pornography with the 'obscenification of everyday life' and 'a loss of innocence' (Amis 2003: 289; Groes and Amis 2004: 49), McEwan's work is ambivalent, emasculating the power of pornography by appropriating its imagery and ridiculing it, and by reminding us that repressive morality, idealizations of 'innocence' and a lack of communication can in equal measure lead to disaster. Head thus rounds off Baxter's and Colebrook's discussion of McEwan's pornographic imagination, while also engaging with the debates about McEwan's experimentation with genre.

An important conclusion reached by Head is that McEwan's stretching of the novella genre points to an exhaustion of the genre, and perhaps even a dissatisfaction with writing as a means to represent experience itself. Yet as a reflection of a complex, paradoxical world whose multiplicity constantly perplexes and confounds us, McEwan's fiction too is confusing and ambiguous. This uncertainty reflects the troubled state of the world at the beginning of the twenty-first century – but McEwan's work will continue to explore the answers to the question asked by Perowne at the beginning of *Saturday*: 'And now, what days are these?' (McEwan 2005: 4).

CHAPTER ONE

Surrealist Encounters in Ian McEwan's Early Work

JEANNETTE BAXTER

Chapter Summary: This chapter reassesses McEwan's first three published works – *First Love, Last Rites* (1975), *In Between the Sheets* (1978) and *The Cement Garden* (1978) – in the light of George Bataille's radical Surrealist writings. Tracing the formal and thematic aspects of McEwan's surrealism, it focuses on the pornographic imagination and its interrogation of culturally-prescribed notions of 'obscenity' within contemporary culture; on the challenges posed by 'base materialism' and 'formlessness' to socio-cultural and aesthetic constraints on form; and on McEwan's creation of vertigo in relationship to eroticism, transgression and taboo. Rereading McEwan's early work within the tradition of dissident Surrealism offers a different set of critical and creative contexts for confronting and understanding these compelling detours into the more disturbing textures of the modern imagination.

McEwan's shocking tales of incest, paedophilia, erotic violence, sex and death in *First Love, Last Rites, In Between The Sheets* and *The Cement Garden* not only demand that we, the readers, immerse ourselves imaginatively in every disturbing texture of each narrative, but they also insist, in a sense, that we stay there. As Kiernan Ryan has pointed out, one of the strengths of McEwan's early fictions is the way in which they force the reader into a disquieting process of self-reflection: 'Far from disguising the tainted pleasure they take in their more lurid themes, his best tales confess the ambiguity of their attitude and oblige us to reflect on the mixed motives governing our own response as readers' (Ryan 1994: 13). This essay concerns itself with this unsettling aspect of reading McEwan's early work. How is the reader expected to respond to tales of rape ('Homemade', 'Dead as They Come'); child abuse ('Disguises', 'Butterflies', 'Conversation with a Cupboard Man'); sado-masochistic torture ('Pornography'); and incestuous desire (*The Cement Garden*)? Should we refrain from indulging in these tales of violent transgression, or should we allow ourselves to fall into the textual abyss? How do we even begin to negotiate, or reconcile, our own shifting responses to McEwan's fictions when initial waves of shock, disgust and nausea give way somehow to feelings of confusion and fascination, and laughter?

The uncertainty of response entailed by McEwan's early writing points to a troubling aesthetic of provocation. Although critics have gone some way to exploring this – Ryan labels McEwan's writing an 'Art of Unease' – the creative and critical impulse behind McEwan's aesthetics are better understood when his first three published works are read as experiments in a form of dissident Surrealism. A literary, artistic and political movement born out of the historical and social circumstances of post-First World War Europe, Surrealism set out to subvert established understandings of the modern world as rational, ordered and homogeneous. Through a diverse range of experimental narrative and visual techniques (including collage, photomontage, dream association and psychic automatism), the Surrealist Group, headed by André Breton, developed an aesthetic repertoire with which they could dismantle socially constructed ideas of identity, subjectivity, sexuality and reality, and, in turn, open art, literature, history and politics to unique ways of seeing.

One aspect of the human condition with which the Surrealists were particularly concerned was desire in all of its manifestations. Influenced by Freudian theories of sexuality, Surrealist art and literature engaged in various ways with the 'polymorphous perverse' (masturbation; incest) and, specifically, with the troubling intersection of art, sex and death (Freud 1920: 79). The reader of Surrealist literature was confronted repeatedly with disturbing and often violent imaginary scenarios which jolted him or her into a radically new way of reacting to and thinking about sexual desire. It was precisely this disturbance of the reader's 'historical, cultural, psychological assumptions, the consistency of his tastes, values, memories' (Barthes 1990: 14) which constituted the uneasy pleasures of the Surrealist text.

Although the exploration of sexual desire formed a central part of the Surrealist project, it was also a site of contestation and eventual rupture. Hal Foster notes how André Breton's and Georges Bataille's diverging philosophies on sex, death and art led to a split in the Group in 1929. At the heart of Bretonian Surrealism lay the notion of sublimation, namely the 'diversion of sexual drives to civilizational ends (art, science) in a way that purifies them, that both integrates the object (beauty, truth) and refines the subject (the artist, scientist)' (Foster 1993: 110). Whilst Breton's recuperation of subversive desire encouraged the transformation of matter into metaphor in an ascending movement of sublimation, Bataille's dissident Surrealism encouraged a descent into the dirt. Rejecting Bretonian idealism, Bataille posited a philosophy of 'base materialism' (Breton dismissed this as 'vulgar materialism'), which refused to rise above 'mere matter, sheer shit, to raise the low to high, to proper form and sublimated beauty' (Foster 1993: 12), and which risked elaborating on the intersection of sex and death.

This willingness to descend imaginatively into the precarious territories of desublimation is a hallmark of McEwan's early work. McEwan's admission that that which compels him to write 'is not what is nice and easy and pleasant and somehow affirming, but somehow what is bad and difficult and unsettling' (Ricks 1979: 526) aligns his early aesthetic and philosophical impulses squarely with Bataille's dissident Surrealism. Bataille keeps company with those Surrealist (or quasi-Surrealist) writers, including Jean Genet, Louis Ferdinand Céline, William Burroughs and Franz Kafka, whom McEwan acknowledges as literary influences (Haffenden 1985: 169). I want to explore the formal and thematic aspects of McEwan's Surrealism as they manifest themselves in three distinct yet related areas: the pornographic imagination and its interrogation of culturally-prescribed notions of 'obscenity' within contemporary culture; the desublimating drives of 'base materialism' and their *informe*, or 'formlessness', and the challenges which they pose to socio-cultural and aesthetic determinations of form; and the dizzying presence of vertigo as it relates to eroticism, transgression and taboo, and to the troubling conjunction of art, Eros and Thanatos. By (re)reading McEwan's early work within the tradition of dissident Surrealism, I hope to reveal a different set of critical and creative contexts for confronting and understanding these compelling detours through the more disturbing textures of the modern imagination.

The Pornographic Imagination in *First Love, Last Rites*

In 'The Pornographic Imagination' (1967), Susan Sontag identifies three kinds of pornography within contemporary culture: pornography as a commodity or 'an item in social history', an idea explored by Claire Colebrook in relation to *The Innocent* (see pp. 43–56); pornography as a pathological symptom which, according to traditional views, is a sign of 'sexual deficiency or deformity in both the producers and the consumers'; and literary pornography, 'a minor but interesting modality or convention within the arts' (Sontag 2001: 83). It is in the light of this third form of pornography – the pornographic imagination – that I want to review McEwan's early fiction. According to Sontag, one significant difference between commercial pornographic novels or 'pot-boilers', and serious works of literary pornography, is the latter's compulsion to elaborate on extreme forms of human consciousness (Sontag 2001: 84). The power of literary pornography is not to be measured by the power to titillate, then, but by 'the originality, thoroughness, authenticity, and power of that deranged consciousness itself, as incarnated in a work' (Sontag 2001: 94). For Sontag, this urgent need to explore the most disturbing states of human feeling and consciousness is articulated in the pornographic writings of Georges Bataille: *The Story of the Eye* (1928), *Madame Edwarda*, (1941), and *Ma Mère* (published posthumously in 1962). Focusing on Bataille's first novella, *Story of the Eye* (1928), a provocative meditation on sexual perversion (paedophilia, necrophilia and incest amongst others), which is intertextually resonant with McEwan's own pornographic writings, Sontag argues that works of literary pornography should not be seen as 'tokens of radical failure or deformation of the imagination' (Sontag 2001: 98). Instead, she insists that literary pornography boasts an imagination which is at once creative and critically mobilizing; the pornographic imagination risks taking up positions on the frontiers of consciousness, in other words, in order to place our conventional thinking about sex, death and art on trial.

In 'Cocker at the Theatre', McEwan makes a dramatic feature of one of the key issues raised in Sontag's polemic, namely, the nature of 'obscenity'. The story offers a behind-the-scenes glimpse of a group of actors as they prepare to simulate a series of sexual encounters; its content flaunts the characteristics we commonly associate with pornography. What is striking about this pornographic tale, though, is not so much its salacious content, but its tone:

> Dale the choreographer moved a girl from the middle and replaced her with a girl from the edge. She did not speak to them, she took them by the elbow, leading them from this place to that place [. . .] She fitted the legs together of each couple, she straightened their backs, she put their heads in position and made the partners clasp forearms. (McEwan 1997a: 67)

The reader is ineluctably cast as a voyeur. Whilst the third-person narrative voice establishes a detached and neutralized tone, the repeated collective pronouns ('they' and 'them') strip the actors of any semblance of personal identity, so reducing these nameless human agents to interchangeable components within an anonymous sexual collective. The choreographer's schematic attempts to stylize the sensuous emphasizes, furthermore, the insensate nature of the reified and sexualized body; assembled and reassembled like mannequins for voyeuristic consumption, McEwan's pornographic troupe are mere prototypes in a potentially inexhaustible and largely affectless sexual exhibition.

I say largely affectless because McEwan's deadpan presentation of simulated sexual encounters is designed to provoke the reader to laughter by means of parody. A common form of pornographic writing, parody works in 'Cocker at the Theatre' to interrogate conventional notions of obscenity, and to open up a line of questioning about the imbrication of sex, art and consumer-capitalism. In an extremely funny turn of events, for instance, two actors transgress the boundaries of pretence by engaging in a real and 'sinuous' sex act (McEwan 1997a: 69). The artistic director's response is telling: 'It's disgusting and obscene [. . .] Well, Cocker, you and the little man stuck on the end of you can crawl off this stage, and take shagging Nellie with you. I hope you find a gutter big enough for two' (McEwan 1997a: 70). The director posits a skewed sense of moral outrage, and, in so doing, gives weight to Sontag's suspicion that 'obscenity' is nothing more than a 'fiction imposed upon a society convinced there is something vile about the sexual functions and, by extension, about sexual pleasure' (Sontag 2001: 103). Furthermore, a resonant irony is born out of the director's continued attempts to couch his own sex show, a cheap pornographic commodity which spectacularly lacks imagination and desire, in artistic terms – 'This is a respectable show' (McEwan 1997a: 65). As the director's hilarious address to the actor's offending member confirms, this particular kind of commercial pornographer is only used to dealing in well-worn clichés and a style of personification which aggressively dehumanizes and fetishes the sexualized body.

McEwan advances this line of enquiry by exploring the standardization and commodification of sexuality in 'Homemade', a disturbing tale of violent sexual fantasy whose title smacks of the 'ready-made' forms of sexual desire in circulation within the contemporary consumer culture. A self-confessed consumer of pornographic literature – 'top shelf' magazines, 'under-the-counter' videos, and 'the more interesting parts of Havelock Ellis and Henry Miller' – the anonymous narrator boasts 'a connoisseur's taste for violence and obscenity' (McEwan 1997a: 27). Indeed, his first experience of masturbation occurs in the cellar of a 'bomb-site' (McEwan 1997a: 26). In the absence of any 'longings or private fantasies' (McEwan 1997a: 27) of his own, the adolescent narrator feeds his imagination on a diet 'of timeworn puns and innuendo, formulas, slogans, folklore and bravado' (McEwan 1997a: 30) which he inherits from popular literary and visual forms, and from the workmen who gather to exchange salacious tales in the local café. The missing ingredient from the narrator's self-styled sexual education, however, is knowledge: 'All the way home I thought about cunt [. . .] And for all this I still did not know just exactly what a cunt was. I eyed my sister across the table' (McEwan 1997a: 35). This last sentence jolts the reader, for now the full implications of the title of this story become clear; Connie, the narrator's ten-year-old sister, is the 'homemade' object of her brother's sexual obsessions.

The suggestion that the adolescent narrator will seek sexual knowledge in his younger sister (her name is a 'translinguistic pun' on knowledge – *connaissance* [see Broughton 1991]) is clearly unpalatable to the reader, and yet the text only proceeds by exacerbating our developing sense of unease. Inviting her to play 'Hide and Seek', for instance, the boy's transgressive thoughts manifest themselves in a double discourse which is playful and insidious – 'I covered my eyes and counted to thirty [. . .] I shouted "Coming" and began to mount the stairs' – before it collapses into unequivocal intent: 'I had decided to rape my sister' (McEwan 1997a: 36–37). It is this uncompromising move to 'advance one step further in the dialectic of outrage' that marks McEwan's early writings out as explorations of the Surrealist pornographic imagination. McEwan strives to make his work revolting and aims to trigger the reader's rejection of it by confronting him or her with the promise of incestuous rape.

By immersing his readers in this offensive textual scenario, McEwan sets out to defamiliarize and disorientate us. What quickly emerges from the siblings' game of 'Mummies and Daddies' is that McEwan not only foregrounds the boy's filial desires, but he simultaneously offers this uneasy desire up as an antidote to conventional socio-sexual relations. At the same time that readers are horrified by 'one of the most desolate couplings known to mankind, involving lies, deceit and humiliation' (McEwan 1997a: 43), we are also unnerved by the 'dreary, everyday, ponderous banalities, the horrifying niggling details of the life of our parents and friends' (McEwan 1997a: 38), all of which are subverted by the central incestuous encounter. It is this transgressive drive to counter-repressive cultural systems which McEwan's writings inherit from Bataille. Reading 'Homemade', and McEwan's provocative early fictions in general, is akin to reading Bataille's meditation on transgression and taboo, *Eroticism* (1957). Situated within a dialectic of interdiction and transgression, eroticism is 'the domain of violence, of violation', which always 'entails a breaking down of established patterns [. . .] of the regulated social order' (Bataille 2001: 8–16). In tension with this is the prohibitive mechanism of interdiction, a repressive and regulating force which maintains the equilibrium through order and restraint.

Oscillating between transgression and interdiction, the reader of 'Homemade' experiences a range of ambiguous emotions. Initial waves of shock and disgust give way to fascination and even laughter when the sexually inept narrator struggles to wriggle from his underpants in order to achieve a 'gnat's orgasm' (McEwan 1997a: 43). The reader's ambivalent response is indicative of the disquieting energies of McEwan's writing, and of a rupture of the conventional paradigm of reader and text (within which the reader is in control) when, out of incredulity, horror or curiosity, the reader feels compelled to read on. It is at this point of re-engagement with the text that the process of reading is pushed to its limits and becomes something resembling performance. In the act of (re)reading, each disturbing textual/sexual scenario is repeated as the reader becomes a participant and performer in McEwan's erotic texts. We are invited to test the limits of our own imaginations – and tolerance – by staging repeated scenes of incestuous rape. Such a process of performative reading has significant consequences: when does readerly participation cross over into complicity?

McEwan foregrounds this question in 'Disguises', a disturbing tale of paedophilia and performance, which also boasts a contest of narrative forms at its heart. On the one hand, the reader encounters the memories of Mina, a retired 'grand dame' of the theatre and 'surreal mother' (McEwan 1997a: 124) to her orphaned nephew, Henry. Pitched against Mina's disjointed and discontinuous surreal narrative is Henry's sequential and conventionally realist narrative, which eschews randomness and chaos in favour of details and facts: 'Henry was not the kind to see the unseen' (McEwan 1997a: 125). It is Henry's faith in surface realities and his inability to perceive the power of the hidden, however, which secures his fate as the object of Mina's perverse desires. Henry's 'new life' resembles a costume drama of sorts, for instance when, each night, Mina dresses him variously as a soldier, lift-boy, monk and shepherd (McEwan 1997a: 128). What the young boy gradually begins to realize, though, is that his surreal mother's sartorial rituals are 'games' which are not really games: 'he sensed some compulsion in it for Mina, he dared not contradict it, there was something dark' (McEwan 1997a: 132). In this context, 'game' reveals itself to be a euphemism for paedophilia.

The intersection of performance and paedophilia is explored most compellingly towards the end of the story when Mina hosts a fancy-dress party for her friends, who come 'disguised as ordinary people' (McEwan 1997a: 153). The events of the party are narrated from Henry's point of view as he wonders and watches from behind a monster's mask. Yet his is not the linear, realist voice which the reader encountered at the beginning of the story. Rather, intoxicated by fear and alcohol, Henry's narrative becomes non-sequential and chaotic as he witnesses his friend, Linda, a bewildered 'Alice in Wonderland', being abused by one of the male guests:

> Was it the monster who fell to the ground or Henry, who was to blame? it came back to him now, dressed like somebody else and pretending to be them you took the blame for what they did, or what you as them do . . . did? (McEwan 1997a: 156–157)

Henry's fractured syntax not only belies the trauma of witnessing sexual abuse, but it also sets up a series of intricate questions about agency and moral responsibility. Henry's own sense of complicity (he invited Linda to the party), together with his subsequent desire to shift the blame from his proper to performative self, manifest themselves in a linguistically fraught narrative. The temporal collapse of the verb 'to do' emphasizes the boy's confusion about where culpability lies. Is he to blame, or is the monster? And who, precisely, is the monster? Is it the boy in the 'Mummy' mask, the paedophile hiding in plain sight, or the reader of the story who, however vicariously, participates in and indeed performs the text's disturbing events? It is precisely this line of self-questioning which makes the act of reading McEwan's early dissident fictions so disquieting and so necessary.

In Between the Sheets: Vulgar Materialism and the Politics of Formlessness

McEwan's early writings are littered with waste of every kind. Whilst traces of urine, vomit, semen, snot, spit, pus and blood wet and stain almost every page of his short prose fictions, accumulations of refuse, shit, abandoned buildings and rotten organic forms threaten to clutter the reader's vision. Critical attention has only been paid so far to McEwan's cataloguing of waste and excess within the context of male adolescent sexuality (earning him the title of 'chronicler' of 'snot and pimples' [Haffenden 1985: 173]). In this section, I want to read McEwan's materialism within a dissident strain of Surrealist writing, advanced by Bataille, known as 'base materialism'. Bataille's fascination with waste, rot and decay – *Story of the Eye* (1928) is sodden with semen, urine, tears, egg yolks and cat's milk, whilst his writings on La Villette Slaughterhouse are saturated with images of blood and unidentifiable bundles of visceral excess – led to Breton deriding him as an 'excremental philosopher': 'M. Bataille professes to wish only to consider in the world that which is vilest, most discouraging and most corrupted [. . .] so as to avoid making himself useful for anything specific' (Breton 1972: 181). I would like to challenge the accusation that base materialism is nothing more than an act of apolitical indulgence, suggesting rather that this dissident Surrealist practice is a form of socio-historical critique which disconcerts idealist aspirations before something 'base' precisely in order to place received notions of order and form on trial.

It is in the notion of the *informe*, or 'formlessness', that base materialism finds its most suggestive expression. An assault on the conventional organization of knowledge and reality into neat and definable terms, formlessness is a term 'serving to declassify' and dismantle traditional notions of form by affirming 'on the contrary that the universe resembles nothing at all and is only formless' (Bataille 1995: 27). One of a number of terms (including abattoir, dust, eye, materialism) which Bataille included in his parodic 'Critical Dictionary', formlessness is nonetheless never defined. Rather, it is given a function: informed by the task of bringing things 'down in the world', formlessness will challenge all formal constraints and reject structure and procedure. Repudiating the idealist trajectory of sublimation, formlessness confronts the reader with a variety of difficult and disquieting encounters which can only be experienced on their own, desublimating terms. As Rosalind Krauss has argued, formlessness 'does not propose a higher, more transcendental meaning through a dialectical movement of thought'. The 'boundaries of terms are not imagined' by the dissident Surrealist artist as 'transcended', but 'merely as transgressed or broken, producing formlessness through deliquescence, putrefaction, decay' (Krauss 1986: 65).

The post-apocalyptic landscapes of 'Two Fragments: March 199–' provide a fitting point of entry into this discussion. In these bleak, proleptic tales, McEwan presents the reader with a radically defamiliarized vision of London:

> The Ministry rose from a vast plain of pavement [. . .] The stones were cracking and subsiding. Human refuse littered the plain. Vegetables, rotten and trodden down, cardboard boxes flattened into beds, the remains of fires and the carcasses of roasted dogs and cats, rusted tin, vomit, worn tyres, animal excrement. An old dream of horizontal lines converging on the thrusting steel and glass perpendicular was now beyond recall. (McEwan 1997b: 39)

A dialectical tension is present within this urban snapshot, namely a tension between 'architecture', which connotes order, system and structure (the Ministry is a metonym for Government), and 'formlessness', which erodes any sense of structure and regulation. What is particularly striking about this description of urban excess, however, is what we might call the trajectory of its energy. Everything is collapsing downwards: buildings are subsiding; rotten matter is trodden down; boxes are flattened; fires have burnt down; car tyres are worn down. The dominant movement in this passage charts a fall from a vertical axis (sublimation) on to a horizontal axis (desublimation). Indeed sublimation, the idealist promise that, in the context of this narrative, governing structures will lift society up and out of the dirt, is nothing more than 'an old dream' (McEwan 1997b: 39). In reality, the Ministry is a massive public convenience which the city's inhabitants visit daily 'to squat on the wide concrete rim of the fountain and defecate' (McEwan 1997b: 40).

With its imaginative descent into formlessness, 'Two Fragments' can be read as a biting indictment of the social, economic and historical contexts of the story's production. Certainly, McEwan's bleak imagery is consonant with the apocalyptic tone of social and cultural commentators of the time. As Tom Nairn put it, the 1970s was a decade of 'rapidly accelerating backwardness, economic stagnation, social decay, and cultural despair'; in short, British society had 'decayed to the point of disintegration' (Nairn 1977: 51, 67). One thing to stress about Nairn's response is that it does not merely operate on a metaphorical level. During the 'Winter of Discontent' (1978–9), a year-long period of widespread strikes by trade unions contesting pay restraints, the British landscape was in a literal state of decay: 'sewage disposal ceased, rubbish piled on the streets, the dead lay unburied' (Bradbury 1993: 418).

These historico-social realities manifest themselves imaginatively throughout McEwan's early fictions. In the second of the 'Two Fragments', for instance, one character bemoans the declining state of British industry: 'We no longer craft things [. . .] Nor do we manufacture or mass-produce them. We make nothing' (McEwan 1997b: 49). Meanwhile, the protagonist, Henry, is placed in a socially compromising situation when he realizes that his act of kindness towards a Chinaman is to be paid in food which the immigrant family simply cannot spare. Embedded in this awkward encounter are complex narratives of economic migration, social deprivation and cultural difference which McEwan's own narrative refuses to sublimate. Rather, the food which Henry is forced to eat out of politeness is a formless, 'dun-coloured' mass which the Chinaman's daughter variably identifies as 'muck' and 'piss' (McEwan 1997b: 57). Holding back his own vomit, the only response available to Henry is to depart the scene, to descend the 'steep flight of stairs' and turn out the paraffin lamp, thus plunging himself and the reader down into the darkness of the 'black street' (McEwan 1997b 57–8).

Another critical impulse behind McEwan's explorations of formlessness speaks to the condition of British fiction (and especially the novel) in the 1970s. As Malcolm Bradbury so bluntly put it: 'After the Swinging Sixties, the Sagging Seventies' (Bradbury 1993: 416). Such was the anxiety surrounding the fate of the British cultural imagination in 1970s Britain that a *New Review* symposium took place which focused exclusively on the quality of novelistic practices (Moore-Gilbert 1994: 2). Artists, commentators and writers, including McEwan, gathered to express their doubt over the future of the novel form. McEwan believed 'fiction to be less vital than other cultural forms in contemporary Britain' (Moore-Gilbert 1994: 2), an authorial anxiety which resides at the heart of 'Reflections of a Kept Ape':

> Was art then nothing more than a wish to appear busy? Was it nothing more than a fear of silence, of boredom, which the merely reiterative rattle of the typewriter's keys was enough to allay? In short, having crafted one novel, would it suffice to write it again, type it out with care, page by page? (McEwan 1997b: 32)

McEwan's short prose can be read as a deliberate strategy for revitalizing the state of British fiction. As Bradbury points out, not 'since Angus Wilson [McEwan's teacher] had a major career started with two volumes of stories rather than a novel' (Bradbury 1995: 437). As I have been arguing throughout, though, it is McEwan's reinvigoration of British fiction along Surrealist lines of influence which distinguishes his fictions as so innovative and imaginative. Following a small number of British writers, including J. G. Ballard and Angela Carter, who also turned to literary and visual Surrealism in varying ways in the post-war period, McEwan's early work gives body to Moore-Gilbert's assertion that the 1970s was not a decade of closure, but a period alive to the influences and innovations of the previous decade. The avant-garde of the 1960s, he argues, had given shape to what he terms a post-avantgardism of the 1970s in which traditional aesthetic models and more radical formal innovations co-existed (Moore-Gilbert 1994: 15).

McEwan makes a dramatic feature of this formal convergence in 'Dead as They Come', a snapshot of sadistic and fetishistic desire which derails the circumlocutory direction of postmodernism in order to take art in another direction altogether. 'Dead as They Come' boasts the desubli-matory account of representation which lies at the heart of the dissident Surrealist project. Representation is 'less about formal sublimation than about instinctual release' or, as Bataille put it: 'Art [. . .] proceeds in this way by successive destructions. To the extent that it liberates libidinal instincts, these instincts are sadistic' (quoted in Foster 1993: 113). This compulsion to deform traditional aesthetic form, to bring art 'down' in the world, reaches a powerful climax at the end of 'Dead as They Come' when, having raped and vomited over the 'corpse' of his mannequin 'lover', the narrator destroys his 'precious' art collection: 'Now I was running like a naked madman from room to room destroying what-ever I could lay my hands on [. . .] Vermeer, Blake, Richard Dadd, Paul Nash, Rothko, I tore, trampled, mangled, kicked, spat and urinated on' (McEwan 1997b: 77). Notably, this particular act of artistic deformation is not absolute. Indeed, in the style of Andy Warhol's 'Oxidation Art', an artistic practice which promoted formlessness by demoting the canvas from a vertical position (wall, easel) to a horizontal one (floor) in order to piss on it, McEwan's dissident artist creates a post-avant-garde site of aesthetic contestation as 'formless' expectorated bodily fluids (spit-tle, urine) and base matter (dirt) mix with traditional materials and vio-late accepted form (Martin 2005). Whilst these radically altered works of art provoke new ways of seeing in a literal sense (the spectator must now look downwards, at the floor), they also initiate radical methods for thinking differently and disturbingly about art, sex and death, and the point at which these energies converge. This is a line of disquieting interrogation which I want to pursue further in the final section.

The Cement Garden: Vertigo and the Surrealist Turn

As David Lomas has argued, the term 'vertigo' appeared with remark-able frequency in the writings of the dissident Surrealists. From the French *vertere*, meaning to *turn*, vertigo is defined as 'a perturbation in the subjective orientation to space which generally takes the form of a gyratory or oscillatory sensation but can manifest as feelings of ascent or descent' (Lomas 2007). Common symptoms of vertigo include loss of balance, light-headedness and the feeling of the ground moving, or giv-ing way, beneath one's feet. I want to trace symptoms of vertigo as they manifest themselves across McEwan's short debut novel, *The Cement Garden*. I will focus upon the complex interplay between vertigo and Bataille's notion of eroticism, that transgressive and disequilibriating form of sexual desire which, in 'assenting to life up to the point of death' (Bataille 2001: 11), elaborates on the marriage of sex and death.

The Cement Garden pivots on the ambiguous conjunction of Eros and Thanatos. Whilst Jack's opening flirtations with parricide – 'I did not kill my father, but I sometimes felt I had helped him on his way' (McEwan

2006: 9) – gesture to the son's growing sexual energy and the demise of his emotionally sterile father (who drops dead at the moment at which Jack achieves his first orgasm), the death of his mother initiates a descent into a series of erotic transgressions. Rereading the science fiction fantasy which his younger sister, Sue, had given him for his birthday, Jack alludes to the erosion of order which his mother's death signifies: 'Now that we do not have gravity to keep things in their place [. . .] we must make an extra effort to be neat' (McEwan 2006: 82). This loss of stability manifests itself most strikingly in the makeshift tomb which the children construct in the cellar of their house in order to bury the traumatic memory of their mother's death and simultaneously preserve her as 'an invisible foundation of their lives' (Ryan 1994: 20). The ambiguity of the home-made tomb is not confined to the children's psychic need to intern their mother, however. In French, the word for tomb, *tombe*, has a double-meaning: on the one hand it refers to a large underground vault for the burial of the dead; on the other hand, it means 'fall'.

When he first learns of his mother's death Jack succumbs to an experience of vertigo: 'For a moment I thought of snatching the key, but I turned and, lightheaded, close to blasphemous laughter, followed my sister down' (McEwan 2006: 52). Oscillating between fear and desire, tears and laughter, Jack's ambivalent response reflects the uncertainty of knowing how to negotiate trauma. Equally, though, his vertiginous descent of the stairs (he is close behind Julie) also gestures symbolically to the siblings' imminent fall into incest. This act of filial desire is couched in vertiginous terms: 'I [Jack] felt weightless, tumbling through space with no sense of up or down. As I closed my lips around Julie's nipple a soft shudder ran through her body' (McEwan 2006: 135). In violating the incest taboo, Jack and Julie transgress the limits of what Bataille would call their 'discontinuity'. It is important to recognize that this excursion into eroticism is asking that 'the erotic lure in things that are vile and repulsive' is not 'dismissed as mere neurotic aberrations' (Sontag 2001: 103–4). Rather, in contrast to Derek's stock response – 'It's sick [. . .] he's your brother [. . .] Sick!' (McEwan 2006: 136) – the reader is provoked into considering the possibility that extreme sexual practices might just be understood as troubling resources for breaking through the limits of consciousness. The 'whole business of eroticism' is, after all, to 'destroy the self-contained character of the participators as they are in their normal lives' (Bataille 2001: 17).

The suggestion that McEwan's imaginative transgressions into the domain of eroticism could also be read in terms of a socio-cultural critique is borne out in the pages which describe Julie and Jack having sex. Notably, the emphasis is not placed on the sexual act itself – they both end up laughing and 'forgetting what we were about' (McEwan 2006: 137). Importance is placed, instead, on the fact that brother and sister talk urgently and incessantly to one another prior to, during and after sex (McEwan 2006: 133–136). Having stripped naked, an act which is the 'decisive action [. . .] shorn of gravity' (Bataille 2001: 18), Jack and Julie share their memories and fears in a vertiginous verbal exchange ('For a long time we talked about ourselves' [McEwan 2006: 134]) which stands out against the rest of the predominantly flat narrative. In this context, nakedness reveals itself to be 'a contrast to self-possession, to discontinuous existence [. . .] it is a state of communication revealing a quest for a possible continuance of being beyond the confines of the self' (Bataille 2001: 18).

Within McEwan's version of eroticism incest is offered up as a disquieting antidote to the acute levels of physical, emotional and psychological isolation which characterizes this desolate, 'familial' tale. Whilst the moral implications of this are potentially troubling for the reader, it is important to note that McEwan is not imagining transgression as a merely subversive act. Rather, he presents transgression and taboo as inherent components of one another: 'transgression does not deny the taboo but transcends and completes it' (Bataille 2001: 62). In other words, transgression ensures the effectiveness of taboo by demonstrating an awareness of the law of sexual prohibition. In *The Cement Garden*, this formulation translates into a dissident narrative that risks breaching the incest taboo in order to prevent stagnation and, at the same time, to maintain stability. The intrusive sound of 'two or three cars pulling up outside, the slam of doors and the hurried footsteps of several people coming up [the] front path' (McEwan 2006: 138) which breaks the children's dream-like existence suggests that a sense of moral and social order will be reinserted into the narrative. This is not to say that the ascendancy of interdiction at the end of *The Cement Garden* should be read in dialectical or sublimatory terms. Instead, the text demands to be read in dynamic and desublimatory terms or, as Bataille puts it, when 'a negative emotion has the upper hand we must obey the taboo. When a positive emotion is in the ascendent we violate it' (Bataille 2001: 64). This vertiginous process of reading is borne out in the reader's final ambivalent response which, oscillating between relief and frustration, dares to imagine the creative and critical implications of the children falling back asleep and tumbling once more into the domain of eroticism.

CHAPTER TWO

'Profoundly dislocating and infinite in possibility': Ian McEwan's Screenwriting

M. HUNTER HAYES AND SEBASTIAN GROES

Chapter Summary: A considerable proportion of McEwan's creative energy, above all in his early years, was channelled into original screenplays and adaptations. Yet it has become commonplace to view McEwan's screenwriting as a process of apprenticeship or as an excuse for collaboration. In contrast, this chapter explores the dialogic relationship between the tele- and screenplays and the prose fiction. It analyses the postmodernism practised by McEwan in the seventies, considers the 'hinge' provided by *The Imitation Game* (1981) within the wider *oeuvre*, and argues for the recognition of a powerful triptych directed against Thatcher and Thatcherism: *The Ploughman's Lunch* (1983), *Soursweet* (1988) and *The Good Son* (1993).

Introduction: Moving Abroad

In the foreword to *A Move Abroad* (1989), the volume containing his libretto 'Or Shall We Die?' and the screenplay for *The Ploughman's Lunch*, McEwan compares writing in other genres or forms to visiting a foreign country:

> Choosing a new form in which to write bears some resemblance to travelling abroad; the sense of freedom is no less useful for being illusory and temporary. The new place has its own rules and conventions, but they are not really yours, not quite yet. What you first notice is the absence of the old, familiar constraints, and you do things you would not do at home. (McEwan 1989: xxi)

Other nations have subtle and distinct cultural and social characteristics, McEwan suggests, just as different forms or contexts for writing entail divergent rules of representation. By 1989, it was certainly the case that McEwan had become established as one of the pre-eminent novelists of his day, so the analogy between writing for the screen or stage and a journey to a distant land seems apt. Yet it is also the case that during the years of his emergence as a writer he was, as it were, a well-travelled writer, working widely across a variety of genres, and he was particularly ambitious in terms of his writing for television and film. 'I thought it would be a simple matter of sending it to the BBC and they'd send me a cheque by return of post' (Hamilton 1978: 15), he remarked sardonically of a television play written during his time as an undergraduate at Sussex University. An adaptation of a Thomas Mann story, the work joined several other early projects including a stage play, a radio play and a novel, in never finding either publication or production, but the anecdote is instructive. A considerable proportion of McEwan's creative energy, above all in his early years, was channelled into original screenplays and adaptations, ranging from short television projects such as 'Jack Flea's Birthday Celebration' (1976) to Hollywood productions such as Joseph Ruben's *The Good Son* (1993).

One way of approaching McEwan's relationship with television and film would be to note the readiness with which McEwan's work has been adapted for the screen – Harold Pinter adapted *The Comfort of Strangers* (1990), McEwan adapted his novel for John Schlesinger's *The Innocent* (1993), which McEwan called 'the only real dud' (Edemariam 2008), Joe Penhall rewrote *Enduring Love* (2004) for Roger Michell, and Christopher Hampton received an Oscar nomination for his screenplay for Joe Wright's *Atonement* (2007). Alternatively, one might argue that screen projects were an expression of McEwan's interest in the representation of complex historical reality marked by his fierce attack on Thatcherism in *The Child in Time* (1987), the attention to the politics of gender and sexuality which saturates his fiction during the late 1970s and early 1980s, and his explorations of the Second World War in *The Innocent* (1990), *Black Dogs* (1992), and ultimately *Atonement* (2001). One might also suggest that formally and stylistically the attention to detail, above all visual perspective and point of view, which is the hallmark of McEwan's writing, from the gruesome specificities of *First Love, Last Rites* (1975) and *The Cement Garden* (1978) to the *tour de force* of the balloon scene at the opening of *Enduring Love* (1997), and the elaborately constructed episode by the fountain in *Atonement* (2001), suggests an imagination schooled in the demands and conventions of visual media. All these approaches view McEwan's screenwriting as a process of apprenticeship, or as a writerly exercise, or even as an excuse for collaboration. This approach regards the scripts always as something of a subsidiary interest, which increasingly falls away as his reputation – and income – as a novelist becomes secure. In the 1970s the novel form seemed in many ways exhausted as a means to explore the kind of subversive and disturbing themes which were his preoccupation (the breaking of conventions, codes and taboos, an attention to incest, sado-masochism, rape, pornography and the murder of children); it is only with hindsight that his work for other media appears marginal.

In this chapter, we will argue that McEwan's writing for the screen provided far more than the mere groundwork for his central concern, the writing of novels. Although by the later 1980s it is already clear that it is as a novelist that he will make his mark, McEwan's fascination with television and cinema is nonetheless longstanding and intense. In this account, the early experimental work, which includes 'Jack Flea's' and 'Solid Geometry' (1978), gives way eventually to the masterful anti-Thatcherite triptych described previously. We will explore how the tele- and screenplays not only share the socio-political and cultural concerns which characterize the novels and short stories, but, in the range of generic and formal possibilities and challenges they present, they have served to invigorate and even determine McEwan's (re)turn to the novel with *The Child in Time* (1987) in the mid-1980s.

McEwan the Postmodernist: 'Jack Flea's Birthday Celebration' and 'Solid Geometry'

McEwan's earliest published screenwriting produced two teleplays: 'Jack Flea's Birthday Celebration' (1974), and an adaptation of his own short story, 'Solid Geometry' (1978). Both these plays are archetypal contributions to what we now consider 'postmodernism' in that these works problematize history, address their own status as fiction via playful metafictional commentary and self-reflexivity, decentre received conceptions of social categories (class, ethnicity and gender), and highlight the ways in which power is embedded within writing and discourse. 'Jack Flea's Birthday Celebration' tells the story of David Lee, an infantile 'young-looking twenty' who lives with his lover, a 36-year-old teacher called Ruth (McEwan 1981: 23), having run away from home. David's parents, both in their fifties, are attending his birthday party, at which they meet Ruth for the first time. After hesitant, *petit-bourgeois* chit-chat, wine is consumed in abundance, and David pretends to read a chapter (called 'A Birthday Celebration') from his semi-autobiographical novel, *Jack Flea's Birthday Celebration*. David makes it clear that the 'stifling, sinister attentions of his mother' have driven him into the arms of an older woman (Hermione, who clearly is Ruth), who makes Jack Flea into her fantasy child (McEwan 1981: 38). However, when Mrs Lee snatches the piece of paper from David, it is 'completely blank' (McEwan 1981: 39), creating the sense that David is making it up on the spot. Indeed, there is a fundamental uncertainty about the extent to which the reader/viewer must treat the narrative as a game: when David during dinner enacts his role as the archetypal Oedipal child by offering food to his mother and throwing a spoonful into his father's face, 'RUTH *smacks him and he drops the spoon. He starts to cry and nuzzles against* RUTH. *Imperceptibly his crying and her comforting noises turn to laughter'* (McEwan 1981: 46). The story swings back and forth between subverting conventional family relationships, and being a mere fantasy thereof. When the mother and Ruth fight for possession of David, Ruth clearly triumphs:

> He doesn't let anyone else put him to bed. Only me [. . .] He's my little boy now. I'm his Mummy now. I play with him for hours, I take him for walks, I give him his tea, I change him, I tuck him up at night. Sometimes he comes and curls up in my lap and closes his eyes and I feed him milk (MRS LEE gasps) [. . .] from a baby's bottle [. . .] yes, my little Jack Flea sucks and remembers he's only a tiny little boy, my little boy. (McEwan 1981: 46)

Although this appears to be a teasing, drunken fantasy, at the end of the play Ruth does tuck up David, after his parents have left; he is *'lying in a large cot'* (McEwan 1981: 49). This final twist locates 'Jack Flea' in the context of the early, dark stories, as McEwan's own later reflections on the piece suggest:

> [I] felt familiar with television's 'grammar', with its conventions and how they might be broken. [. . .] [I] was attracted by its scale, its intimacy. The possibilities and limitations presented by the thirty, fifty, or even seventy-five minute television play seemed very close in some ways to those presented by the short story: the need for highly selective detail and for the rapid establishment of people and situations, the possibility of chasing one or two ideas to logical, or even illogical, conclusions, the dangers of becoming merely anecdotal. (McEwan 1981: 9)

The close relationship between short fiction and teleplay is immediately apparent. Short stories are conventionally determined by temporal and spatial singularity, and have relatively flat characters and a clear building of narrative tension towards either a final closure, or a disconcerting twist.

However, 'Jack Flea' also contains moves away, in significant ways, from both the recurrent patterns and the concerns of McEwan's stories, and from what one might expect from television as a medium, namely, relatively short and realistic programmes with domestic topics and a production value rooted in pragmatism, aimed at a wide, general audience. The teleplay contains two distinct but opposing visual discourses; McEwan argued that his objective had been 'to take a television cliché – a kind of family reunion, a dinner party – and to transform it by degrees and by logical extension to a point where fantasy had become reality' (McEwan 1981: 11). Social-realism in the manner of directors such as Ken Loach and Tony Garnett is yoked together with the techniques of self-conscious, self-reflexive or absurd drama more readily associated with Bertolt Brecht's alienating 'epic theatre' (with its distinctive undermining of realist convention and challenges to naturalist expectations), or Samuel Beckett. Indeed, 'Jack Flea' contains several allusions to Beckett's work. Mr and Mrs Lee ('Yesterday? Yesterday? [. . .] What a memory' [McEwan 1981: 31]) are reminiscent of Nag and Nell in *Endgame* (1957). There is an overt reference to *Malone Dies* (1951) in the presence of a certain Mrs Malone (McEwan 1981: 44).

The teleplay's opening makes a bravura use of mirrors as a device for moving between the story's two locations: Mr and Mrs Lee's bedroom and David's bedroom. The mirror above Mrs Lee's dressing-table reflects both her husband and the sheet of paper displaying the title of David's novel, an autobiographical novel which offers a metafictional commentary on the story we are watching. The title refers at once to David's novel-in-progress and to the teleplay itself, further disrupting any easy division between fiction and reality and thwarting the audience's capacity to suspend disbelief.

In this respect, the teleplay differs significantly from the short stories of the same period, even while approaching similar themes. The latter contain surrealist elements, but they are written predominantly within the bounds of realistic representation, in naturalistic language, and take place in specific geographical locations (London's Soho and Finsbury Park; the River Ouse in East Anglia). This appearance of quotidian normality and domesticity serves to heighten the impact of the child rape, incest and castration which the narratives describe. The realism of the teleplay is subverted from the outset, which is also evident in the disparate collection of street names mentioned by Ruth: 'Outside here I cross the road and go down Bluebell Lane, and then I turn right into Kabul Avenue till I come to the roundabout, straight over and down Rawalpindi Road, past the Lamb and Flag and into Khyber Pass Road' (McEwan 1981: 29). The names actually refer to places McEwan visited after completing his Masters degree, but it is evident that he exploits television's inherently naturalistic aesthetic both to challenge its conventions and to defamiliarize the habitual viewing experience and expectation; in short, 'to kick over the traces' (McEwan 1981: 10).

The complex relation between teleplay and short story in McEwan's early career is thrown into particular relief by examining his adaptation of his own short story 'Solid Geometry' (1975). The tale is unique in McEwan's early phase for its concern for the status of an earlier, historical narrative. It is concerned with the failing relationship, in the present day, between Albert and Maisie, and the issues in sexual and gender politics this involves; it is also a mystery story, a gothic reworking of the Faustus story concerning the hubristic ambition of nineteenth-century scientists, an aspect of the tale which also questions the underlying gender politics of scientific knowledge. Albert is editing the diary of his great-grandfather, a Victorian amateur scientist, with a view to solving the mystery of the disappearance of his (the great-grandfather's) close friend and collaborator Maxwell, and, before him, of an 'obscure young mathematician from the University of Edinburgh, David Hunter' (McEwan 1981: 75). The disappearances seem to be connected to an obscure series of calculations relating to the possibility (logically impossible) of the 'plane without a surface' (McEwan 1981: 78), the discovery of which would 'invalidate everything fundamental to our science of solid geometry' (McEwan 1981: 75). As he becomes increasingly obsessed with his eccentric ancestor, Albert neglects Maisie, behaviour which prefigures the 'pathological rationality' of Joe Rose in *Enduring Love* (1997). In the penultimate scene he re-enacts the convoluted set of actions delineated in his great-grandfather's diary, and Maisie herself disappears. The final scene, which resolves the mystery of Maxwell's disappearance, returns us to the Victorian sage's study, in which the bemused great-grandfather simply *'sways slightly before the empty settee'* (McEwan 1981: 93). Central to the narrative is a jar that contains a penis acquired by Albert's great-grandfather at an auction – an ambivalent metaphor for power relationships between the sexes. The phallus stands both for Albert's admiration of masculinity and the dominance of male scientific discourse, but also for female power and the processes of castration and emasculation, which McEwan also explored in the story 'Pornography' (1978). Ironically, given McEwan's reputation at this time, his exploration was seen as introducing additional 'grotesque and bizarre sexual elements in the play' (McEwan, 1981: 14), presumably the discussion of the position of the clitoris, which love-making positions give the best orgasm, onanism and menstruation, which ultimately resulted in the BBC calling a halt to production. Twenty-five years later the story was filmed by Denis Lawson, starring Ewan McGregor and Ruth Miller, and the film premiered at the Edinburgh International Film Festival in 2002.

McEwan's changes to the story during the process of adaptation are subtle but revealing, and reinforce its underlying themes. First, there is a shift from the first-person, subjective narration by Albert to the objectification, or third-person narration, that comes with the camera's point of view. Whereas the reader of the story, to an extent tricked into, perhaps naively, 'identifying' with the narrator, is forced to make decisions about the ways in which Albert controls his story and the reader (and about how the great-grandfather's diaries in turn control Albert), the television audience is given a different but equally problematic position. Although the viewer stands outside the narrative, which would allow for a more independent position, the passivity associated with television as a 'hot medium' (in that it uses both sound and vision), on the contrary, would perhaps lead to a more inactive role, which is precisely what McEwan is attempting to challenge. Second, there is a clear shift from Albert's diegetic narrative (his narration of the historical actions) to the play's mimesis (it directly shows the actions) within the opening scene: whereas Albert narrates the great-grandfather's acquisition of the penis, the teleplay shows this, thus giving an urgency and immediacy to the event. Although the short story is unspecific about the details of the auction, the teleplay shows the great-grandfather entering a frenzied bidding war that not only suggests his own eccentricity, but also adumbrates Albert's own psychotic behaviour, thus linking the two men. However, whereas the story notes that the great-grandfather 'was keen' on also purchasing Lady Barrymore's private parts (McEwan 1976: 25), the teleplay shows Albert's relative being ushered away by Maxwell while protesting.

This shift from diegesis to mimesis heightens the sense of realism, which is then subtly undercut and problematized within the teleplay. The scene depicting mathematicians at a convention in Vienna in the late nineteenth century, for instance, ends with Maisie interrupting Albert, who is reading the diary account of the convention. When she knocks on Albert's door to bring him some tea, all the '*mathematicians, HUNTER included, drop their guise and become interrupted actors. They turn towards the door*' (McEwan 1981: 79). Although it appears that the present intrudes upon the past, the viewer actively engaged in the story should here assume that it is Albert's reading of the diary that is interrupted. Whereas in the story the great-grandfather's diary is a story buried within McEwan's text, the teleplay self-consciously emphasizes that it is the diary that acts as the bridge between the historical period and the contemporary narrative: '*The same diary. A different table, one hundred years later*' (McEwan 1981: 57). McEwan further foregrounds the diary as a connection between two worlds by giving directions such as the following: '*Through the medium of the diary we are back in* ALBERT*'s study*' (McEwan 1981: 76). Both the short story and teleplay thus argue, in a typical postmodern fashion, the principle that the past is a discursive construct only accessible through the great-grandfather's writing, which is interpreted subjectively by Albert. In both versions, then, Albert's editing of his great-grandfather's manuscripts is a way of recuperating an apocryphal narrative ignored by the mathematicians whose knowledge and scientific materialism is questioned: when Hunter disappears, '*The mathematicians are stunned.* [. . .] *Uproar*' (McEwan 1981: 83–84).

However, whereas the relationship between writing and reading as a creative and imaginative act is implicit within the short story, the teleplay portrays the writer-reader relationship as fantastic and magical. McEwan's teleplay is much clearer about the parallel between, on the one hand, writing and reading as imaginative acts of creation and, on the other hand, the plane without surface theory as an imaginative form of the 'de-creative'. Yet the visualization of the disappearance of Hunter, Maxwell and, finally, Maisie defies the rules of the screen: '*He lies on the couch and with* GOODMAN*'s help puts his body through a series of contortions. These must seem improbable – use tight close-ups and other people's legs!*' (McEwan 1981: 83) Similarly, the transition from the present to the past, set up with a special effect rendered by '*The page glows* *whiter . . .'* (McEwan 1981: 60), suggests McEwan at one and the same time exploits television's technical possibilities and overcomes the problem of the improbable: television's 'dazzling electronic techniques were on hand [. . .] in moving us from one time level to another through the medium of the glowing page of the diary' (McEwan 1981: 13).

The levels of the improbable are foregrounded also by the important rewriting of the original story's ending, which alters the narrative structurally, but obscures its historical concerns. In the short story Maisie is folded into the 'plane without a surface' by Albert, but the play ends with Maxwell's disappearance in the great-grandfather's study. This intervention perfects the structural symmetry between the relationships of, on the one hand, Albert and Maisie and, on the other, the great-grandfather and Maxwell, but it also stresses the historical continuities between the great-grandfather and Albert, and Maxwell and Maisie, as characters. Thus, again McEwan uses the mirror as a metafictional device that flaunts the artifice of the structural neatness, simultaneously exposing the anti-mimetic nature of the representation. McEwan's adaptation is useful, then, for offering him the opportunity to emulate his own material, while it also confronts him with the question of how to address and structure historical reality in relationship to the present – a question he was to explore in a more directly political context in the early eighties.

McEwan's Historical 'Turn': *The Imitation Game*

Towards the end of the seventies, McEwan refocused his ambitions by writing a full-length television film, *The Imitation Game* (1981). This play forms an important 'hinge' in McEwan's wider *oeuvre*, because it allowed him to break away from both the solipsistic protagonists and narrow subject matter, and the temptation towards experimentation, that were part of the early writing. McEwan also exploited the possibilities offered by the feature film, the more intricate plotting and development of characters, in order to break out of his engagement solely with the private, domestic sphere and to refocus on historical subject matter and public concerns, and he later acknowledged that this 'was the novel [he] had wanted to write' (McEwan 1981: 20).

McEwan's ingenious transplantation of a contemporary issue – the possibility of women's emancipation – into a past setting complicates the topical narrative of feminism, suggesting that the emergence of new aspirations and hopes which attended what has been called 'first wave feminism', in fact involved contradiction and even regression in the specific historical context of the war. In his introduction to the teleplay McEwan argued: 'The Women's Movement had presented ways of looking at the world, both its present and its past, that were at once profoundly dislocating and infinite in possibility' (McEwan 1981: 16).

The play opens in the summer of 1940, in 'the modest, suburban house of the Raines, on the edge of a small southern town' (McEwan 1981: 99), amid widespread unease about the possibility of a German invasion, a public discontent that forms an allegory for the personal aspirations of the protagonist, the piano player Cathy Raine. She abandons a job in a munitions factory '[m]aking shells and bombs' (McEwan 1981: 101) in order to join the Auxiliary Territorial Service (ATS), which, despite its promise of gender equality during wartime service, entails only an illusive appeasement of the women who threaten to invade the ranks and privileges of male soldiers. Although Cathy imagines herself as 'our special operator behind enemy lines' (McEwan 1981: 129), she never makes it beyond her role as wire operator writing down Morse codes for her male colleagues to decipher. After a scrap with a publican, who assumes she is a prostitute using his public house to pick up clients, Cathy ends up doing general duties at Bletchley Park, the centre of Allied code breaking operations symbolic of male-dominated knowledge and power. Cathy's attempt to enter this male bastion, and to obtain access to knowledge, is thwarted after a sexual encounter with a young code breaker, John Turner, who might have been able to assist her in this objective, leads to her incarceration. The war, which has often subsequently been represented as a period of women's emancipation, and which at the time seemed to offer so much liberatory potential for women, in this case effectively perpetuates, and even exacerbates, the opposition between the sexes.

Cathy is frustrated by the lack of opportunity to use her talents and intelligence for an active rather than a support role. Women must remain passive, she says later, because it creates the illusion that invests wars with their moral justification: 'The men want the women to stay out of the fighting so they can give it meaning. As long as we're on the outside and give our support and don't kill, women make the war possible [. . .] something the men can feel tough about' (McEwan 1981: 174). Through the play's conceptual pairing of conflict in gender-based social spheres and a martial war – the eponymous 'imitation game' analogous to the one that Turner describes, which involves 'a triangulated relationship of strategic deception and assistance between men and women' (McEwan 1981: 153) – McEwan dramatizes the incongruity between men, who are able to project and live out their fantasy within reality, and women, who find a great divide between their reality and their imagination.

This conflict reaches a crisis precisely at the moment when Cathy attempts to gain sexual knowledge. Instead of remaining passive after agreeing to Turner's clumsy proposal of sexual intercourse that will lead to her defloration, Cathy becomes the aggressor. For Turner, her actions appear inconsistent with his image of her as a virgin, a fact that owes as much to his own virginity as to his perception of sexual stereotypes, and this breach of the sexual order leads to an embarrassing moment of impotence. The inversion of the gendered innocence-experience dynamic between men and women resurfaces in *The Innocent* (1990), while the disastrous consequences of an unsuccessful deflowering adumbrates the wedding night of Florence and Edward in *On Chesil Beach* (2007).

However, here McEwan, for the first time in his career, gives his material a complex historical dimension. He engaged in extensive historical research into Alan Turing and Bletchley Park. The title of the play is derived from Turing's experiment on artificial intelligence, the eponymous 'imitation game', which, as Dominic Head notes, is 'underpinned by a preconceived expectation of gender traits [and] clearly a metaphor for the imposition of set gender roles' (Head 2007: 55). Yet the title also indicates that McEwan's screenwriting again draws attention to the artifice of its composition by means of metafictional commentary. McEwan thus declares Aristotle's classic concept of imitation as part of the construction of realism to be merely a game, and, as *imitatio* is enshrined in Western rhetorical traditions, he undercuts the play with an anti-realistic subtext. Indeed, the title points to McEwan's interest in natural history, and in particular to a book that McEwan has acknowledged he admires, which had a tremendous impact upon public debates in the late seventies, namely, Richard Dawkins' *The Selfish Gene* (1976). Dawkins argues that human behaviour can be explained as an interplay between ruthless selfishness and calculating altruism, driven by our genetically programmed need to disseminate our genes. We hear echoes of Dawkins, for instance, in a shocking speech when an ATS officer states to soldiers:

> Women will always reciprocate once their trust is given. It is a natural instinct with them to live up to what someone whom they like thinks of them. It should be remembered that 'rumour' plays a bigger part with women than with men. Their capacity for magnifying and altering any rumour which reaches them is incredible [. . .] Tears are natural with some women, and are frequently genuine [. . .] The worst type is the woman who can turn tears on and off, according to the effect gained. With these an attitude of slightly amused detachment will work best, as it gets under their self-esteem. But do not let them get away with it because they cry. Women have a fairly good instinct for justice and respect it, even at their own expense. (McEwan 1981: 124–5)

Building upon Dawkins' assertion that 'ideas propagate themselves by imitation' through imitative units which Dawkins terms 'memes' (Hutcheon 2006: 176), one of the key theorists of the postmodern condition in an Anglo-American context, Linda Hutcheon, explains this idea in relationship to textual imitation and transmission:

> Memes are not high-fidelity replicators: they change with time, for meme transmission is subject to constant mutation. Stories too propagate themselves when they catch on; adaptations – as both repetition and variation – are

their form of replication. Evolving by cultural selection, traveling stories adapt to local cultures, just as populations of organisms adapt to local environments. (Hutcheon 2006: 177)

Whereas Cathy seeks to alter her environment so that it can accommodate her desires, her true challenge, according to Dawkins, is to adapt her desires to the context. After Cathy is locked up in her cell, she begins to read the score of her favourite piano piece, Mozart's *Fantasia, K475*: '*We watch* CATHY *from a jailor's point of view – through the barred window of her cell. She reads the score. The music plays*' (McEwan 1981: 175). We leave Cathy forced to retreat into the realm of the imaginary, literally and figuratively imprisoned and excluded from reality.

The Anti-Thatcherite Triptych: *The Ploughman's Lunch*, *The Good Son* and *Sour Sweet*

After 'The Imitation Game', McEwan begins to politicize the relationship between the present and the past by producing a series of works that could be considered a triptych directed against Thatcher and Thatcherism. The title of the first work, *The Ploughman's Lunch*, refers to a grand historical deception: the invention by advertisers of the cold meal comprising a piece of (local) cheese, pickle, bread and butter, as a reminder of an authentic pastoral English heritage. This '[t]raditional English fare' (McEwan 1989: 106) forms 'a controlling metaphor for self-serving fabrications of the past' (McEwan 1989: 26). The film is set during the Falklands War – a detail incorporated during the production process to root the film into its period. Another sign of the filmmakers' engagement with the contemporary and the mixing of fact with fiction occurred when the crew illegally shot scenes during the actual Tory Party conference in Brighton. McEwan remembers:

> [W]e sneaked in under the auspices of another organization. [. . .] I was amazed how easily we could insinuate our actors. Jonathan Pryce was very bold in walking under the platform where Michael Heseltine was speaking (no one recognised him as an actor), and doing it about six or seven times, since we had to do several takes. (Haffenden 1985: 185)

Whether McEwan's 'actor' refers to Jonathan Pryce's Penfield or to Heseltine is not clear, but the directness and urgency of the film's portrayal of the cultural and socio-political climate in the early eighties is striking.

The play narrated the story of a BBC journalist, James Penfield, who is writing a revisionist account of the 1956 Suez crisis, a debacle commonly regarded as the moment when the end of Empire, already begun with the loss of overseas dominions at the end of the war, and the decolonization of India, became vividly apparent. Penfield does not uncover historical facts but engenders 'facts' which accord with his own yuppie ambitions by expunging from the historical record 'all the moralising and talk of national humiliation that is now the standard line on Suez' (McEwan 1989: 5). The film appropriates Suez as a means of criticizing the Thatcherite ideology of greed, materialism and individuality, with its concomitant but vacuous revival of 'moral' values, another example of a fabricated tradition.

Penfield's falsification of the historical record diminishes him ethically, and the flaws in his revision of the Suez crisis serve also to expose the moral and ideological failings of a contemporary justification of the Falklands War. His lack of fidelity to history is reproduced in his personal life. In a move away from the Oedipal psychology that characterized the early work, Penfield neglects his dying mother in order to pursue an ambitious young woman, the successful television researcher Susan Barrington. Nonetheless, the film does not simply represent Penfield as a lone egotist or as a foil for other characters' goodness, as such a schematic account might suggest, but positions him as no better or worse than a whole cast of corrupt characters. Barrington herself has little moral or political scruple when it comes to the position of other working women. During a dispute about women's rights in the workplace, Barrington votes against her female colleagues:

> [I]n many ways I'm right behind the women's movement. But sometimes I wish they'd get on with it instead on moaning on [. . .]. [As] a human *being* and a *television* researcher, as a *professional*, I could just sense they'd got it all wrong. I could see there were two paths I could go down, power and not-power. Down the no-power path was lots of sisterly feeling, masochism and frustration. Down the other path, I could keep working. So of course I voted with the men and the other women all resigned. I think they're mad, don't you? (McEwan 1989: 41)

Barrington's speech, which reinforces the stereotype of women as 'mad', cleverly ends in a pernicious rhetorical question which prevents James from answering. This undercutting of male power by silencing the man is paradoxically reinforced by her siding with men and rationality: Barrington's speech emasculates whilst ironically denying any grounds of solidarity with her female colleagues.

Barrington's refusal to sleep with Penfield drives him, however, into the arms of her mother, the famous historian Ann Barrington, who had years before abandoned a book on Suez. Ann is one of a number of characters, including anti-war protesters at an airbase in Norfolk, who have not wholly surrendered their idealism in favour of Penfield and Susan Barrington's greed and individualism. In 1985, McEwan said of the character: 'I do still see Ann Barrington as a sympathetic character, one based loosely in her ideas around E. P. Thompson, but with the great difference that E. P. Thompson has in fact moved in the opposite direction, from theory to practice' (Haffenden 1985: 188–9). Indeed, Ann emphasizes the value of cultural memory and a deep historical awareness within all citizens:

> If we leave the remembering to the historians then the struggle is already lost. Everyone must have a memory, everyone needs to be a historian. In this country, for example, we're in danger of losing hard-won freedoms by dozing off in a perpetual present. (McEwan 1989: 47)

While Ann's distrust of historians as curators of cultural memory reminds us that the past affects everyone, her idealism is also curiously complicit with the manipulative actions of the other characters, including Penfield and his aptly named publisher (and prefiguration of Charles Darke in *The Child in Time*), Gold. Her analysis of Thatcherism as symbolic of a post-historical condition, a 'perpetual present', is itself flawed because the present is in fact harder to find or capture through increased acceleration, and her longing to rewrite history to shift the emphasis and alignment of perspective mirrors Penfield's own actions. However, Susan's authority as a moral beacon in the film is undercut in other ways: not only does she admit that her position as a research professor is motivated by the desire for bourgeois comfort, but her seduction of Penfield is itself driven perversely by his resemblance to her dead brother (McEwan 1989: 101–2).

Rather than asking viewers to identify with these characters, McEwan seems to be provoking us into a wholesale rejection of Thatcherite ideology, and he represents Thatcherite Britain as a culture deprived of any redeeming qualities. On the one hand, the representation of yuppie types such as Penfield, Hancock and Barrington satirizes their modes of strategic partnership, and exposes the danger involved in their manipulation of history. On the other hand, Ann Barrington's belief that an objective history is nonetheless retrievable is undermined by McEwan's ambivalent representation of her character. *The Ploughman's Lunch* insists that, although history needs to be recovered and rewritten constantly to take account of our changing times and perspectives on the past, and although that it is every citizen's duty to remember, these actual acts of retrieval and narrative are always fraught with difficulties and uncertainties. In the penultimate scene Gold proposes a toast to Penfield's successful book:

> GOLD   It's everything we wanted. A very good read. A terrific piece of work. So, here's to you and Suez.
> JAMES   And to history. (McEwan 1989: 118)

Under Thatcher, history, memory and time have become commodities that can be packaged, manipulated, and shaped for financial gain, which is reinforced by the final scene, when we find Penfield at the funeral of his mother. While his father is 'immobile with grief', James remains 'expressionless' as he *'glances at his watch'* (McEwan 1989: 118). This grotesque ending suggests the dehumanizing effects of Thatcherism upon the social fabric, its corrosive impact on traditional family structures, on social and sexual relationships, but it also brings to the fore a fundamental change in our experience of the world through the death of social connectedness, and the commodification of time, which is now at the mercy of free-market forces.

Mourning also lies at the heart of *The Good Son*, completed by McEwan in 1987, which continues with the political tone of *The Ploughman's Lunch*, albeit in a less satirical mode. The film tells the story of an only son, Mark Evans, who, following the loss of his mother to cancer, stays with his cousin's family. This family is coping with a loss of their own, the death of the eldest son in mysterious circumstances. The aunt/mother, Susan Evans, in particular, is inconsolable. Mark's cousin, Henry Evans, soon involves Mark in a series of increasingly dangerous, and ultimately deadly, games, which include threatening to shoot a dog, throwing a life-size doll on to a busy road, and Henry's 'accidental' attempted murder of his sister, Connie, by making her skate on thin ice. These events lead to a solution to the mystery of the boy's death.

McEwan's screenplay provides a characteristically gothic critique of the forms of masculinity and materialism which dominate middle-class family life in Reagan's free-market America. Not only does Mark's father desert his son during the mourning process to 'close a deal in Tokyo', but Henry's father, Wallace, urges his wife to give up her dead son's bedroom, which she has turned into a 'museum', and to 'get on with life' in order to project a comfortable image of the family to small-town America, the locale in which the film is set.

Henry's lust for torture and killing also forms a dark parallel to the domineering and aggressive, deregulated capitalism of the 1980s, whilst also reflecting the preoccupation with serial killers in literature and films of the 1990s – including Bret Easton Ellis's *American Psycho* (1991) and Jonathan Demme's *Silence of the Lambs* (1991). McEwan's script also anticipates the transgression of another taboo, namely the recent phenomenon of the killing of children by children, such as the murder of the Merseyside toddler, James Bulger, in 1993; the massacres at American high schools such as Columbine (1999); and the shooting of 11-year-old Rhys Jones in Liverpool (2007).

The Good Son was critically unsuccessful for a variety of reasons. The piece was rewritten to suit the commercial requirements of its Hollywood producers, which banalized the film's thematics. McEwan withdrew from the project because of the predominant influence of *Home Alone* star Macaulay Culkin and his family, whose demands distorted McEwan's original objectives, trivializing his complex investigation of evil by appropriating the film as a vehicle for redirecting Culkin's stereotype as the goofy innocent to a darker character. The film's most significant difficulty, however, lay in the way the complex and challenging renegotiation of the classic Oedipal scenario in McEwan's original script was destroyed by the realistic aesthetic of the movie, and the absence of a 'knowingness' demanded by the intricate narrative. The disruption of the stable Oedipal triangle (see Claire Colebrook's analysis of *The Innocent* in the next chapter, pp. 43–56) caused by the death of Mark's mother is restored by finding a substitute mother figure in his aunt. *The Good Son* thus continues the psychological paradigm of 'Jack Flea' and *The Ploughman's Lunch*, in which the protagonists also exchange their mothers for alternative maternal figures. This in turn destroys the Oedipal relationships within Henry's family, and opens up the possibility of rescuing the movie from the simplistic reading of Henry and Mark as archetypal Oedipal children fighting for the sole claim over their mother (figure): the film in fact goes beyond this logic to express ideas about innocence and experience, justice and punishment that precede familial relationship. Indeed, at the climax of the film, which mocks the Hollywood cliffhanger cliché by presenting it in a bizarre context, the mother is confronted with the counterintuitive choice between acknowledging Henry's crimes and saving him. She chooses the good son, and does so against an Oedipal psychology that blinds us to potential harmful elements and dark issues within the family, society, and history, and which must be destroyed.

Soursweet (1988) returns us to McEwan's comparison between writing in a different form and moving to a different country. McEwan's adaptation of Timothy Mo's original novel, *Sour Sweet* (1982), occupies a distinctive place within McEwan's *oeuvre* as his only extended engagement with the problems of ethnic identity. Mo's original novel narrates the story of a Chinese family, the Chens, who in the 1960s emigrate to northwest London's Burnt Oak, where they open a Chinese takeaway restaurant. They soon run into trouble with another 'family', the Chinese mafia, the Triads, who control Chinatown through extortion and physical brutality, with an ultimately tragic outcome for the Chens.

Despite portraying himself as 'the hooligan builder' who aggressively converts Mo's novel, 'a splendid mid-nineteenth century mansion', into 'a roofless shack' (McEwan 1988: v), McEwan remains faithful to the spirit of Mo's novel and its realistic mode. There are some minor but significant changes, however, that draw attention to McEwan's acuity as a screenwriter. McEwan contracts the two words of the original title, which foregrounds both the novel and the film as a tragic-comedy, re-emphasizing the familiar theme of food as a culturally specific way of assimilation: while the protagonists Chen and Lily open a Chinese takeaway and show no interest in the British society around them, her sister, Mui, is pregnant with an illegitimate child by a British man, and, at the end of the novel, opens a fish and chip shop. *Soursweet* is concerned, then, with the problems of socio-cultural integration and adaptation that Asian immigrants undergo in post-war Britain.

Family is another important topos within *Soursweet*, and it presents a problem that McEwan has frequently explored in his own work. Rather than focusing on the three generations of the Chen family living under one roof in relationship to the Chinatown community and its underworld, McEwan's script foregrounds the relationship between Lily and Chen as the vehicle for narrating the story. This alteration is established by McEwan's incorporation of a sequence that depicts the Chens' wedding at the film's opening, a watershed moment when the couple change their social roles, but also move abroad and become geographically divorced from their wider family circle and culture. Yet, due to the structural symmetry that exists in the novel between, on the one hand, the Chen family and, on the other hand, the Triad 'family', McEwan's focus on Lily and Chen forces him to reduce the role of the Chinese gang, by focusing on the actions of individual gang members such as Jackie Fung, Red Cudgel and Night Brother. One further effect of this opening sequence is a heightened sense of the characters' origins, which in turn clarifies the narrative's trajectory.

McEwan also set the film in the contemporary period. This temporal change is made clear at the outset, when Chen announces they have been granted permission to move to the United Kingdom: 'The Secretary of State, in exercise of the powers conferred by the British Nationality Act 1981, hereby grants this certificate of naturalization to the person named below who shall be a British Citizen from the date of this certificate' (McEwan 1988: 5). One of the issues McEwan's screenplay highlights, then, is the discrepancy between the official and the unofficial, gradual and sometimes unsuccessful inscription of the immigrant into Western culture via their economic and cultural assimilation, which involves the entire trajectory of the film. The narrative about opening a takeaway thus inadvertently becomes a part of a tragi-comic, and critical, investigation of how a family from an ethnic minority group famous for its entrepreneurial spirit inscribes itself into modernity, but also of how, in Chen's case, this may have destructive consequences. Similar issues are foregrounded by, for instance, Hanif Kureishi's screenplay for Stephen Frears's *My Beautiful Launderette* (1985), and McEwan's screenplay should, together with *The Ploughman's Lunch* and *The Good Son*, be considered as marking a specific moment within Britain's wider cultural examinations and criticism of Thatcher's Britain and Reagan's America.

In conclusion, his screenwriting has been of great importance to the development of McEwan as writer. The playful, postmodern work for television in the seventies allowed him to redirect his creative energies at a point in time when the possibilities of fiction seemed exhausted. The screenwriting in the early eighties formed a catalyst within McEwan's trajectory towards the later work, with its interest in history, and its continuous aptitude in exploring forms of realism. This change takes place not only *in* screenwriting but also *because of* screenwriting. In his Foreword to *Soursweet* McEwan stated that a 'novelist may play

God with imaginary characters and situation. The screen writer has the chance to play God with the real world' (McEwan 1988: vi). It seems, however, that his experimentation within, and mastery of, the screen-writing, and his subsequent discovery of its limits, expedited a fruit-ful return to the possibilities offered by fiction as both a freedom of expression, and an expression of freedom.

CHAPTER THREE

The Innocent as Anti-Oedipal Critique of Cultural Pornography

CLAIRE COLEBROOK

'The lost child was everyone's property.'
— Ian McEwan, *The Child in Time* (1987)

Chapter Summary: This chapter explores the meanings of childhood in *The Innocent* (1990) by looking at the ways in which the problem of innocence — understood as a collective fantasy — informs McEwan's work. *The Innocent*'s images of childhood are read in the light of critical theories of cultural pornography and anti-Freudian psychoanalysis. McEwan's fiction argues that as long as we see adult life as suffering from the loss of an original innocence, we will also always imagine politics as a relation to a master or authority. McEwan also presents the work of art as the consequence of a drive for an organic totality that is childish in its desire for godlike control, and which therefore prevents rather than offers self-knowledge. Therefore, McEwan is not a conservative or reactionary author. His anti-Oedipal narratives are a diagnosis of conservatism, which McEwan subverts by historicizing and politicizing the image of the child. In doing so, he deconstructs oppositions between adult and child, between knowing and not-knowing, and between science and art, by foregrounding the relationship between subjectivity, subjection and the cultural pornography of the child.

Cultural Pornography: an Introduction to the Geography of Childhood

Although much of McEwan's work is concerned with innocence, *The Child in Time* (1987) and *The Innocent* (1989) are explicitly about what it means to be a child and what it means to lose one. The latter novel offers a profound critique of what could be called the cultural pornography of the child, an idea earlier explored through the prism of Surrealism in

Chapter One (see pp. 15–23). I will argue that *The Innocent* prefigures in intensified form a collective fantasy that we have witnessed in the British media over the past decade: the images of missing or murdered children, often displayed alongside images of grieving parents or suspected perpetrators. In the case of Madeleine McCann (2007), for example, the media offered viewers posters that could be downloaded and placed in positions of prominence. Posters were displayed in areas as unlikely as rural Scotland and suburban Melbourne, as though it were possible through repetition and display of solidarity to create a form of vigilance – after the event – that might have prevented the initial trauma.

Such images effect a multiple investment in childhood as at once perfectly innocent – a world unto itself of unreflective joy, rendered poignantly in the photographs of abducted children whose gaze (prior to their loss) can bear no intimation of their now tragic disappearance – and horrifically fragile. There is a simple temporality at work in the intense display in the media of the lost child: the repeated, circulated, downloaded images are rendered ceremonial and funereal through practices of mourning and experienced as final, frozen and spectral – presenting a paradoxical mode of life as at once fully open and yet tragically unfulfilled. The collective viewing of these images of missing children becomes a form of 'working through': following an irreparable loss, the repetition of a mourned absence allows for an eventual recognition, if not restoration, of the damage done to the psyche.

Cultural, or social, pornography is distinctly different from child pornography, which purveys erotic images of children for private, secret and devalued enjoyment. The term cultural pornography describes the ways in which a certain image, fantasy and structure of the child frames our experience of time, history, cultural difference, violence and normativity. Cultural pornography of the child is a public obsession with figures of infant innocence that is also permanently threatened by the intrusion of an adult world of suspicion. Jennifer Wicke defines social pornography as the public and legitimized circulation of pornographic images that has become increasingly intense in a putative and moralizing opposition to the threat of pornography. She already gestures to the way in which the anxiety surrounding the sexualization of children, and the adult's relation to that sexuality, has allowed an increase in the dissemination of images of vulnerable, threatened and abused children:

> Social pornography is the best phrase [. . .] for the substitutive collective pornographies our culture produces; social pornography is the name for the pornographic fantasies the society collectively engenders and then mass-culturally disseminates, usually in the cause of anti-pornography. The past decade's fascination with explicit and imaginary child sexual abuse is the best example, although there are many others, not the least of which is the public discussion of pornography, which allows for pornographic enactment in the most explicit if mediated forms. (Wicke 1991: 54)

Wicke's work is directed against an academic and high-brow moral critique of the passive consumption of reifying images because the intensity of cultural pornography, as a mode different from the conventional meaning of pornography, is intrinsically tied to its publicity and moral rectitude. Far from being a form of therapy that would repair a wound in our collective psyche, we at one and the same time enjoy the image of the innocent, unselfconscious and temporally frozen gaze of the child *and* we wallow in the pleasure of moral elevation as we view the horrific possibility of a corrupter or intruder into this necessarily fragile world.

This curious and complex figure of the child allows us to open McEwan's work away from the private realm of family relationships to the public realms of politics and history. Deleuze's and Guattari's criticisms of psychoanalysis and ideology in *Anti-Oedipus* (1972) insist that politics, in the sense of a power that produces an imaginary dimension which structures society and masks oppression, begins with the world of the child. For Deleuze and Guattari, *and* for McEwan, there is no such thing as the dutiful Oedipal child who experiences life and history as a series of familial submissions and repetitions. Instead, the familial world of the child already involves ethnicity, history and culture, and the child is therefore directly political.

This makes McEwan a profoundly anti-Oedipal writer, because his work, at the level of form and narration, displays a libidinal economy that goes beyond the imaginary and the familial. Placed within McEwan's work is the Freudian image of bounded organic life, what Freud refers to as 'His Majesty the Baby':

> The child shall have things better than his parents: he shall not be subject to the necessities which they have recognized as dominating life. Illness, death, renunciation of enjoyment, restrictions on his own will shall not touch him; the laws of nature, like those of society, are to be abrogated in his favour; he is really to be the center and heart of creation, 'His Majesty the Baby', as we once fancied ourselves to be. [. . .] Parental love, which is so touching and at bottom so childish, is nothing but parental narcissism born again. (Freud 1959: 48–49)

McEwan's work exploits this curious, seductive and paradoxical Eros by tying the fantasy of the work of art to a fantasy of childhood. The child gives us the image of a world closed in upon itself, not yet subject to the imperatives of normativity, history, self-consciousness or the violence of competitive adult life. In *The Child in Time*, this vision is voiced by one of the members of a sub-committee on reading and writing, who states:

> 'By forcing literacy on to children between the ages of five and seven, we introduce a degree of abstraction which shatters the unity of the child's world view, drives a fatal wedge between the word and the thing that the

word names [. . .] It is in effect, Mr Chairman, nothing less than a banish-
ment from the Garden, for its effects are lifelong.' (McEwan 1988: 76–7)

The work of art – including, and, perhaps, in particular, the narratives
that give sense to and order the world – offers itself as a well-wrought
whole, and creates a pause in the chaotic movement of time and intensity to form a point of equilibrium.

However, it is precisely this Freudian and Oedipalized image of life
that McEwan's process of narration challenges, for the child is not simply the object of nostalgic and parental fantasy; the child lives its position within the family as historically, politically and libidinally open.
In other words, McEwan's narratives are fascinated by the image of a
world that is blissfully and autonomously enclosed, while, at the same
time, they tear such images of organic unity apart.

McEwan's destruction of organicism intersects with a number of formal features and motifs, the most important of which is narration: the
narrative voice that presents a sequence of events also interprets those
events from a later point of view. *The Innocent* is retrospectively framed
by the postscript which narrates Leonard's return to Berlin in 1987, from
which point the narrative looks back on a (putative) moment of plenitude from a fallen present, in which the loss in the present is recognized as having existed potentially in the past. This is not actually so:
temporality is established retroactively: the lived past is not closed, but
it is, through continual revisitation and memory, constantly disclosing
aspects of contamination and rupture. Childhood innocence is never
lived – by the child – *as* innocent, but constructed as such afterwards.
Paradise can be recognized as prelapsarian and completely self-present
only after its loss.

However, McEwan's texts do not create a temporality in which the
origin is only lived as original after its loss or absence. On the contrary, the retroactively posited and fantasmatic origin is, in its constant
reinvention, invocation and re-living, shown to harbour an enigmatic
and seductive malevolence. The clearest example of this we find in
Atonement (2001), where Briony's desire to narrate, to tell stories, is simultaneously typical of the infantile sense of omnipotence that does not yet
acknowledge a world of negotiation and others, *and* an object of desir-
ing spectacle for the adults viewing and reading narrations (including
the reader of *Atonement*), as Alistair Cormack explores in Chapter Five
(see pp. 70–82). McEwan connects art with narcissism, but not in the
classic Freudian manner whereby the difference between the artist's
fantasy and that of the everyday individual is that the artist manages
to give a form to his desire and present his narcissism in a consumable
form so that others can experience it. Rather, the artwork is an image of
self-devolving unity and an image of poised time, where the relations
among elements are internal, not part of or subject to a world other than
itself. Contemplation of the artwork is contemplation of a closure that

every subject who has lost the world of childhood lives. In *Atonement*, as elsewhere, McEwan shows the ways in which narration, composition or performance present themselves as alluring images of a wholeness and organicism that has liberated itself from a world of relations, negotiation and ambiguity.

Therefore, McEwan's fiction demonstrates that confusing childhood with biological infancy is missing the true sense, and problem, of childhood innocence. As *The Child in Time* and *The Innocent* show, that state of innocence is made possible only through a strangely retroactive temporality, a seductive relation of submission, and a dialectic between narrative progression and regressive fascination. Whereas *The Child in Time* presents the loss of the child and its connection with politics literally – for the central character's search for his abducted daughter is intertwined with an account of a government enquiry into child development – *The Innocent* presents childhood as a transcendental condition: we are always children in relation to authority, and authority establishes its force through producing fantasies of subjection. These conditions allow McEwan to pose the problem of infancy in a historical sense: just as the child is a fantasmatic structure of adulthood, so understanding oneself as human is intertwined with a mythic narrative of human, historical and civilized progression.

In *The Innocent*, the problem of innocence – understood as a collective fantasy – informs McEwan's other reflections on seduction, transgression, time and narrative. McEwan offers an aesthetic challenge to Oedipal organicism that is deeply political: narrative is an alluring wholeness that precludes our drive for comprehension, presenting a world unto itself that resists all appropriation and demystification. In *The Innocent*, McEwan intertwines and juxtaposes the drive to mastery through a totalizing systematization (science, narration, communication) with the resistance of that which holds itself apart from comprehension and consumption. He continually presents the work of art at once as the consequence of a drive for totalization that is childish in its desire for godlike control, and as resulting in an object or wholeness that, as McEwan acknowledges in the interview included in this volume (see pp. 123–24), remains outside self-knowledge, self-narration and temporal synthesis. McEwan's writing deconstructs the opposition between knowing and not-knowing, between science and art, between adult and child, between sexuality and innocence, not so much because he fragments the subject but because he foregrounds the profound relation between subjectivity, subjection and the cultural pornography of the child.

The Innocent: Europe versus America

There is a tradition in modern English literature of exploring the structure of childhood through relations of distance, relations that are also

historical, sexual and class-based. The clearest example of this fig-
ural complex we find in the fiction of Henry James, who presents the
new world of America as, in part, the regaining of the state of childhood. However, this regained state is always viewed, nostalgically
and longingly, from the point of view of a European adult who simultaneously yearns for that historically unburdened naiveté, while, at
the same time, being disturbed by the tendency for that innocence to
fall all too easily into the corruptions of a late capitalism of unbridled
immediacy.

James often sublates this opposition between Europe and America –
between the tired Old World laden with history, morality and propriety, and the new world that is nothing more than material for exchange
and self-promotion – with the figure of woman or of the innocent
child. In *Daisy Miller* (1879), James presents the figure of the girl who
is alluring precisely because of her seeming ignorance of issues of propriety. Continental Europe acts as a site of an encounter between the
historic and class-conscious normativity of England and the liberated
world of American capital; Daisy is neither the restricted adult of manners who can only view the world as it is seen by morally-burdened
others *nor* the vulgar American whose world is so new and devoid of
sense that it is nothing more than a commodity. Daisy is seen as cap-
tivatingly unaware of social codes; she is incapable of acting improp-
erly precisely *because* she fails to see the class and sexual connotations
that would render her actions – her spontaneity and artlessness – as
vulgar. Class identity in this scenario is a profoundly political phenomenon: for class is not a category of social analysis so much as an
experience of *proper place* – one's already determined position in a
system of social meaning that transcends any action or perception of
the individual.

The historical context of *The Innocent*, set in post-war Berlin amid the
secret Anglo-American partnership that spies on the Communists by
tunnelling into the Russian sector in order to undermine Soviet communication, marks the point at which the child-adult relation between
Europe and America is reversed. Once seen as the very figure of a childlike origin of the world in relation to a historically over-burdened Europe,
America is now closer to being a street-wise and awakened adolescent
enlivened by knowledge acquisition. English culture is now presented
as being in a position of childlike subjection, puzzlement and seduction
in relation to the adult world of post-war America, which has become
self-creative, liberal and immediately intimate: 'He was suddenly a son
again, not a lover. He was a child' (McEwan 1990: 157). The early days in
Berlin of the protagonist, Leonard Marnham, are marked by a series of
adjustments in his appearance that aim to reduce the difference between
his received English formality and the Americans' open bravado: 'Like
Glass, Russell wore his shirt open to reveal a high-necked white T-shirt
underneath. As they pulled away, Leonard fingered his tie knot in the

darkness. He decided against removing the tie in case the two Americans had already noticed him wearing it' (McEwan 1990: 37). When Leonard returns to London he experiences the propriety and grammar of English convention, making him yearn for the free self-creation of America, embodied in his superior, the foul-mouthed Bob Glass: 'Leonard missed the near rudeness of the American's speech, the hammer-blow of intimacy, the absence of the modifiers and hesitancies that were supposed to mark out a reasonable gentleman' (McEwan 1990: 155).

The Innocent ties this position of infantile subjection to the specific modes of post-war politics and sexuality. The English characters, and Englishness in general, occupy a position of unwitting, dull and subjected naivety, while American characters and culture seem to open out to the future, to sexuality and to knowledge. In the tunnel in which electronics engineer Markham works, though built by the English, American technology is used to decode and convey messages, messages picked up and passed on by the English, but which only the Americans can read, and this because of technology which they have kept secret. As John MacNamee explains to Leonard:

> 'So, very generously, we let the Americans into our tunnel, gave them facilities, let them make use of our taps. And you know what? They didn't even tell us about Nelson's invention. They were taking the stuff back to Washington and reading the clear text while we were knocking our brains trying to break the codes [. . .] Now that we're sharing this project, they've let us in on the secret. But only the outline, mark you, not the details. That's why I can only give you the simplest account'. (McEwan 1990: 93)

This is the structure of time and experience in *The Innocent*, where Leonard receives information regarding relative disclosure and secrecy, at once being privileged with knowledge while also knowing that he remains distanced from the full story, held back by his American colleagues who are sexually, politically and technologically dominant.

It is only when he has left England that Leonard views himself as an adult reader, but he does so both with a sense of simulation *and* with the sense that the adulthood he is feigning comes from a primarily English past: 'He could never read a paper, especially this one [*The Times*], without feeling he was imitating someone else, or in training for adulthood' (McEwan 1990: 146). One is always a child taking on the signs of adulthood, knowledge and mastery, but those signifiers of adult sophistication are also always those of the child. McEwan not only locates the fantasy and structure of childish innocence as an ideal that can be possessed by wistful adults, who look back upon a time of unself-consciousness that is no longer possible. He also sees the idea of adult knowledge, mastery and sexual competence as itself fantasmatic and political, and constantly traversed by unmastered and atavistic motifs that return us to a past and aggressiveness not our own.

Modern Power Structures of Infantilization

The structure of Cold War politics in *The Innocent*, very much like today's War on Terror, is formed around secrecy. The world is lived as threatened, monitored, and as subject to a logic one can never fully grasp. *That* there is potential violence or destruction of one's being is lived as certain, but just who or what might embody or represent that possible transgression is unknowable. *The Innocent* at once presents a new political logic of secrecy and seduction at the same time as this specifically twentieth-century phenomenon is offered as an actualization of a deeper and more essential logic of subjection. Politics is not a public domain of disputes, claims and contestation, but is lived asymmetrically: there is always the sense of an order, system, logic or command to which one is subjected but which will never be disclosed – not only because the logic is held in secret, but because the centre of command is no longer master of itself. Indeed, the novel itself offers a putative explication of its title, where the Americans regard themselves as innocent or unknowing in relation to the disenchanted and overly formal Russians:

> And that's how it went on. They never smiled. They never wanted to make things work. They lied, they obstructed, they were cruel. Their language was always too strong, even when they were insisting on a technicality in some agreement. All the time we were saying, 'What the hell, they've had a crappy war, and they do things differently anyhow.' We gave way, we were the innocents. We were talking about the United Nations and a new world order while they were kidnapping and beating up non-Communist politicians all over town. (McEwan 1990: 41)

Russell's analysis of proto-Cold War relations indicates that a new structure of innocence replaces the initial frank openness of the Americans, and their new world order that has been duped by the technical and violent Russians. Russell goes on to say, 'It took us almost a year to get wise to them' (McEwan 1990: 42), and it is that second 'wise' position that is encountered by Leonard. Knowing that they were innocent, facing an opponent of centralized, executively violent and bureaucratized power, the American mode of politics becomes one of decentred, distributed and disciplinary tactics. Far from power operating in some sovereign position above the body politic, where subjects would be childlike and innocent citizens, power in its post-war and American mode abandons the myth of innocence and bodies subjected to sovereigns. Instead, power operates through local gestures, networks, tunnels, communicative routes and passages.

If, today, we use words such as 'Kafkaesque' to describe a relation to a bureaucracy that is present everywhere but visible nowhere, this is because Kafka, like McEwan after him, recognized that modern power structures of infantilization express a tendency that may be exemplified in specific institutions but that is also present in the very condition of being a self in relation to a knowledge one does not have.

There is a directly sexual investment in this model of secrecy. It is only once he returns to the torpor and self-evidence of an unknowing England that Leonard recalls the excitement of both the practices and physical structures of networks and circuits; not the knowledge or content of what he has received, but its mode of dissemination and mediation: 'He missed the perfection of the construction, the serious, up-to-the-minute equipment, the habits of secrecy and all the little rituals that went with it' (McEwan 1990: 154–55). This shift from an imposed and external authority to a diffuse, silent, distributed power that is felt everywhere but visible nowhere, mirrors a structure of sexual knowledge. Sexuality 'begins' as an intrusive and alien signifier: as Freud's notion of *Nachträglichkeit,* or deferred action, makes clear, the child experiences a scene that is initially enigmatic but that later takes on the meaning of sexual content. At first sexuality is experienced as a domain of knowledge and experience that is hidden, and one is seduced by this very veiling or enigma of a knowledge held by a masterful and mature other, an other who will grant me my desire.

In addition to Russell's earlier definition of innocence, there is a later use of the term (and its reversal) in a scene of sexual encounter. Leonard, now the supposedly wiser and knowing sexual master, wants to warn Maria's friend Jenny about the predatory nature of Russell's sexual desire (and this scene in turn connects with the narrative's eventual trajectory of men exchanging women, of mastery achieved and threatened through networks of communication). Maria, as in the earlier scenes of sexual initiation, laughs at Leonard's innocence, for she is all too aware of Russell's sexuality. It is the woman who will play and control this system and not, as Leonard naively thinks, be its victim:

> 'Jenny looks after herself. Do you know what she was saying when the [*sic*] Russell came into the room? She said, "That's the one I want. I don't get paid till the end of next week and I want to go dancing. And," she said, "he has a beautiful jaw, like Superman." So, she goes to work, and Russell thinks he did it all by himself.'
>
> Leonard put down his knife and fork and wrung his hands in mock anguish. 'My God! Why am I so ignorant?'
>
> 'Not ignorant. Innocent. And now you marry the first and only woman you ever knew. Perfect! It's women who should marry the virgins, not men. We want you fresh –' [. . .]
>
> Maria raised her glass. He had never seen her so beautiful.
>
> 'To innocence.' (McEwan 1990: 173)

Maria's claim to mastery here is a seductive lure; for it is precisely at the moment that one believes oneself to be in command of the system that one places oneself in a position of innocence. For all her laughter and attributions of innocence in relation to a Leonard who is all too easily seduced and lured, it is Maria who becomes the final token of exchange, and who lives a life of married respectability in order to cover over the scandal that occurs when Leonard murders her ex-husband. Indeed, far from Leonard being a sexual and social *tabula rasa*, an innocent who can only relate to the worldy-wise Americans in an attitude of wonder, he finds himself becoming increasingly determined by desires for domination and mastery – eventually finding himself to be a mirror or double of Maria's violent ex-husband. Those desires are lived by Leonard as intrusive and alien, as radically other than his proper and innocent self.

McEwan thus represents sexuality as a double and conflicting tendency within those who would once again be a child, and the adult who (always remaining a child) lives adult life as a fantasy of mature mastery:

> It was the sort of face, the sort of manner, onto which men were likely to project their own requirements. One could read womanly power into her silent abstraction, or find a childlike dependency in her quiet attractiveness. On the other hand, it was possible she actually embodied these contradictions. (McEwan 1990: 59)

On the one hand, sexuality is an outward drive to take what is alien into the self in order to reduce the self's exposure, risk and vulnerability – a principle of constancy where the self's energy remains constant insofar as its needs are met. On the other hand, sexuality is a return to zero insofar as the self desires to end its state of living tension. The adult is exposed to a world that must be read and mastered, while also regarding him or herself as once having been a childlike unity before such submission.

Between Knowing and Not-knowing: Fiction-making

Where is narrative in this relation? Narrative is both a work of art that, like science, masters all that is other than itself, and also like music: an alluring wholeness that stuns or precludes our drive for comprehension. The opposition between science and art is analogous to an opposition between adult communication and childhood secrecy, between a world that is open to relations, systematization and mastery and some point of stillness or resistance that holds itself beyond the mastery of narration. These oppositions are, however, exposed by McEwan as both deeply embedded and impossible: just as the child lives its world as already structured by adult desires, and the adult is always reliving its fantasized lost childhood, so art and fiction strive to dominate and master the world, while science possesses an irreducible mythic and imaginative drive.

McEwan intertwines and juxtaposes the drive to mastery through systematization throughout his *oeuvre*. In *Amsterdam* (1998), Clive Linley composes a work that will synthesize the disorder and dissonance of existence, but that very act of composition is also a turn away from life and the demands of others, and an awareness of his own position in relation to time and consequences. In *Saturday* (2005), Matthew Arnold's poem 'Dover Beach' (1851) enters the novel as a fragment from a past time when art could still yearn for a lost plenitude. However, the poem also acts as an object that disrupts the impending violence of the present, against the disenchanted and violent perspectives of Perowne and Baxter respectively. In *On Chesil Beach*, the relative sexual, social and political maturity of Edward (the husband) is undermined when he hears his wife, Florence, performing in a string quartet. 'Later, on the train home, he was able to tell her with complete honesty that he had been moved by the music, and he even hummed bits to her.' (McEwan 2007: 126) Edward has, until that point in the narrative, imagined her as unaware and incapable of passion, but is then captivated and mesmerized by the music's expression of an intensity that appears beyond comprehension.

Thus McEwan's writing deconstructs the opposition between knowing and not-knowing, between science and art, between adult and child, between sexuality and innocence. The condition for knowing, speaking, narrating or adopting an adult viewpoint of mature relations is a recognition that the world is not one's own, that relations to others are mediated and that we are subjected to a system not of our own making. The position of the adult is, therefore, an abandonment of childish narcissism or omnipotence. At the same time, however, the very idea of an original presence, a time before our subjection to relations, others, language and secrecy – the myth of the child – is constitutive of the adult world of resignation. In *The Innocent*, McEwan deploys a series of ostensible oppositions only to show the ways in which each term will always appear as the other's parasite or supplement. McEwan's work constantly shows that our moments of supposed clarity and mastery are our moments of greatest blindness.

In a similar manner, *The Innocent* shows that such political modes of care and solicitation are also the moments of extreme paternalism and violence, for it is precisely through monitoring, documenting and educating that one is creating the other as nothing more than an image of oneself. The child is always the lost child from the point of view of adult disenchantment, but the child itself – that world of lost innocence – is a world already traversed by the fantasy of a father, sovereign or master who 'knows' the secret. The Berlin tunnel, now mastered by the more knowing Americans, reminds Leonard of his childhood, where he takes part in his father's power while at the same time experiencing that maturity as given by others. It is as though, for Leonard, the Americans now take over the bestowal of authority and know-how that he had once received from his father:

> It was hard not to feel proud of the tunnel. Leonard lent a child's token assistance, fetching a trowel, taking a list to the hardware shop and so on. When it was all finished, and before the breakfast table and chairs were moved in, he stood in the new space with its plaster walls, electrical fittings and homemade window, and he felt quite delirious with his own achievement. (McEwan 1990: 94)

The image of the circuit, the tunnel, the passage or the path all act as fantasy figures for communication, for communication is at once the creation of relations or paths that allow for the circulation of sense and disclosure, and also the very creation of a network that (like language) means that sense, experience, privacy and secrecy are only possible because there is already a system that allows one to figure the private and hidden to oneself. Leonard states: 'To confront her [Maria] he needed privacy and several hours. Then she could be furious, then accusatory, then sorrowful and finally forgiving. He could have drawn an emotional circuit diagram for her. As for his own feelings, they were beginning to be simplified by the righteousness of love' (McEwan 1990: 126). However, the supposed position of mastery that the tunnel would enable is exposed, at the end of the novel, to have been always already redundant. Politics takes on the structure of the open secret; nothing is truly held apart, and there is no ultimate sense or truth that is contested. What must be maintained, though, is the fantasy of communication – that tunnels, codes, passages and networks are ultimately subtended by a prior truth. Similarly, sexuality is always promised as a scene that might disclose the truth or sense of all the signs and suggestions one heard as a child. In *The Innocent*, the sexuality that would ultimately yield the sense of the secret and allow one to mature is always traversed by signs of an otherness one can never master.

The broader political implications of this deconstruction are explored in, for instance, *The Child in Time* and *Saturday*. In the former novel, Stephen, an author of children's books, has lost his daughter – her absence being a constant and haunting present throughout the narrative, which prevents time from moving forward. Simultaneously, Stephen's friend, Charles Darke, moves from the world of publishing to politics, which he eventually leaves to become a child again: Stephen finds him playing in a tree-house. On the one hand, we could see Charles's becoming-child as a retreat from truth and politics. However, the narrative destroys a series of borders that would make such a reading possible. First, Stephen's debut novel, initially intended as a novel of coming-to-adulthood and transgression entitled *Hashish*, stalls in its first part and remains a children's book, called *Lemonade*. It is as though the forward movement and time will always be drawn back to some already disturbed and lost childhood. The success of Stephen's book demonstrates a mode of political infantilism, a refusal to face a world of contingency, loss, otherness and destruction. Second, set in conservative Britain, *The Child in Time* presents the politician's concern with childhood – demonstrated in the government report on child development – as ultimately libidinal and infantilizing. The process of consultation and dialogue is a deception, for the paternalistic solutions have already been determined. Not surprisingly, the Prime Minister eventually seeks out the boyish Charles as a forbidden love object (McEwan 1988: 188).

Finally, the opposition between science and childish myths of timelessness is destroyed in Stephen's conversation with Charles's wife, Thelma. The physicists' accounts of time also suggest that the forward movement of chronological time is an illusion, and that time cannot be grasped or mastered by the simple narrative or human forms. What appear at first glance to be conservative and passive gestures turn out to be a profound mode of politics of secrecy, authority and paternalism that demonstrate our tendency to illusion, our seduction by authority, and our fantasies of infantile omnipotence.

It is that childish belief in a world that could be just as one wishes that McEwan often aligns with the artist's belief in, or illusion of, omnipotence. In *Saturday*, the case for and against the Iraq war is seen as an Oedipal battle between the musician-son and poet-daughter, on the one hand, and the scientific and disenchanted father-surgeon, Henry Perowne, on the other. In our youth we believe in the possibility of saying no to violence and conflict, and in the pure present of aesthetic enjoyment. From the point of view of Perowne the anti-war demonstration is a self-righteous and morally jubilant objection to *Realpolitik*, the narcissism of which is exemplified in the placard slogan of 'Not in my Name' (McEwan 2005: 72).

As in all of McEwan's oppositions between scientists and artists, art stalls and freezes time, and presents the possibility of a liberation from life's inevitable and necessary destruction of bounded form. By contrast, the father's scientific point of view places the all too human belief in individual life and organic beauty in a recognition of broader unbounded processes that go well beyond agency, cognition, personality and human historical narratives. It is therefore possible to read *Saturday* simultaneously as a psychologization of a political content (rendering the relation between resistance and conservatism as a relation between fathers and children) and as a dehistoricization: in the face of the grand evolutionary struggle between life and chaos the wars of nations matter little. It is the neurosurgeon, not the street demonstrator, who grasps – literally in *Saturday* – the truth of ethics. Only by attending to the forces of life from which we are composed, and not through the narcissism of political movements, can we achieve any form of amelioration. By displaying political struggles as familial dramas, and those dramas in turn as consequences of some broader imperative of 'life', McEwan might appear to be the most self-castrating of novelists: presenting art as a seductive deception that will ultimately preclude us from the recognition that poetry makes nothing happen.

Conclusion: To Remain a World unto Oneself

One of the charges that might be directed at McEwan's fiction, today, is its conservatism, both at the level of form and content. At the level of content, a character such as Perowne seems to point to the futility and atavism of political endeavour. At the level of form, we might note that McEwan's novels are hardly experimental, and usually bear a narrative trajectory that, through the use of flashbacks and shifting points of view, may be rendered somewhat complex.

However, this conservatism presented *in* the novel and the conservatism of the fiction's style is ultimately radical, especially if we consider the sense of the terms conservatism and radicalism. Conservatism is a desire for remaining the same, for maintenance, for non-change, for a being not subjected to threat, contingency, exposure or infraction. Images of children dominate McEwan's fiction precisely because he sees that desire for perfect stillness and self-enclosure as ultimately political: it charges all our images of humanity, of communication, of selfhood and time. McEwan's work is therefore a sustained political critique of cultural pornography. True radicalism would not be the simple opposite of this illusory closed and self-perfecting wholeness; radicalism would not be the emergence from childhood into a position of mastery, progression, pure becoming and knowledge. Instead, mastery may be more radical – closer to the root of the political – by examining the fantasies of power, wholeness, domination and mastered time. Similarly, at the level of form, it might be more radical to present and render explicit the drive to conservation, the drive to remain a world unto oneself. This would yield a fiction that could be read at one and the same time as the most alluring and seductive of narratives, while also presenting the politics and desire of being seduced into the image of organic wholeness.

CHAPTER FOUR

Words of War, War of Words: *Atonement* and the Question of Plagiarism

NATASHA ALDEN

Chapter Summary: In 2006, Ian McEwan was accused of plagiarizing parts of *Atonement* (2001) from the autobiography of the recently deceased novelist Lucilla Andrews. The wider intellectual implications of this row sparked questions about the relationship between history and fiction, and the ways in which novelists can draw upon (historical) sources. By reconsidering postmodern theories of historiographical metafiction, this chapter responds to some of the issues by focusing on McEwan's use of source material in *Atonement*. The chapter argues that McEwan's regard for historical veracity is secondary to his desire to create a particular atmosphere that affects his characters. *Atonement* demonstrates what fiction *can* do with history that history *cannot*. McEwan establishes these narratives as a direct challenge to the national, still prevailing myth of Dunkirk, and as a wider critique of a society at war, while invigorating our understanding of the relationship between history and fiction.

Introduction: A Weighty Obligation to Strict Accuracy

Historical fiction tends not to make the front pages of national newspapers. Yet in 2006, when Ian McEwan was accused of plagiarizing parts of *Atonement* from the autobiography of the recently deceased novelist Lucilla Andrews (1919–2006), the nature of historical narrative suddenly became news. In a lengthy *Mail on Sunday* article on Andrews's life, and her reaction to discovering that *Atonement* (2001) was, in part, based on Andrews's autobiography *No Time for Romance* (1977), Julia Langdon detailed the parallels between the two texts. Andrews's agent and brother were quoted voicing their disquiet at McEwan's use of Andrews's writing and about his not having contacted her (Langdon: 37). On the front page of the following day's *Guardian*, McEwan responded by stating that he had used Andrews as an inspiration and a source, and that he had recognized his debt to her in the Acknowledgements to *Atonement*, but had not copied her writing (McEwan 2006: 1). His extensive use of sources, he explained, was due to a concern for historical accuracy, born out of respect for the suffering of the characters' generation.

The *Mail* directly charged McEwan with plagiarism in a second article by Glenys Roberts, less than subtly titled 'Plagiarism (or why I need atonement) by Ian McEwan', whereupon a variety of academics and novelists came to McEwan's defence (Roberts: 26). Erica Wagner wondered if originality in literature was even possible, given that all stories are to some extent recycled, and likened *Atonement* to novels that 'talked to' other novels, such as Zadie Smith's *On Beauty* (2005), which is in part a response to *Howards End* (1910) by E. M. Forster (Wagner: 3). Smith herself took a different view; *Atonement*, she suggests, is not 'in dialogue' with Andrews's work, but only uses it for historical background information (Smith in Lyall, E1). Rose Tremain pointed to McEwan's ability to transform his source material into something 'singular and new' as a defence against the suggestion of improper usage, while Thomas Mallon argued that the case raised two separate issues: whether McEwan's use of Andrews's phrasing amounted to plagiarism (he concluded that it does not), and the less clear-cut issue of the ethics of using someone else's life story without consulting them (Tremain in Lyall, E1. *Talk of the Nation* 2006). Writing in the *Observer*, Robert McCrumb argued that McEwan only borrowed a few factual phrases, an entirely reasonable and laudable thing to do for a novelist concerned with the historical accuracy of his text (McCrumb: 13).

The debate turned on the phrases of Andrews echoed in *Atonement*, but also drew attention to the ways in which novelists use historical material, particularly historical scenarios. In *Atonement*, McEwan inserts Briony, and her point of view, into Andrews's narrative, which underlies Part Three, to the extent that it arguably could not exist as it is without that element. This means that McEwan relies on Andrews in a different way – to a different extent – than he does on his other sources, and is right to acknowledge her book (as he does). The way McEwan researched and wrote *Atonement* thus raises important broader questions about how novelists use historical material, and suggests that there are no clearly defined rules about how writers can echo another text, about how much of another author's work can be drawn on, or about the sorts of changes writers can make. What can authors do with source material, and, perhaps more importantly, what can they *not* do?

McEwan himself points out that 'Dunkirk or a wartime hospital can be novelistically realized, but they cannot be re-invented'; writers of historical fiction are, he argues, necessarily dependent on 'memoirs and eyewitness accounts' (McEwan 2006: 2). This raises questions about the importance of historical accuracy in historical fiction, and whether any rules could be established. McEwan made his views on such issues clear in his defence against the accusation of plagiarism:

> It is an eerie, intrusive matter, inserting imaginary characters into actual historical events. A certain freedom is suddenly compromised; as one crosses and re-crosses the lines between fantasy and the historical record, one feels a weighty obligation to strict accuracy. In writing about wartime especially, it seems like a form of respect for the suffering of a generation conscripted into a nightmare. (McEwan 2006: 1)

Although the media circus surrounding the debate moved on swiftly, the significant ethical questions remain.

This essay engages with some of these questions. The central conceit of *Atonement* – that the novel is a fiction based on reality created by its protagonist in an attempt to atone – foregrounds questions about how the historical novel creates a version of the past, and explores the narrative potential of this hybrid of history and fiction. The divide between reality and fiction is firmly emphasized because, at the end of the novel, we are told explicitly that the real Robbie and Cecilia are dead; we are told which parts of the story we have just read 'really happened'. Briony's confession foregrounds the consoling power of narrative, while simultaneously emphasizing the difference between fiction and the reality it is based on.

An analysis of *Atonement*'s engagement with historical sources, focusing on a few particular instances in detail, can help us to answer these questions. This careful unpicking of the historical source material, and an examination of the process by which it is 'translated' into a new fictional work, pinpoint the issues that McEwan wants to emphasize, such as 'the collective insanity of war' (McEwan 2001: 353), or the stripping-away of personal identity that war inflicts on those involved. It also allows us to trace how the novel practises the relationship between history and fiction, while revealing McEwan's view of the creative drive of *Atonement*, namely, to demonstrate what fiction *can* do with history that history *cannot*. McEwan actively distances himself from narratives that, true to the radical ontological doubt of historiographical metafictions from the nineteen-eighties and nineties, suggest history and fiction are inseparable, and – as Briony's brutal revelation about Robbie's and Cecilia's deaths emphasizes – shows they are all too separate.

But What *Really* Happened? Historiographical Metafiction Revisited

Atonement is a story *about* stories, our own and other people's. It is a meditation on how we tell stories, and what they can do. Does *Atonement* have a happy ending? It depends on your view of the power of story. Briony thinks it is not impossible that Robbie and Cecilia could be present at her 70th birthday celebrations. This comes pages after the revelation that both died in 1940. Any reader hoping for a happy ending should also remember Briony's earlier question: '[H]ow can a novelist achieve atonement when, with her absolute power of deciding outcomes, she is also God?' (McEwan 2001: 371). In her fiction Briony may be able to bring Robbie and Cecilia back to life and grant them a happy ending, but, as she notes, 'a certain kind of reader will be compelled to ask, But what *really* happened?' (McEwan 2001: 371).

The fact that the question 'what really happened?' is being asked of a novel at all is an indication of the complex metafictional nature of *Atonement*. McEwan asks important questions about the ways in which we write about ourselves and others, and, in particular, about the ways in which we write about the past. The novel is a complex double hybrid: firstly, Briony's novel is a 'forensic memoir' (McEwan 2001: 370) dedicated to demonstrating Robbie's innocence. Secondly, it forms an attempt to atone further by giving Robbie and Cecilia the happy ending in fiction denied them in real life. McEwan's novel is a novel-within-a-novel that reveals the (rewritten) stories behind stories; it brilliantly shifts between ontological levels and epistemological parameters, deliberately confusing the reader to the extent that we no longer know whose text we are reading.

Recent critical work on historiography and the writing of fiction has emphasized the constructed nature of narrative. This emphasis on artificiality challenges history's claim to empirical certainty and replaces it with a doctrine of competing narratives. Linda Hutcheon's *The Politics Of Postmodernism* (1988) groups together recent novels such as Salman Rushdie's *Midnight's Children* (1981) and Julian Barnes' *Flaubert's Parrot* (1984) that self-consciously attempt to redefine the relationship between fiction and history. Hutcheon labels them historiographical metafictions and argues that, in contrast to 'traditional' historical novels which are less self-reflexive and do not question their ability to accurately relay the past, such metafictional historiographies foreground the artificial, and therefore problematic, nature of narrative, including historical and literary stories.

Amy J. Elias revises Hutcheon's work in *Sublime Desire* (2001), which argues for a spectrum of ontological doubt within historiographical metafiction, ranging from profound radicalism to fiction that aims for verifiable historical accuracy. Elias suggests, for instance, that postcolonial writers who use postmodernist historiography to explore forgotten or marginalized voices have a political and often personal investment in writing these forgotten narratives 'back into' history, and tend therefore towards the conservative end of the spectrum of ontological doubt.

As the son of a Second World War veteran who served at Dunkirk, McEwan has a personal, biographical investment in the story told in *Atonement*, trying to re-imagine what it was like to be a soldier, or to nurse the wounded. A second-generation post-war writer, McEwan wants to tell a particular story and to 'put the record' straight about Dunkirk in particular, and about our nostalgic view of the war in general. He establishes these stories as a direct challenge to the national myth of Dunkirk that still prevails, and also as a wider critique of any society at war. As Alistair Cormack argues in the next chapter (see pp. 70–82), McEwan rejects a postmodernist relativism which suggests that there is no difference between history and fiction because both are mediated narratives. The form and plot of *Atonement* refute this thinking, as does McEwan's own insistence on historical accuracy wherever possible. In other words, the novel is not historiographical metafiction, nor is McEwan naively unaware of the complex questions that the form of its narrative raises.

However, this is not a clear-cut rejection of such postmodernist ideas. McEwan's text does not suggest we can have unmediated access to the past, or to any form of reality. The creation of Briony's Dunkirk narrative, for example, is dissected in 'London, 1999'. Here we are shown how the narrative is corrected, purged of factual errors and mistakes. Thus, the constructed, mediated and fallible nature of the narrative is emphasized. This, McEwan and Briony say, is what it *might* have been like. *Atonement* is still a metafictional novel, but McEwan is reasserting the history/fiction divide, broken down by postmodern historiography, in order to interrogate it, while retaining the freedom fiction gives the author to explore the past – to go *beyond* the factual record. Fiction allows McEwan to recreate these arenas of war, and enables readers to imagine themselves in the past. Briony atones by using fiction to portray thoughts and events she has no actual access to, and thus to 'reach' Robbie and Cecilia. She exploits, as McEwan does, the contradiction inherent in historical fiction, that of being simultaneously fictional *and* based in reality.

Working Atmosphere to a Sufficient Pitch: *Atonement*'s Use of Historical Source Material

As the son of a veteran, McEwan is especially concerned with presenting his vision of events in as historically accurate a way as possible; therefore he uses a vast amount of research material of varying kinds in *Atonement*. In Part One, set in the 1930s, Briony's prose style is modelled on that of contemporary writers – Rosamond Lehmann (1901–1990) and Virginia Woolf (1882–1941) in particular – partly because Briony is influenced by them, and partly because this modelling gives the prose a 'period' feel. Part Two, which chronicles Robbie's Second World War experiences and Briony's time as a probationer nurse at St Thomas' hospital in London, has a more modern style: McEwan weaves into the narrative details about the retreat to Dunkirk from histories, letters and diaries by eyewitnesses (including his father).

The earlier part of Part Three, describing the discipline of Briony's training, and particularly the terrible injuries sustained by soldiers from Dunkirk, is based very closely on two memoirs. The first, Lucilla Andrews's *No Time for Romance* (1977), describes the author's training at St Thomas' in 1941. (As McEwan needs Briony to be in London in order to see Lola, Marshall, Robbie and Cecilia, as well as to create tension by harnessing the reader's awareness of the imminence of the start of the Blitz in September 1940, he has Briony become one of the very last probationer nurses to be trained in London before the hospital was evacuated.) McEwan expands on Andrews's descriptions of the difficulty of keeping up her writing in her limited spare time, and of needing to be careful about what she wrote because she had nowhere to lock her notebooks.

McEwan's second source is 'The Memoir of Mrs A. Radloff', an unpublished typescript in the Imperial War Museum's collection. This memoir describes Radloff's training at St. Thomas' in London and Basingstoke, where, like Andrews, she looked after casualties from Dunkirk and from the *Lancastria*, a Cunard liner which was sunk on 17 June 1940 while attempting to evacuate British soldiers from France. At the time of the Dunkirk evacuation, Andrews and Radloff were both working in the sector hospitals to which the majority of St Thomas' staff had been evacuated: Andrews near Salisbury Plain and Radloff in Basingstoke.

Both women are slightly older than Briony and they both write in a pithy, clear-sighted manner that resembles the older Briony's prose style. The sequence of events of the first four sections of Part Three is based almost exactly on Andrews's autobiography – it begins shortly after Briony has begun her training, and demonstrates the hard work and intense discipline required of her. Both memoirs chronicle the steady build-up to the evacuation of Dunkirk. The details of wards being cleared and extra supplies delivered come from Andrews. The jaundiced sailors are the last patients before the arrival of the waves of casualties in both hospitals, and both Andrews and Briony finally realize what is happening in France by reading between the lines in newspaper reports.

McEwan remains faithful to the chronology of Andrews's narrative of nursing the wounded from Dunkirk, but rewrites history a little, transplanting her experiences to London. In reality, both Radloff and Andrews worked in outlying bases, and none of the wounded from the evacuation of France were sent to St. Thomas'. Briony herself explains this conflation, describing how she merged her experiences of working at Alder Hey, the Royal East Sussex and St Thomas' in order 'to concentrate all my experiences into one place' (McEwan 2001: 356).

However, in Part Three we are told that Briony intended to see Cecilia, but that she actually 'never saw [Cecilia and Robbie] in that year. [Her] walk across London ended at the church on Clapham Common [and] a cowardly Briony limped back to the hospital, unable to confront her recently bereaved sister' (McEwan 2001: 370–71). This places Briony in London after Robbie's death on 1 June and before Cecilia is killed in the Blitz in September. Therefore Briony cannot be conflating her own memories when she describes the men from Dunkirk and the *Lancastria*. This shows that McEwan's regard for historical veracity is secondary to his desire to create a particular atmosphere, which becomes clear earlier in the description of Robbie's journey to Dunkirk.

McEwan creates the atmosphere in the hospital – the depersonalization, the relentless hard work, the incomprehensible rules – almost entirely by means of details taken from the two memoirs. The stripping away of identity Briony experiences is, for instance, illustrated by a story from Radloff:

> The dragon who met us (sister) thrust a tray of labels disdainfully at my front and without looking at me [. . .] It was marked N. Reeves. Naively, for I didn't realize that I now had no identity, I protested that my initial was A. 'Stupid girl, do not you know that N stands for Nurse?' (Radloff: 1)

The Sister's reply to Briony's making the same mistake is politer, but no less alarming:

> This was how it was going to be. She had gone up to the Sister to point out courteously that a mistake had been made with her name badge. She was B. Tallis, not, as it said, on the little rectangular brooch, N. Tallis.
> The reply was calm, 'You are, and will remain, as you have been designated. Your Christian name is of no interest to me. Now kindly sit down, Nurse Tallis.' (McEwan 2001: 275)

Sometimes McEwan deviates for specific reasons. The senior nurses frighten Briony, Andrews and Radloff, but whereas the real-life nurses work with a variety of other staff, 'Briony often [thinks] that her only relationship was with Sister Drummond', and that her life on the wards is 'largely dependent on how she stood in the Ward Sister's opinion' (McEwan 2001: 274, 275). Sister Drummond appears to be the only senior nurse on Briony's ward; McEwan uses her to personalize the discipline depicted by Andrews and Radloff, and concentrates Briony's life down to a very small, very intense set of contacts.

Briony's daily routine is similarly curtailed, drawn from selected parts of Andrews's and Radloff's memoirs. After listing Briony's menial tasks, McEwan adds a short list of her medical experiences – '[she had] dabbed gentian violet on ringworm, aquaflavine emulsion on a cut, and painted lead lotion on a bruise' (McEwan 2001: 277). This list is derived from Andrews, and differs only in the tense used and in omitting the next item on Andrews's list, namely, taking patients' temperatures. Andrews's list continues: 'very occasionally doing a minor surgical dressing or removing a few stitches, sticking on and removing strapping plaster, and handing out doses of Gee's Linctus by the gallon, M. and B. tablets by the dozen, and the troops' beloved A.P.C. tablets by the gross' (Andrews 1977: 67). While McEwan cannot assume, as Andrews does, that his readers will know what these abbreviations mean, truncating this list also gives a stronger impression of how menial and boring Briony's work is.

McEwan picks up on details of the privations of the nurses' routine scattered throughout Andrews's and Radloff's accounts, and concentrates them together in three major sections that establish atmosphere. McEwan describes how the nurses' lives are regulated by the chimes of nearby Big Ben, a detail borrowed from Radloff: 'Big Ben dictated our routine, we dreaded his frequent reminders that we were late' (Radloff: 2). In *Atonement*, McEwan uses this idea to exacerbate the feeling of tension: 'The chimes of Big Ben marked every change of the day and there were times when the solemn single note of the quarter hour prompted moans of suppressed panic as the girls realised they were supposed to be elsewhere' (McEwan 2001: 283). Bedpans feature heavily in Briony's nursing, and McEwan borrows details from Andrews and Radloff that not only emphasize how disgusting emptying them is, but also stress the bizarre attitude the nurses, who are adapting to hospital discipline, are expected to have towards this task. In Radloff's memoirs, the nurses are told the following: '[Nurse], don't carry your bedpans like tennis rackets – carry them to the glory of God!' (Radloff: 2, 3) In Briony's account this appears as:

> The day therefore began with bedpans. Sister did not approve of them being carried down the ward 'like tennis rackets'. They were to be carried 'to the glory of God', and emptied, sluiced, cleaned and stowed by half past seven, when it was time to start the morning drinks. (McEwan 2001: 283)

Briony is told off for running in the corridor with the phrase: 'Only haemorrhages and fires were permissible reasons for a nurse to run' (McEwan 2001: 283). This is derived directly from Andrews, who is told: '"Please remember a nurse may only run for haemorrhage or fire"' (Andrews 1977: 161). Briony's technique for dealing with the bedpans is based on Andrews's, who describes herself addressing the bottles: 'Either I have to empty you with my eyes shut and holding my breath or I can't empty you at all' (Andrews 1977: 155). Briony discovers '[t]he trick of emptying them, in fact the only way it was possible for her, was to close her eyes, hold her breath and avert her head' (McEwan 2001: 283). The humour present in Andrews's memoir is missing in McEwan's version: his desire to portray this world as unrelentingly harsh and disciplined means that he adapts, or edits, his sources to fit the desired picture.

Beside such details from the nurses' routine, McEwan picks up particularly odd pieces of information from his sources and uses them to sustain the underlying tone of strangeness. We have the sense that Briony's reality is undercut by a Surrealist experience, as earlier explored in detail by Jeannette Baxter in Chapter One (see pp. 13–25). McEwan adapts Andrews's description of the models used to teach bed-bathing techniques so as to emphasize a curious sexuality, which is hinted at but never made explicit. Andrews describes models who are called 'Mrs Mackintosh, Lady Chase, and George, a baby boy of convenient physique to allow him to double as a baby girl' (Andrews 1977: 151). In *Atonement*, they reappear as: 'Mrs Mackintosh, Lady Chase, and baby George, whose blandly impaired physique allowed him to double as a baby girl' (McEwan 2001: 275). The change from 'convenient' to 'blandly impaired' introduces a note of damaged, or sublimated, sexuality not present in the original, adding to the atmosphere of muffled hysteria in the novel.

Briony's experience of nursing the dying from Dunkirk prompts a change in her that is as important as her development of a concept of realism while watching Robbie's and Cecilia's scene by the fountain in Part One. As McEwan wants to show *how* Briony's personality swiftly undergoes this vital change, he does not have space to show her off-duty. This happens because the narrative pace has to be maintained, and he therefore omits the details of life outside the hospital that Radloff and Andrews incorporate. For Briony's transformation to be dramatically plausible, McEwan has to keep constant and mounting pressure on her, which peaks with the death of the young French soldier Luc Cornet. This is not to say that Radloff and Andrews would not recognize The Nightingale School of Nursing that McEwan recreates, but he does not introduce the stoicism and sense of comradeship, present in their stories, to Briony's until after the death of Luc Cornet. Up till this point, McEwan heaps on borrowed details of the lonelier, harder parts of the nurses' lives, because the reader's focus is meant to be entirely on Briony and her inner life. This is why, unlike Andrews and Radloff, Briony has only one friend, and why McEwan concentrates all the details of the many senior nurses into the single figure of Sister Drummond – his aim is to create a 'spotlight' on Briony's claustrophobically circumscribed world.

Once the atmosphere has been worked to a sufficient pitch, McEwan introduces the first seriously wounded men whom Briony encounters. McEwan is still following the chronology of Andrews's account at this point, but makes occasional changes to serve his narrative ends. He also rewrites Radloff's and Andrews's descriptions of the soldiers' wounds and behaviour – adopting the personal details of soldiers and nurses but making them behave in ways diametrically opposed to their originals. These changes always emphasize the brutality and futility of the fighting. McEwan's soldiers are less stoical and more bitter, and they come across as being more contemporary than Radloff or Andrews's patients. Briony's patients do not have stiff upper lips.

During this episode, McEwan increases the horror Briony faces by having her treat five patients, two of whom are based on patients from Andrews's book, and two from Radloff's. The surreal, nauseating undercurrent of this part peaks in Briony's one love scene in the novel, after which she is never the same again – much in the melodramatic spirit of her early heroines. Briony's first patient was injured building runways in northern France. His story deviates from the original one in Andrews's book to emphasize his helplessness; he is less cheerful and more passive than Andrews's patient. McEwan abridges the soldier's description that 'Jerry kept bombing them every time they had the runway half built' (Andrews 1977: 79), but adds phrases such as 'all over', which emphasize his exhaustion and powerlessness (McEwan 2001: 298). In Andrews's account, the original soldier concludes by saying that '[w]e got shoved so far back we run out of fields, and seeing as you can not build runways on the sea, here we are. What you got to say to that, eh nurse?' (Andrews 1977: 79). McEwan's soldier is less forthcoming, but the grammatical error in Andrews's patient's speech is carried over: 'We drops back [. . .] then it's Jerry again and we're falling back again. Till we fell in the sea' (McEwan 2001: 298).

The next patient is a composite of two patients treated by Andrews and of McEwan's father, who suffered shrapnel wounds on the retreat to Dunkirk. Here McEwan takes medical details from Andrews and adds his father's experience of being reprimanded by a nurse for swearing in pain while the shrapnel fragments were taken out. Briony's patient also swears when she rips out the first fragment. Sister Drummond's reaction is contemptuous:

'How dare you speak that way in front of one of my nurses?'
   'I beg your pardon, sister. It just came out.'
   Sister Drummond looked with disdain into the bowl. 'Compared to what we've admitted these past few hours, Airman Young, your injuries are superficial. So you'll consider yourself lucky. And you'll show some courage worthy of your uniform. Carry on, Nurse Tallis.' (McEwan 2001: 300)

As Briony continues, the soldier's body shakes in pain while he silently holds on to the bedhead. This part of the description is directly taken from Andrews, where the soldier does not swear and behaves as stoically as Sister Drummond expects. Nowhere in any of the sources do the nurses speak with such harshness to a patient, and nowhere do the soldiers behave in the way that McEwan's do. Andrews's patient stays silent until the end of the procedure when the biggest fragment is removed, 'and then he said, "I am thanking you very much, nurse."' (Andrews 1977: 82). In *Atonement*, Briony's patient, staring at a similar fragment, says, '"Run him under the tap, Nurse. I'll take him home." Then he turned into the pillow. It may have been the word home, as well as the pain' (McEwan 2001: 300). This does not alienate the reader – it is hard to imagine reacting differently – but a more significant alteration is McEwan's decision to leave out the exchange between the nurse and patient at the end of Andrews's account, when he is brought a measure of brandy. McEwan is faithful to Andrews's description: the nurse goes to fetch the brandy, but is so shaken that she has to stop to be sick. However, while in Andrews's account the soldier tries to get the nurse, who is visibly upset, to drink the brandy, McEwan rushes the reader straight on to Briony's next patient, omitting the conversation. The editing here has the same function as Briony's invented lie about the shrapnel travelling to the airman's brain if it is left in place; it lessens our sense of there being a personal connection between nurse and patient. This puts McEwan's novel at serious variance with Andrews: where Andrews dwells on the mutual respect and concern between patients and nursing staff, McEwan invites his reader to condemn the rigid hospital rules, which prevent any real personal connection developing. In other words Briony, who is still immature and inexperienced, sees her patient as a problem to be solved as quickly as possible. Sister Drummond's furious response to the soldier swearing in pain is similarly lacking in empathy. Here, McEwan is modifying the source material in order to foreground his criticism of the crippling, dehumanizing rigidity of social and professional protocols that regulate the behaviour and lives of both soldiers and nurses.

Briony's next patient, Luc Cornet, is taken from Andrews's book. Dramatically speaking, he is the most significant patient whom Briony treats. Their interaction reveals the purpose of McEwan's emphasis on the misery of hospital life, bringing Briony and the reader back into a domestic, intimate sphere with sudden and unexpected power. McEwan begins this episode by firmly emphasizing its place within the tiny world encompassed by Briony's relationship with Sister Drummond; Andrews was told to sit with the dying soldier by 'a very senior QA' (Andrews 1977: 98) whom she does not know personally, whereas in *Atonement*, it is Drummond again (McEwan 2001: 305). Both Briony and Andrews are told that the soldier is 'acute surgical, but there's no need to wear a mask' (McEwan 2001: 305; Andrews 1977: 98). McEwan's narrative shifts the emphasis here: unlike Briony, Andrews understands that this means her patient is dying. McEwan also leaves out Andrews's explanation that masks frighten patients, perhaps because this would prevent him from getting straight into his description of Briony and Luc's meeting, and also because McEwan does not want to show just yet Sister Drummond's compassion, which becomes obvious after Luc's death.

The description of Luc Cornet in *Atonement* is much more romanticized than it is in Andrews's memoir. In an interview with John Sutherland, McEwan explained that he altered this scene because he wanted the reader to see 'some eruption of feeling from Briony': 'I saw it as a love scene, even though it's a dying scene – [without this glimpse of her emotional life] there would be something too unreliable about her account of love' (Sutherland 2002). Even so, McEwan does follow Andrews's account: Briony makes the same mistake as Andrews and takes the soldier's gauze dressing off. Both Briony and Andrews are so horrified by his injuries that they recoil, and the dressing begins to fall. The details of what happens next are taken from Andrews, though McEwan changes Luc's injuries slightly, as he wants him still to have both eyes, while in Andrews's account the soldier has lost one. McEwan also adds the detail of Briony catching the bloody sterile towel before it hits the floor, furthering our sense of horror.

The most immediately apparent difference between the two passages is that in Andrews's version the soldier is English, whereas in McEwan's he is French. McEwan has used French in intriguing ways before (see Baxter in this volume, p. 24, and Broughton 1991). Here, it has one functional advantage; Briony's schoolgirl grasp of French forces her to translate nurse as 'sister', which leads to a discussion of Cecilia, and then to their discussion of love. John, Andrews's patient, seems a polite public schoolboy. His language is more dated than Luc's; at one point he says 'I say – jolly decent of her' (Andrews 1977: 99). McEwan does follow the events as Andrews describes them but John talks about school and the army, which Luc does not, and when Andrews asks him his name, he gives his surname and army number. Luc, by contrast, seems a boy rather than a soldier. He is already more delirious than John is when Briony first meets him; this forces Briony into a more intimate conversation, which gestures more obviously towards the domestic, family life that Briony has lost and that Luc is about to lose absolutely. The details of Luc's ramblings are different from John's, concentrating more on his sister, and then on Briony. Although Briony weakly protests that she does not know him and that he is in hospital in London, Luc thinks they have met before, and draws her into a conversation about his bakery and his family. While this is all McEwan's invention, the detail of the 'grating sound at the back of his throat' (which signals that more is wrong than Briony has noticed) and the description of his tight grip on her hand are both from Andrews (Andrews 1977: 99, 100). Luc deteriorates and starts thinking they are a couple, which gives the scene a very personal intimacy that Andrews's account does not have. Briony realizes that Luc is dying and behaves accordingly. Like John, Luc asks her to loosen his bandages, and like Andrews, Briony does not expect to see half of his head and face shot away. This is the moment when Briony is shocked into adulthood. Shortly afterwards, Luc and John die, suddenly sitting bolt upright, making Briony and Andrews both catch them in their arms. Both are unaware for a moment that the soldier has died.

The ending of this episode is significant for its dramatic inversion, which underscores Briony's new-found adulthood. While McEwan follows Andrews's narrative and even takes the basis of the dialogue from her account, he reverses his previous tactic of portraying Sister Drummond as a cold and distant character by making her more sympathetic and humane than the original. In other words, Briony's quick mental change and empathy allow her to reinterpret the cold, harsh environment. We can see further evidence of this in McEwan's brief comment about Briony emptying bedpans. Both Radloff and Andrews never minded changing bedpans: the patients were so humiliated by them that the nurses would have felt self-indulgent complaining themselves (Andrews 2005: 2). For Briony, it is now a task which 'she had never minded [. . .] less' (McEwan 2001: 297). Thus, McEwan uses details from Radloff and Andrews to create a dramatically coherent atmosphere and narrative trajectory that are satisfying from a literary point of view, and which, while adapting the source material, are not wholly historically inaccurate.

Conclusion: Between History and Fiction

Can we draw any general principles about McEwan's use of historical source material in *Atonement*? Or is it perhaps the case that the rules are made, and unmade, by authors themselves? Rules about the mechanics of using source material in fiction are, and may perhaps remain, notoriously hazy: unlike other forms of writing, there are no agreed rules as to what kind of details can be used, or how; no rules governing the use of phrasing, or scenario, or background detail. Does it make a difference if an author uses a single source extensively, or builds a narrative out of a number of stories, or facts, from different sources? Is the extent to which an author relies on a single source significant, and, if so, how might an author properly acknowledge this? Fiction, after all, is not held to the same standards of objective truth as history, but will we find footnotes spreading into novels in the future?

   If we read *Atonement* as an answer to such questions, the novel offers a passionate ethical argument against postmodern fabulism, reasserting the difference between historical and fictional forms of narrative, and creating a new form of historiographical metafiction. By rejecting postmodernism's erasure of the difference between history and fiction, McEwan extends the debate about truth in narrative from the level of the plot to the form of the novel itself, and historical fiction in particular. This form, because of its difference from that of historical narrative, can take us towards an understanding of the past that the source material alone might not achieve. *Atonement* partakes of both the empiricist and postmodern traditions, creating a dynamic tension that is both explored and challenged in the next chapter, which investigates the form of *Atonement* in great detail.

CHAPTER FIVE

Postmodernism and the Ethics of Fiction in *Atonement*

ALISTAIR CORMACK

Chapter Summary: In *Atonement* (2001), Ian McEwan performs a complex examination of novelistic discourse. The narrative involves a collision between different styles and modes of representation; in particular, the 'Englishness' of the novel's setting and its self-conscious references to a pantheon of canonical English writers seem at odds with its jarringly postmodern conclusion. This chapter investigates this dissonance. It begins by looking at the tradition of English fiction through a consideration of F. R. Leavis, after which postmodernism is discussed. Finally, a reading of *Atonement* will be presented that looks at how the novel overlays these complex and contradictory discourses. It seems that McEwan has written a novel that passes through modernism and postmodernism to arrive back at a more traditionally realist form. The chapter concludes by arguing that McEwan rejects the moral indeterminacy of postmodern poetics, and pits against it a tradition of English empiricism.

The Great Tradition: McEwan and Leavis

Atonement is haunted by a host of English novelists. We encounter Jane Austen, L. P. Hartley, E. M. Forster, Rosamond Lehmann and Virginia Woolf among others. McEwan engages with and updates Forster and Austen, and the effect is to render newly significant their concerns. Implicit in this account is the conviction that to name Forster and Austen is adequate shorthand for the 'historical layers of English fiction' (Lee, 2001: 16). One might argue that this is a rather narrow definition: English fiction also contains *Tristram Shandy* (1760–67), *Frankenstein* (1817), and *Wuthering Heights* (1847), novels that suggest very different traditions, and modes of writing that are absent from *Atonement*. When critics talk of McEwan's debt to 'English fiction' they are invoking a certain set of novels, a certain set of values.

One way to approach the values implicit in the works referred to in *Atonement* is to look at F. R. Leavis's influential work on English fiction, *The Great Tradition* (1948). Though Leavis's list of great writers – Austen, George Eliot, Henry James and Joseph Conrad – is not identical to those referred to above, those he specifically excludes – Laurence Sterne, Emily Brontë and James Joyce – match those excluded by McEwan. Leavis, as we shall see, even makes an appearance in *Atonement*, and clearly represents more than mere period colour. In talking of the central figure in his pantheon, Austen, Leavis outlines what he considers to be central to the greatness of a novelist:

> [W]hen we examine the formal perfection of *Emma*, we find that it can only be appreciated in terms of the moral preoccupations that characterize the novelist's peculiar interest in life. Those who suppose it to be an 'aesthetic matter', a beauty of 'composition' that is combined, miraculously, with 'truth to life', can give no adequate reason for the view that *Emma* is a great novel, and no intelligent account of its perfection of form. It is in the same way true of the other great English novelists that their interest in their art gives them the opposite of an affinity with Pater and George Moore; it is, brought to an intense focus, an unusually developed interest in life. For, far from having any of Flaubert's disgust or disdain or boredom, they are all distinguished by a vital capacity for experience, a kind of reverent openness before life, and a marked moral intensity. (Leavis 1948: 17–18)

George Moore, Walter Pater and Gustave Flaubert are guilty of 'aestheticism', by which Leavis means an overdeveloped interest in style at the expense of morality in the sense of a 'reverent openness before life' and a concern for what Plato calls 'the good life'. The great English writer, instead, has a particular interest in the representation of reality: their interest in their art is in fact an interest in 'life' itself. This interest is indicated by a personal investment in the investigation of right conduct, or practical morality. The novel, considered in this way, is a vehicle for the convincing portrayal of individual ethical choice in a social setting created with unobtrusive verisimilitude. The sort of writers who are not 'Great' are non-mimetic, and are thus either amorally interested in form or didactically interested in allegory.

There are two philosophical positions that go together to create the foundation for the art that Leavis endorses. On the one hand we find humanism, the belief that humanity has an unchanging essence and therefore that the central concerns of life – the search for love and meaning perhaps – are the same for all people at all times. On the other hand we find empiricism, the notion that only what is made evident to the senses, or is directly experienced, can be trusted. What these ideas have in common is a distrust of anything that betokens abstraction, which explains Leavis's distaste for the 'aesthetic', even within criticism itself. His 'Englishness' is one in which common sense dominates the mode of representation and orders moral perceptions; Leavis himself represents Englishness in his own refusal to adopt an intellectual or critical vocabulary. In the passage quoted above, the terms 'life' and 'moral' are not examined or challenged; the reader should know what is meant. It is no coincidence that they are a sort of non-intellectual way of announcing empiricism ('life') and humanism ('moral'), and although it could be noted that Leavis is self-conscious about their unhelpfulness, it is this tradition to which *Atonement* refers by its many implicit quotations.

As the Pompidou Does its Escalators: Postmodernism

Along with the attention paid to the 'Englishness' of *Atonement*, critical responses have also sought to explore the novel's postmodernism. The striking metafictional twist that ends the novel, in James Wood's words, 'makes the book a proper postmodern artifact, wearing its doubts on its sleeve, on the outside, as the Pompidou does its escalators' (Wood 2002). Looked at in one way, postmodernism indicates a periodization and a style of art; most obviously we can describe it as that which came after modernism. This simple approach is important when reading *Atonement* because the poetics of modernism are a subject for speculation throughout the novel. However, in a broader sense modernity is not a limited moment of experimentalism in the arts, but a project in science, politics and culture that issues from the Enlightenment, which stands for the belief that the natural world can be finally understood through experiment, and that human life can be organized along rational and equitable lines. Postmodernism represents the rejection of this belief, or at least the sense that it has failed or is limited.

Whereas the Leavisite tradition of English fiction presents us with a set of convictions about reality and morality, postmodernism brings a rejection of certainties. Since there is no unmediated reality there can be no certain truth; since there is no truth, there is no ground on which to base universal moral principles. We are moving towards the second approach to postmodernism. The doubts that arise in postmodernism about absolute claims to truth reflect a sense that the accounts of human activity that have offered complete explanations are fatally tainted by a desire for order and power. Thus, widely different systems of knowledge – Christianity, Marxism and the scientific notion of progress – are all attacked as generalizations that serve to occlude difference and suppress dissent. Postmodernism becomes a rejection of the Enlightenment and counters with the sense that the end of scientific exploration is nuclear weaponry, and that any attempt to control social life is inevitably fascistic. Art that derives from this position is often understood to foreground the constructedness of narratives that claim the status of clear and self-evident truth. Once again fiction can claim a renewed significance; by exposing its own processes of storytelling, novels reflect how knowledge of all types is formed. As we will see, there are aspects of *Atonement*'s representation of war and its questioning of the truth of Briony's accounts that seem to fit into the paradigm of postmodernism just outlined. However, the exact way in which this tessellates with the novel's Englishness still requires explanation.

From Modernism to Postmodernism: Fictional Fictions

Modernist novels are characterized by the absence of omniscience in their narration and its replacement with a variety of fragmentary subjective perspectives. The first section of *Atonement*, set in 1935, seems to embody just such a modernist poetics. Although delivered by a third-person narrator, each chapter is closely focalized through the consciousness of one character, except Chapter Five, which is shared by the villainous duo of Marshall and Lola. For example, Chapter Six follows the thoughts of Emily Tallis, the mother of Briony, Cecilia and Leon. Suspecting she will suffer a migraine, she has withdrawn to her darkened bedroom; like Virginia Woolf's Mrs Dalloway, she is weighed down with concerns about the social event taking shape around her. She hears feet on the stairs and reflects that 'by the muffled sound of them [. . .] they must be barefoot and therefore Briony's' (McEwan 2001: 66). Her ability to deduce this fact, we learn, comes from practice:

> Habitual fretting about her children, her husband, her sister, the help, had rubbed her senses raw; migraine, mother-love and, over the years, many hours of lying still on her bed, had distilled from this sensitivity a sixth sense, a tentacular awareness that reached out from the dimness and moved through the house [. . .] a conversation that penetrated a wall, or, better, two walls, came stripped of all but its essential twists and nuances. (McEwan 2001: 66)

Emily surmises that she can hear Briony stomping off in a mood and Cecilia belatedly taking flowers to Marshall's room; she can also smell her older daughter's illicit cigarette, imagining that 'she would be wanting to impress Leon's friend, and that in itself might not be a bad thing' (McEwan 2001: 67). The staging of the scene seems designed to flaunt a novelistic discourse settled on the cornerstones of modernism: the hypersensitive consciousness, in darkened solitude, attentive to each creak of the house; the maternal solicitousness, offering a persuasive but finally partial interpretation of the sounds and smells she encounters. The way in which the narrative attends to individual perception seems almost *too* impeccable. Indeed, as we will see, there are further clues that the exemplary modernist text we encounter is being subtly subverted.

Most of the chapters in the first section are given to 13-year-old Briony Tallis. To begin with, it appears strange that her perception of events should be the most significant. However, as the story progresses we realize that she has a role, in both the plot and its telling, that brings to mind L. P. Hartley's *The Go-Between* (1953), a novel also narrated by a figure who as a child had been involved as intermediary in a tragic class-traversing love affair in a country house. An event which proves central to the novel occurs when Briony glimpses from an upstairs window the sexually charged encounter between Robbie and Cecilia by the fountain. Briony is already a creator of fictions, and she muses on what she has witnessed as an aesthetic problem:

> [S]he sensed she could write a scene like the one by the fountain and she could include a hidden observer like herself. [. . .] She could write the scene three times over, from three points of view [. . .] None of these three was bad, nor were they particularly good. She need not judge. There did not have to be a moral. She need only show separate minds, as alive as her own, struggling with the idea that other minds were equally alive. (McEwan 2001: 40)

We may find ourselves reflecting that we are reading just such a series of scenes. For instance, the presentation of Emily Tallis's thoughts, a backwater of the plot, is primarily to show her independent existence in just the way Briony describes. The proto-modernist insight offered above prompts a jarring break from the primary diegesis; the narration strangely, and suddenly, leaps forward from 1935: 'Six decades later she would describe how, at the age of thirteen, she had written her way through a whole history of literature' (McEwan 2001: 41). Despite this fissure in the surface of the text, on a first reading of the first section it is easy to be self-deluding and to take the virtuoso display of modernism at face value. Wrapped up in the drama of what Briony refers to later as the 'crime' and the frequent psychological insights with which we are presented, the reader does not attend too much to the role as writer which the text has assigned to the youngest Tallis.

However, in the third section of the book we are forced to reconsider what we have read. It is 1940 and Briony is now a nurse. In the period immediately before her training she has written a novella entitled – we find out later – *Two Figures by a Fountain*. Reflecting on her literary practice, Briony argues:

> The age of clear answers was over. So was the age of characters and plots. Despite her journal sketches, she no longer really believed in characters. They were quaint devices that belonged to the nineteenth century. The very concept of character was founded on errors that modern psychology had exposed. Plots too were like rusted machinery whose wheels would no longer turn. . . . It was thought, perception, sensations that interested her, the conscious mind as a river through time [. . .] She had read Virginia Woolf's

The Waves three times and thought that a great transformation was being worked in human nature itself, and that only fiction, a new kind of fiction, could capture the essence of the change. (McEwan 2001: 281–82)

It is decidedly unsettling for a reader engrossed in a novel that scrupulously recreates 'the conscious mind as a river through time' to find a character musing on precisely this topic. The full force of this self-referentiality is not felt for another 50 pages. Briony has sent her story to a magazine called *Horizon*, whose editor (who signs off 'Yours sincerely, CC', referring to the magazine's editor Cyril Connolly) writes an appreciative rejection letter. The letter corrects a variety of infelicities of style and implausibilities of action. As Frank Kermode points out, changes from novella to novel can be tracked; for example, in the original Cecilia goes fully dressed into the fountain, the vase is Ming not Meissen, and the Tallises' fountain has been described as a copy of one in the Piazza Navona (Kermode 2001: 8). More importantly, in the novel the real impetus of the event has been restored to it. Briony's first attempt, Connolly thinks, was rather dry:

> Your most sophisticated readers might well be up on the latest Bergsonian theories of consciousness, but I'm sure they retain a childlike desire to be told a story, to be held in suspense, to know what happens. (McEwan 2001: 314)

Connolly's reference is to Henri Bergson's theory, so influential on modernist aesthetics, that the consciousness is never static, and that instead it is constantly changing due to present impressions integrating with past memories. The letter makes us aware of our own collusion in the postmodernism that takes us beyond the focus on the representation of consciousness to the exclusion of action. It is not enough for us to witness passively the flow of a mind at work; we desperately want to know what has happened. Briony, it turns out, was wrong when she argued that there need not be a moral.

There are several aspects of this narrative 'trick' that can be described as postmodern. First we have historical personages (Connolly and Elizabeth Bowen) who write for a real magazine commenting on a fictional fiction, indeed on specific phrases we have already read. More importantly, we now realize that we have been duped. We are forced to return to the scene at the fountain – indeed to the whole first section – and regard it as pastiche: what we read in good faith in the first section as a Woolf-like modernism – a piecing together of 'what actually happened' from a variety of perspectives – we must now regard as an imitation by an absent author-demiurge (McEwan) of one character's own modernist reconstruction of the event, which occurs entirely within the fictional boundary of *Atonement*. That this is the story of a novelist, not a 'teller' of any other type, and a modernist novelist at that, seems sufficient grounds to argue for the formal postmodernism of *Atonement*. However, in the epilogue, dated 1999, we have further evidence. Briony addresses us in the first person for the first time and makes an argument that seems, in postmodernist style, to challenge the notion of an independent reality: 'When I am dead, and the Marshalls are dead, and the novel is finally published, we will only exist as my inventions' (McEwan 2001: 371). What right, she asks, does reality have to arrogate to itself the primary ontological position? However, if this is postmodernism, it is not the postmodernism of the type that revels in fragmentation and celebrates moral relativism. Although there is plenty of evidence of self-reflexiveness and pastiche in *Atonement*, the sort of airy exhilaration that often characterizes works in this mode is absent from McEwan's novel. If it is postmodern, it is not postmodernism of the playful celebratory type. At the end of the novel both Briony Tallis, our narrator, and we, her readers, are profoundly troubled by the uncertainties we face.

Postmodernist and Leavisite Readings of *Atonement*

It is plain that *Atonement* is postmodern in the sense that it comes after, and explicitly criticizes, modernism. Many critics have extended this reading to suggest that it participates in the broader postmodern critique of the Enlightenment and representation. Brian Finney has argued that *Atonement*'s two time frames are on either side of a huge cultural divide:

> In 1935 the West was suffering from a collective myopia in the face of the rise of fascism, which only a minority on the left seemed prepared to confront. Robbie is typical of the collective delusion at that time with his fantasies of a future life spent as a family doctor and casual reader. The West is about to be hurled into a war that will usher in a radically different, postmodern era to which this narrative, completed in 1999, belongs. (Finney 2002: 77–8)

This view might seem surprising given the comfortable familiarity of the country house setting. Attentive readers will have noticed, however, that McEwan has undermined conventional expectations: the 'ambience of solidity and family tradition' (McEwan 2001: 145) is misleading in a house only a few years old; the folly overlooking the lake, though picturesque at a distance, at close inspection has a 'mottled, diseased appearance' and 'exposed laths, themselves rotting away', which resemble 'the ribs of a starving animal' (McEwan 2001: 72). This is an England whose tradition is a visibly decomposing fake.

Finney poses his argument against those reviewers who, perhaps ignoring its unsettling undertones, enjoyed the first section of the novel, but were disappointed by what they considered the 'gimmicky' nature of the novel's metafictional conclusion. He points out that the metafictional

element is present throughout – both through the self-conscious narration of Briony and through the novel's obtrusive intertextuality – and
argues that literary self-consciousness is at the heart of what the novel
is trying to achieve. The reader is being refused the comforts of classic
realist narrative:

> To draw attention to the narrative process is not an act of self-indulgence on
> the part of the metafictional novelist [. . .] It is central to the book's concerns
> [. . .] [W]hen novelists force us to understand the constructed nature of their
> characters, they invite us simultaneously to reflect on the way subjectivity
> is similarly constructed in the non-fictional world we inhabit [. . .] [T]he use
> of metafiction in the book serves to undermine the naturalization of social
> and economic inequalities that especially characterized British society in
> the 1930s. (Finney 2002: 76)

Finney argues that the novel forces us to see how we ourselves make
sense of the world through the very processes of narrative that Briony
has revealed to be so misleading. Furthermore, he implies that the way
in which tradition is shown to be a barely convincing artifice exposes it
as a means through which people are oppressed.

Though there is much to recommend the reading offered by Finney,
there are two main problems with his argument.In the first place,
Finney adopts Catherine Belsey's criticism of the naturalizing function
of 'histoire' in the classic realist text (see Finney 2002: 70–71 and Belsey
1980: 72). However, *Atonement* could never really be read in this way:
the first section is not an undermined classic realism, but an undermined modernism. This is key: classic realism is characterized by a
mediating discourse – what Colin MacCabe influentially named 'meta-
language' – whereas modernism presents its consciousnesses without
an overarching and containing discourse (MacCabe 1979: 13–38). This
sort of 'point of view' modernism is what we encounter in the first section and is commented on by Briony's novella *Two Figures by a Fountain*.
McEwan is thus not using his novel to challenge the ideological functions of a novelistic discourse assaying verisimilitude, but rather to
attack static, morally disengaged, plotless modernism. McEwan criticizes the two poles of writing: the moralistic simplicity of melodrama
in Briony's naive *Trials of Arabella* and the amoralistic disengagement of
modernism in her later work. It is worth noting here that in its distaste
for the didactic and the aesthetic, *Atonement* is very much in accord with
Leavis's view of art. It is important that we grasp *Atonement*'s rejection
of modernism, as it is modernism that critics like Belsey and MacCabe
present as a felicitous alternative to classic realism. They argue that
modernism's refusal to produce a hierarchy of discourses meant the
reader could not situate herself in the text in a stable subject position.
If *Atonement* is an attack on modernism it cannot be so easily co-opted
to a Belsey-like critical position: that is to say, the novel cannot be a

criticism of our reification of a shared ideological construction of the real, but is rather a criticism of a certain novelistic form. In a sense, there is a narrow literary dimension to *Atonement*, which critics have been rather reluctant to note.

A far more important problem with Finney's argument concerns how the ending of *Atonement* works. He argues that the force of the criticism implicit in the novel is against the naivety of the bad reviewers who want 'the simplified wish fulfillments of classic realist fiction' (Finney 2002: 81), and in favour of the postmodern notion that we are *all* narrated. In the following passage there is a break in the logic of the argument:

> From the start, [Briony's] powerful imagination works to confuse the real with the fictive [. . .] The young Briony suffers from the inability to disentangle life from the literature that has shaped her life. She imposes the patterns of fiction on the facts of life. To complain about the metafictional element in the book is to fail to understand that we are all narrated, entering at birth into a pre-existing narrative which provides the palimpsest on which we inscribe our own narratives/lives. (Finney 2002: 78–9)

It is true that Briony is guilty of imposing fiction on reality and that her confusion of literature and life causes her 'crime'. It is less clear that the implication of this insight is that 'we are all narrated'. McEwan suggests that there is an overarching thing called the 'real' beyond the narratives we construct about our lives, and that we are morally obliged to know that 'real' so that we can distinguish it from our fantasies. If 'we are all narrated', there is no exterior reality which can be used to judge the inaccuracy of Briony's literary imagination. McEwan's insistence on the real over our illusions is the opposite of a postmodern insight. The crime in *Atonement*, as McEwan points out, is generated by the 'danger of an imagination that can't quite see the boundaries of what is real and what is unreal' (Reynolds and Noakes 2002: 19). In answer to some of the questions raised by Natasha Alden in the previous chapter (see pp. 57–69), it could thus be argued that the effect of the metafiction is not to undermine certainty about the real, but to present a critique of the processes by which the imagination works. Rather than belonging to the uncertain postmodern era, *Atonement* belongs to a world in which Enlightenment thinking, far from being in crisis, is confident enough to chastise fiction and its fripperies: an identifiable real world lies beneath, and casts a critical eye on, the fictional surface created by the novel's narrator.

This takes us back to the tradition of English empiricism outlined earlier, which, McEwan suggests, finds its most important source in the work of Jane Austen:

> What are the distances between what is real and what is imagined? Catherine Morland, the heroine of Jane Austen's *Northanger Abbey*, was a girl so full of

the delights of gothic fiction that she causes havoc around her when she imagines a perfectly innocent man to be capable of the most terrible things. (Reynolds and Noakes 2002: 20)

However, *Sense and Sensibility* (1811) offers an even more fruitful comparison to *Atonement* than *Northanger Abbey* (1803), from which *Atonement* derives its epigraph. *Sense and Sensibility* takes its title from contemporary debates about knowledge and right action; the notion of sense as it relates to sense impressions (and thus empiricism) is linked to the idea that good sense recommends adhering to orthodox social codes, propriety and manners. Briony is an inheritor of Marianne Dashwood, someone guilty of sensibility understood as the selfish indulgence of internalized emotions and imagination. The question of Englishness turns out to be relevant after all: McEwan has written a story that passes through modernism and postmodernism to return to the heart of the 'Great Tradition' of English novelists.

McEwan has asserted that not only Briony but 'Robbie too has a relationship, a deep relationship with writing and storytelling' (Reynolds and Noakes 2002: 19). Indeed, in two significant passages involving him, this relationship is coupled with the opposition of sense to sensibility. In the first, Robbie is reflecting on his decision to become a doctor:

> There was a story he was plotting with himself as the hero, and already its opening had caused a little shock among his friends. [. . .] Despite his first, the study of English literature seemed in retrospect an absorbing parlour game, and reading books and having opinions about them, the desirable adjunct to a civilised existence. But it was not the core, whatever Dr Leavis said in his lectures. It was not the necessary priesthood, nor the most vital pursuit of an enquiring mind, nor the first and last defence against a barbarian horde [. . .] [H]is practical nature and his frustrated scientific aspirations would find an outlet, he would have skill far more elaborate than the ones he had acquired in practical criticism, and above all he would have made his own decision. (McEwan 2001: 91)

We must carefully trace the levels at work here. McEwan is writing as Briony, who in turn is ventriloquizing Robbie's thoughts as part of her act of atonement, while these thoughts are themselves 'a story he was plotting'. At first glance this would seem the epitome of a critical postmodernism, investigating the ways in which narrative functions in literature and life. Nevertheless, there is no sense in which the 'truth' or 'life' disappears. Beneath the accreted layers of narrative the manifest content of the passage is, rather, simply an attack on the imagination. Robbie suggests that literature has merely a peripheral role as part of a 'civilized existence'; claims for its centrality are absurd. Dominic Head has argued that, in light of these comments, the implication of Robbie's fate is 'the need for a more urgent re-evaluation of cultural work than

Leavis can offer' (Head 2007: 173). However, Robbie's 'story' is one leading him away from literature and into 'life'. Head's criticism of Leavis is thus rather unfair, for the implicit empiricism (Robbie's 'practical nature') that informs the decision is entirely consistent with Leavis's own position that literature is only valuable when in service to morality and reality. That is to say, while in the diegetic world of *Atonement* Robbie may be opposed to Leavis, as a character in a novel he is a device – a means by which Leavisite aesthetics may be promoted. Robbie, in the English tradition, rejects the sensibility of literature for the sense of a career in medicine.

Part Two forms the key to *Atonement*. It extends the critique of storytelling into the public arena. The act of mediation is complex in the first example, but it becomes even more complicated, and of even greater urgency, in the next. Here, Robbie is drifting off to sleep at the end of the Dunkirk episode:

> They would be forming up in the road outside and marching to the beach. Squaring off to the right. Order would prevail. No one at Cambridge taught the benefits of good marching order. They revered the free, unruly spirits. The poets. But what did the poets know about survival? About surviving as a body of men. No breaking of ranks, no rushing the boats, no first come first served, no devil take the hindmost. (McEwan 2001: 264)

If Briony must learn to rid herself of her literary imagination then British culture must, too, divest itself of its controlling myths. In this case, the notion of the 'Dunkirk Spirit' is savagely demythologized; the retreat is replayed in all its contingent horror. The idea of a cohesive 'Spirit' is replaced by an event marked by division between the services (an airman is attacked [250–53]) and between classes. The passage quoted above suggests a degree of self-accusation on both Briony's and McEwan's part: 'What did the poets know of survival?' (264) Robbie asks and the two authors hover above him anxious and indicted. They may do their best to imagine, but the success of their version depends on a trickery involving the apparently random deployment of convincing detail – what Briony terms, in the last section, the 'pointillist approach to verisimilitude' (McEwan 2001: 359). Once again empiricism implicitly demolishes the value of literature, for even the most random and demythologizing account of war can never offer an experience that approaches its reality. The reader, too, is indicted as party to the vampirism of 'war literature'.

However, the passage goes beyond these implications. In Marilyn Butler's influential *Jane Austen and the War of Ideas* (1975) she characterized her subject as 'anti-jacobin': Austen's writing displays affinities with much late-eighteenth century British writing which reacted to, and rejected, liberal ideas and threats that emerged from the French Revolution. Such fiction provided an opposition to sentimental writing, which assumed that human instinct is essentially good and preferred the individual over established institutions and conventions. Butler's account of *Sense and Sensibility* offers a way into this debate:

> Jane Austen's version of 'sensibility' – that is, individualism, or the worship of the self, in various familiar guises – is as harshly dealt with here as anywhere in the anti-jacobin tradition. [. . .] Mrs. Ferrars's London is recognizably a sketch of the anarchy that follows the loss of all values but self-indulgence. In the opening chapters especially, where Marianne is the target of criticism, 'sensibility' means sentimental (or revolutionary) idealism, which Elinor counters with her sceptical or pessimistic view of man's nature. (Butler 1975: 194)

In Robbie's association of poets with 'unruly' freedom, he aligns the imagination with selfishness. The alternative is the good order that guarantees survival. Throughout McEwan's novel the imagination is portrayed as dangerous, untrustworthy and originating in self-interest. *Atonement* has thus inherited an updated form of anti-jacobinism. McEwan returns to Austen's conservative notion that knowledge of the self and the principles on which moral action is based must be mediated through conventional social obligation.

The final place in which we must test this anti-postmodern reading is at *Atonement*'s close, when the text's self-consciousness is most obvious. We are told that the section in Balham is a fabrication – that Robbie and Cecilia are dead – and are forced to recognize the constructedness of the world in which we have been immersed. As McEwan has stated, the novel is less about the 'crime' than 'the process of atonement' through writing (Reynolds and Noakes 2002: 20). However, this does not clarify the implications of Briony's confession. Although *Atonement* certainly wants us to feel the force of its ambiguity, as readers we feel sympathy for Briony and admire her candid self-analysis while feeling desolated by Robbie and Cecilia's death. However, in the end there seems little uncertainty. For the novel to belong to the world of the postmodern – for it to argue, as Finney suggests, that constructing false fictions is unavoidable – there has to be doubt about what really happened. Here, there is none. The real, against which Briony struggles, as she did in the case of the rape, is the unavoidable truth of the lovers' death; depicting them has not brought them back to life or enabled her to assuage her guilt. Fiction is presented as a lie – a lie that, if believed, comforts, distorts and finally produces unethical action. There is no atonement and fiction is necessarily a failure because Briony knows what is true.

The status of fiction in *Atonement* is clearest in the passage in which Briony is explaining why she has to wait for her death before publishing:

> The Marshalls have been active about the courts since the late forties, defending their good names with a most expensive ferocity. They could ruin

a publishing house with ease from their current accounts. One might almost think they had something to hide. Think, yes, but not write. The obvious suggestions have been made – displace, transmute, dissemble. Bring down the fogs of the imagination! What are novelists for? (McEwan 2001: 370)

The last two-and-a-half sentences are Briony's quotation from an imaginary friend, publisher or editor advising her on how she might publish without becoming open to litigation – in itself ironized, given the plagiarism row traced in Chapter Four of this book. However, the view of literary production put forward here is consistent with the implicit view held throughout *Atonement*. The imagination is a fog, something that obscures facts and misleads the unwary. The answer to her own question 'What are novelists for?' is surprisingly damning. Whether they are fairytale fabulists, scrupulous modernists, or self-conscious postmodernists, they are here to lie.

Atonement's metafiction is not there to present the reader with the inevitable penetration of the real with the fictive. Instead the novel serves to show that the two worlds are entirely distinct: there is the world of the real and the world of literature, and woe betide those who confuse the two. For the novel to be postmodern there would have to be ontological uncertainty rather than the overwhelming confidence about what is true with which we are confronted.

McEwan has a profound interest in the ethical dimension of the processes of reading and writing fiction, but this does not mean that he is tempted to believe that we are all narrated. This latter position is tainted with a moral indeterminacy that his work consciously rejects. The brunt of the criticism of the imagination implicit in *Atonement* falls not on Briony alone, however. By referring to Austen, the novel implicitly attacks postmodern novelists and their celebration of the fictive. These latter-day Jacobins – one thinks perhaps of Angela Carter and Salman Rushdie, and, ironically, McEwan's earlier self, who wrote *The Child in Time* – are guilty of making over-elaborate claims for the novel, and the literary imagination in general. Against the dangers of relativism and self-delusion implicit in postmodern poetics *Atonement* pits a tradition of English empiricism.

CHAPTER SIX

Ian McEwan's Modernist Time:
Atonement and *Saturday*

LAURA MARCUS

Chapter Summary: At the heart of all Ian McEwan's fiction is a concern with time and the experience of temporality. This chapter examines McEwan's interest in 'modernist time' – the explosion of interest in dynamic temporalities and variable time caused by scientific progress – in *Atonement* (2001) and *Saturday* (2005). It analyses modernist time by examining *The Child in Time* (1987) and moves on to explore McEwan's narration of time via his engagement with Virginia Woolf. McEwan brings her work back into the fold because she plays out a movement between the dissolution and recreation of character in the novel, and she explores the interrelationship of individual consciousnesses. McEwan's fictions ultimately confound absolute distinctions between 'realist', 'modernist' and 'postmodernist' writing, while at the same time revealing the most acute awareness of the particularities of times and of histories.

At the heart of all Ian McEwan's fiction is a concern with time and the experience of temporality, from the time of the fiction – narrative duration, the looping backwards and forwards in the temporalities of memory and anticipation – to the ways in which characters and readers themselves experience time. McEwan's signal narrative technique is his representation of the extended temporalities entailed in a singular occurrence: a car-crash; the collapse of a hot-air balloon; the approach of menacing dogs in an isolated landscape; a struggle by a fountain over a vase; the flight-path of a burning aeroplane. In *The Child in Time* (1987), the central protagonist, Stephen Lewis, successfully steers his car to safety after a collision and, as he becomes aware of the ways in which time has contracted and expanded, marvels at 'how duration shaped itself round the intensity of the event' (McEwan 1987: 95). From novel to novel, McEwan's characters come up against this experience of time and its shaping and warping: it also becomes the essential matter of the reader's experience.

McEwan's fiction is further preoccupied by the relationship between public and private histories, and with the ways in which our individual experiences occur in tandem, or at odds, with historical events. Testing the concept of 'collective' experience and the extent to which the time-sense of the individual is aligned with that of the group or mass, a number of his novels represent public and historically-charged events which take place within the public sphere of the modern city: demonstrations, celebrations, protests. In *Black Dogs* (1992), the narrator, Jeremy, and his father-in-law, Bernard, a former member of the Communist Party, travel to see Berlin for themselves as the wall surrounding West Berlin comes down in 1989, and division cedes to the promise of unity. It was Bernard who had first alerted Jeremy to the events taking place, in a phone call which interrupts Jeremy and his wife Jenny's love-making. They resume, for it was important 'that we maintain the primacy of the private life [. . .] But the spell had been broken. Cheering crowds were surging through the early morning gloom of our bedroom. We were both elsewhere' (McEwan 1998: 69). They turn on the television and watch as '[t]he camera bobbed and weaved intrusively into wide-armed embraces' (McEwan 1998: 69). The relationship and, at times, tension between the private life and the public event are intertwined with the question of story-telling, the piecing together of lives in the biographical form, the complexities created by competing accounts of events, and the need to shore up the past through narrative and in the face of memory's losses.

In *Atonement* (2001) McEwan's preoccupation with the experience and representation of time is intertwined with his explorations of the nature of fiction and the fictive. This entails complex negotiations with the work of modernist writers and with 'modernist time' – the exploration of dynamic temporalities and variable time caused by scientific progress in the nineteenth and early twentieth centuries. The novel both inhabits this time and articulates its cultural and temporal distance from it. This temporal 'double consciousness' has its parallel in the double nature of *Atonement*'s engagement with the relationship between experience and representation, and with the imbrications of reality and fiction. Its fictive self-reflexivity is achieved within an apparently realist framework in which the reader becomes fully engaged in the immediacies of the depicted events which are retrospectively revealed to be fictional. 'I think that I'm always drawn', McEwan has stated, 'to some kind of balance between a fiction that is self-reflective on its processes, and one that has a forward impetus too, that will completely accept the given terms of the illusion of fiction' (Noakes and Reynolds 2002: 20). The achievement of *Atonement* is to bring these two dimensions together so seamlessly, and to integrate the 'forward impetus' with the 'posthumous ironies' (McEwan 2002: 48) of retrospective narration.

Saturday, in its representation of a day in the life of a man and a city, is indebted to the great modernist city texts of James Joyce and Virginia Woolf – *Ulysses* (1922) and *Mrs Dalloway* (1925). The nature of this debt or legacy is, however, by no means straightforward. Like other contemporary novels which rewrite earlier fictions – Michael Cunningham's re-imaginings of Virginia Woolf's life and fiction in *The Hours* (1998) is a central example – *Saturday* enacts a split between the text's 'knowledge' that it is a repetition of a fictional predecessor and the novel's characters' unawareness of this fact. Living their lives as if for the first time, they are nonetheless caught in the literary webs of echo, allusion, reference. McEwan has on occasion adopted a critical attitude towards what he has perceived as Woolf's refusal of 'character' in her novels, but his recent fiction, in particular, is profoundly engaged with the forms of time, narrative and consciousness which lay at the heart of her fictional experiments: the one-day novel; the irruptions of the past into present time; the distinction between external and internal time – 'time on the clock and time in the mind' (Woolf 1992a: 95), in Woolf's phrase – and the variable temporalities that result from this disjunction; the construction of a 'passage' or tunnel through which time travels. McEwan explores and deploys these temporal and narrative structures, but he does not attempt merely to reproduce the modernist text, nor to create a parody or pastiche of it. His later novels are, rather, in dialogue with the structures of modernist fiction, which revolutionized the ways in which stories could be told. He acknowledges the debt even as he calls attention to the necessary and inevitable distance between his own time and that of the modernist novelist.

The Temporalities of *The Child in Time*

How do we live in time, and what is the relationship of the individual's time to that of the public and historical event? These questions preoccupied nineteenth-century writers and we could certainly position McEwan as an 'historical novelist' and writer of 'historical fiction', as Natasha Alden asserts in Chapter Four. His 'period' is to a significant extent World War Two and its aftermath: his parents' time. This suggests that we live in, and through, the values of the generation, or generations, preceding our own. To this extent, we are never fully present at and in our own times. This suggestion of an ideological time-lapse or time-lag is realized, in an unfamiliar dimension of experience, in *The Child in Time*, when Stephen travels to visit his wife Julie, from whom he has separated after the devastating experience of their young daughter's abduction. Walking to the cottage in which Julie is living, he passes a country pub through whose window he sees a young man and woman, dressed in the clothing of the mid-twentieth century, engrossed in discussion. Through the window he meets the eyes of the young woman 'who he knew, beyond question, was his mother' (McEwan 1987: 59), but though she seems to look at him – 'she simply returned Stephen's gaze' – she does not appear to see him. This quasi-encounter, and the failure of reciprocity, removes all the security of his being, sending him spinning through a time before, or outside the known structures of, identity and temporality. Stephen later questions his now elderly mother about his experience, and she tells him of the time, early in her marriage, where the recently discovered fact of her pregnancy had seemed an inconvenience to his father, and where the continued existence of the foetus had hung in the balance. She had decided to have the baby when she had seen, as she sat in the pub, 'a face at the window, the face of a child, sort of floating there [. . .] [A]s far as I was concerned then, I was convinced, I just *knew* that I was looking at my own child. If you like, I was looking at you' (McEwan 1987: 175). As Dominic Head argues, 'McEwan here employs the post-Einsteinian conception of the plasticity of time and space to allow his protagonist to intervene in the past and secure his own future' (Head 2002: 235).

In *The Child in Time*, McEwan creates a character, Thelma, an academic physicist whose subject is the nature of time. She serves as the 'theorist' of time in the novel, explaining to Stephen (and us) the ways in which time in the universe is conceived by scientists. The commonplace understanding of time as linear, 'marching from left to right, from the past through the present to the future, is either nonsense or a tiny fraction of the truth. We know this from our own experience. An hour can seem like five minutes or a week. Time is variable' (McEwan 1987: 117–18). It is also possible that time can grind to a halt altogether (as in 'black holes'), or move backwards. The engagement of McEwan's novel with, in Peter Middleton's and Tim Woods' phrase, 'the temporal discourse of the new physics' (Middleton and Woods 2000: 117), connects it to other late-twentieth-century novels – Middleton and Woods instance Margaret Atwood's *Cat's Eye* (1988) and Ursula Le Guin's *The Dispossessed* (1974) – in which physicists of time play significant parts. The highly complex and speculative concepts of time in contemporary physics – which differ radically between theories of relativity (in which time is relative to the observer) and quantum mechanics (in which time is external to the system) – are not, however, easily incorporated into narrative fiction, though they have shaped the directions of 'science fiction' as a twentieth-century genre. In *The Child in Time* Thelma can offer Stephen no explanation for his experience, though its confounding of the ordinary conceptions of the ordering of time bears some relation to the hypotheses at work in the scientist Stephen Hawking's *A Brief History of Time* (1988), which include the possibilities of time lived backwards and travel into the past. She does suggest, however, that:

It was not entirely fanciful to imagine that there would one day be mathematical and physical descriptions of the type of experience Stephen had recounted [. . .] Think how humanised and approachable scientists would be if they could join in the really important conversations about time, and without thinking they had the final word – the mystic's experience of time-lessness, the chaotic unfolding of time in dreams, the Christian moment of fulfilment and redemption, the annihilated time of deep sleep, the elaborate time schemes of novelists, poets, daydreamers, the infinite unchanging time of childhood. (McEwan 1987: 120)

The 'utopian' conceptions of bringing together 'scientific time and social time' (Middleton and Woods 2000: 117) and the languages of science and literature are central to *A Child in Time* as a 'novel of ideas'. They also resonate, however, albeit in different guises, in *Atonement* and, most markedly, in *Saturday*. These novels of 'character' and 'consciousness' are preoccupied not only with time, temporality and duration, but with the competing claims of science/medicine and literature to 'truth'. They also possess an extreme self-consciousness about the stakes and status of fiction and storytelling, and an intense, if often implicit, relationship to other fictional works, in particular those of early- and mid-twentieth-century writers. The remainder of this chapter explores McEwan's preoccupation with the nature of the fictive, as it relates to his negotiations with the work of modernist writers and 'modernist time'.

Time and Knowledge in *Atonement*

The ironies of *Atonement*'s retrospective composition are unlikely to be fully comprehended at a first reading. The intense jolt to the first-time reader occurs at a late stage in the novel when it is made clear that we have been reading the final 'draft' of a novel, written by the central character, Bryony Tallis, who makes her initial appearance, as an aspiring 13-year-old writer, on the novel's first page. The two characters – Cecilia and Robbie – whose destinies have become a matter of such moment, have not survived within historical time. Their lives have been extended only in Bryony's narrative, the consolatory nature of which is presented in coded form in the third section of the novel when Bryony, nursing a dying Frenchman, Luc Cornet, tells him of her sister and the man she is to marry. In readings beyond the first, the insistent use of prospect and retrospect, and the invocation of 'posthumous ironies', will point to a knowledge initially concealed by the power of the narrative drive. Time becomes the medium and instrument of irony and pathos, as the lineaments of the 'present' are imagined from the perspectives of a future which neither Cecilia nor Robbie, the characters who are represented most fully in this mode of anticipated retrospect, will in fact live out – 'the unavailable future', in a phrase used later in the novel in connection with the dead Luc (McEwan 2002: 311). Cecilia envisages a future vantage point from which she will look back at a present which has become the past: 'Cecilia wondered, as she sometimes did when she met a man for the first time, if this was the one she was going to marry, and whether it was this particular moment she would remember for the rest of her life – with gratitude, or profound and particular regret' (McEwan, 2002: 47). Robbie projects himself forward into the man he will never in fact become, imagining his future as he walks to the Tallis's house for an evening whose outcome will be the destruction of every plan he has made: 'The hard soles of his shoes rapped loudly on the metalled road like a giant clock, and he made himself think about time, about his great hoard, the luxury of an unspent fortune. He had never before felt so self-consciously young, nor experienced such appetite, such impatience for the story to begin' (McEwan 2002: 92). Our stories, though, are not always ours for the making.

In the long first section of the novel, which recounts the events of a single day, the third-person narration enters, in turn, the conscious-nesses of four of the characters depicted: Bryony, her sister Cecilia, their mother Emily, and Robbie, son of their cleaning woman Grace Turner. If Cecilia and Robbie, who first become lovers during the evening of this day, are caught in the imaginings of time and subjected to its failed possibilities and ironies, Bryony and Emily inhabit, and are inhabited by, another set of terms, in particular those of knowledge and vision, knowing and seeing. Bryony is explicitly represented as the fabulist, the maker-up, and the writer, of stories. Writing is her way of ordering the world, and its initial pleasures are those of miniaturization – to be com-pared with the satisfaction of her neatly arranged model farm – and the satisfactions of completion. Yet as the day progresses, Bryony begins to understand something of complexity of the role of fiction in represent-ing multiple and conflicting points of view.

An author often cited by McEwan as an influence on his work, Henry James, proclaims: 'The house of fiction has in short not one window, but a million – number of possible windows not to be reckoned, rather' (James 2003: 45). Throughout *Atonement* Bryony, like Henry Perowne in *Saturday*, is represented as a watcher from windows. James, writing at the turn of the nineteenth and twentieth centuries, represented such ways of seeing as central to the 'architecture' of the modern novel. The intense focus, in the work of James and his contemporaries, including Joseph Conrad and Ford Madox Ford, on the relationship between con-sciousness and vision and its multiple perspectives, challenged the idea that there is a single, objective way of viewing and describing events, objects and people. Bryony's witnessing of 'the scene by the fountain' – the encounter between Cecilia and Robbie which lies at the novel's heart – already witnessed by the reader through the eyes of a seemingly omniscient narrator, and her failure to comprehend what she sees, leads to a new understanding of writing: 'she sensed she could write a scene like the one by the fountain and she could include a hidden observer like herself' (McEwan 2002: 40):

> She [Bryony] could write the scene three times over, from three points of view [. . .] She need only show separate minds, as alive as her own, struggling with the idea that other minds were equally alive [. . .] And only in a story could you enter these different minds and show how they had an equal value. That was the only moral a story need have. (McEwan 2002: 40)

Yet this is not a fully or finally achieved vision: Bryony subsequently finds herself unable to deal with contradiction and imposes an interpretative 'order' on events, which has fatal consequences for those around her.

Emily writes nothing and sees nothing from the bed to which illness confines her, yet possesses a form of 'sixth sense', which she describes as

> a tentacular awareness that reached out from the dimness and moved through the house, unseen and all-knowing [. . .] What to others would have been a muffling was to her alert senses, which were fine-tuned like the cat's whiskers of an old wireless, an almost unbearable amplification. She lay in the dark and knew everything. The less she was able to do, the more she was aware. (McEwan 2002: 66)

Lying in bed, she hears the sound of a man's voice in the room in which her niece Lola is staying. She 'beamed her raw attention into every recess of the house. There was nothing, and then, like a lamp turned on and off in total darkness, there was a little squeal of laughter abruptly smothered. Lola, then, in the nursery with Marshall' (McEwan 2002: 69). She is reassured by her identification of the sounds of the house: wrongly so, for it is Marshall who will be responsible for the damage that follows. The novel thus puts into question the very concept of narrative omniscience, of the 'unseen and all-knowing' narrator. Emily is indeed aware that she 'could send her tendrils into every room of the house, but she could not send them into the future' (McEwan 2002: 71).

The terms of 'knowing' and 'seeing/unseeing' are brought together with those of Bryony's 'crime' at the close of the day, the false identification of Robbie as Lola's rapist: 'the understanding that what she knew was not literally, or not only, based on the visible' (McEwan 2002: 169). Bryony's dangerous 'knowledge' results from her need for a story that makes sense of the events she witnessed earlier in the day but whose meaning she has not understood: Cecilia and Robbie at the fountain, the 'obscene' word in the letter she carried from Robbie to Cecilia, their love-making in the library which Bryony interprets as Robbie's assault upon her sister. Throughout the first section of the novel, she understands sexual passion as coercion and violence.

Issues of knowledge and vision function at two levels in the narrative: they relate to the question of what characters know and see, or imagine they know and have seen, and to the question of narration itself and the workings of narrative omniscience. This is brought into relationship with 'telepathy' and 'clairvoyance', the 'shilling's glimpse of the future' (with all the irony that this phrase imparts, in a novel of 'unavailable futures') provided by Robbie's mother Grace (McEwan 2002: 88). 'A story was a form of telepathy', Bryony thinks, as she contemplates the question of 'intention' and of minds other than her own: 'By means of inking symbols onto a page, she was able to send thoughts and feelings from her mind to her reader's. It was a magical process, so commonplace that no one stopped to wonder at it' (McEwan 2002: 37). The thought chimes with Nicholas Royle's argument that narrative 'omniscience' is a misnomer, bringing with it an inappropriate religious baggage, for the ways in which communication occurs between author and character, author and reader – the reading of minds, the entry into the minds of others, and the communication of the contents of these minds to readers – is not 'omniscient', Royle argues, but telepathic. The category of the 'omniscient narrator', so familiar that its presuppositions go unquestioned, conceals the 'magical process', the magical thinking that lies at the heart of literary writing and reading (Royle 2003: 261).

Atonement and Woolf

A further form of communication is the one that occurs between works of literature themselves. Woolf is directly named twice in the novel and her words haunt not only Bryony but the novel itself – or, more accurately, the echoes of Woolf become Bryony's style and signature, covertly alluding to her authorship of the entire work. In the passage quoted above, in which the mother 'beamed her raw attention into every corner of the house', we hear echoes of Woolf's Mrs Ramsay, of the identification between the mother and the house and her 'becoming' the light of the lighthouse: 'She looked up over her knitting and met the third stroke and it seemed to her like her own eyes meeting her own eyes, searching as she alone could search into her mind and her heart, purifying out of existence that lie, any lie' (Woolf 1992b: 70).

The first draft of the novel which Bryony's 'atonement' will require her to write again and again is explicitly linked to Woolf's fiction, as the following quotation underscores:

> Despite her journal sketches, [Bryony] no longer believed in characters. They were quaint devices that belonged to the nineteenth century [. . .] Plots too were like rusted machinery whose wheels would no longer turn [. . .] It was thought, perceptions, sensations that interested her [. . .] If only she could reproduce the clear light of a summer's morning, the sensations of a child standing at a window, the curve and dip of a swallow's flight over a pool of water. The novel of the future would be unlike anything in the past. She had

read Virginia Woolf's *The Waves* three times and thought that a great transformation was being worked in human nature itself, and that only fiction, a new kind of fiction, could capture the essence of the change. (McEwan 2002: 281–2)

The terms 'change' and 'transformation' are central here, echoing their repetition in the novel's first section. Robbie, finally acknowledging his desire for Cecilia, is 'in no doubt that a great change was coming over him' (McEwan 2002: 80); entering a room, and seeing light falling through a glass door 'in fiery honeycomb patterns', he is 'surprised by the transformation' (McEwan 2002: 87). Literature is central to Robbie's imaginings, and the versions of the letter he writes to Cecilia are referred to throughout as 'drafts' which, like Bryony, he works over again and again. The 'obscene draft' which he sends unintentionally is said to have been charged by his reading of Lawrence's *Lady Chatterley's Lover* (1928), a novel whose plot is another ghost in McEwan's narrative of 'cross-class' love and eroticism, above all in Robbie's deliberate and precise usage of the word 'cunt'. Entering Cecilia's consciousness, we are told of the ways in which she also feels herself to be 'changed' and 'transformed' by her years at Cambridge (McEwan 2002: 103). Robbie and Cecilia's subsequent love-making 'marked a transformation', 'changed' their childhood relationships to each other (McEwan 2002: 135). Love is rendered as 'the momentous change they had achieved', as the 'transformation' of the self (McEwan 2002: 137), a topos explored in *Saturday*, and assessed by Sebastian Groes in the next chapter (see pp. 103–6).

The impact of the day's events on Bryony is a bewildering one, but it is underlain by the sense that it has brought about 'changes that had made her into a real writer at last' and 'transformed what had gone before' (McEwan 2002: 121). The repetition of the two terms in these varying contexts, and their later return in Bryony's adult reflections on the change and transformation that has occurred in modernist writing – with its clear echoes of Woolf's playful assertion that 'On or about December 1910 human character changed' (Woolf 2008: 38) – creates a complex nexus of literary values. 'Change' and 'transformation' are to be perceived as dimensions of perception and sensation, and of the alteration in the ways in which the modernist work represents the world, but they are also processes acting upon characters who are, or feel themselves to be, changed and transformed by events and passions. The transformation that is being worked in human nature, McEwan appears to be suggesting, is to be represented through 'character' and not in opposition to it, and this would seem to be the position Bryony comes to adopt as she drafts and redrafts her novel, the final draft of which is given to us whole and entire.

The first draft, by contrast, would appear to have eschewed 'character' and 'plot'. Bryony receives a letter from the editor of *Horizon* magazine (initialled CC, for Cyril Connolly) rejecting the novella, entitled 'Two

Figures by a Fountain': 'Something unique and unexplained is caught. However, we wondered whether it owed a little too much to the techniques of Mrs Woolf' (McEwan 2002: 313). It is suggested that the novella requires 'development', 'the backbone of a story': 'If this girl has so fully misunderstood or been so wholly baffled by the strange little scene that has unfolded before her, how might it affect the lives of the two adults? Might she come between them in some disastrous fashion?' (McEwan 2002: 313) This is, of course, the way in which the novel unfolds. The letter also provides clues that the narrative we have already read – that of the scene by the fountain in the first section – has undergone revisions following the letter's suggestions: the Ming vase has, for example, become a Meissen vase. We are being prepared as readers – and yet when it comes we are not prepared – to be told that the narrative is Bryony's and not the 'impartial' truth of historic narration or *histoire*. The shock of this knowledge, when it comes, exposes the extent of our investment as readers in 'the illusion of fiction'.

The 'fictionalism' of *Atonement* is closely connected to Woolf's writing, and the novel of Woolf's most strongly echoed is *To the Lighthouse* (1927). *Atonement* deploys a version of its tripartite structure: a single day in the house in the country, the middle section – time passes and the war – and, finally, the return to the house, when everything that happens is an attempt to complete what was left unfinished. The trip to the lighthouse, Lily's painting of Mrs Ramsay and, in *Atonement*, the enacting of the young Bryony's play, whose performance was abandoned some six decades previously – these are all gestures of completion which come too late. The questions raised here are those of the relationships between belatedness and atonement, narration and reparation, and of McEwan's novel as 'late Woolf'. McEwan is drawn to the 'redemptive' nature of modernist time, in which the work of art offers compensation for the losses wrought by time and history, but he deploys it with the full knowledge of its identity as a consolatory fiction.

In its central section, *Atonement* gives us the experience of war – the Second World War and the retreat of the British and French at Dunkirk. This section transmutes the empty house and the passage of time in *To the Lighthouse* into an intensely realized representation of war and its impact upon bodies. One might be tempted to say that this is the male novelist, supplementing, or filling in, or giving flesh – albeit of a torn and wounded kind – to the sort of events and experiences at which Woolf would not look directly, in her refusal to 'heroize' the protagonists of a war (in her case World War One) to which she was profoundly opposed. Yet *Atonement* narrates the war (we later learn) through Bryony's imaginings. The women nurses' experiences of war, and their sensations of seeing and touching broken and maimed bodies, occupy the third part of the novel. The distorted, fragmented and surreal perceptions of body parts and faces that characterize the novel's opening section, which are linked to the strange sensations brought about by the heat of the day and the tensions within the household, return in its second and third parts as the realities of warfare.

The connective images of fragmentation also serve to link the 'private' pre-war world of the country house with the depredations of war. 'Change' and 'transformation' operate not only at the level of the individual character and the private life: the sense of something momentous, but unnamed and unnameable, on the point of occurrence is also part of the public history of the mid-1930s, at a time when, as Brian Finney writes in his account of *Atonement*, 'the West was suffering from a collective myopia in the face of the rise of fascism which only a minority on the political left seemed prepared to confront' (Finney 2004: 77). The vase, the central 'prop' in the *mise-en-scène* of the 'Two Figures by a Fountain' – broken, repaired and broken again along its fault-lines – creates a direct link to the preceding war. The post-war years transmute into the inter-war years. The family situation which has led to the presence in the household of the Tallis's cousins – Lola and her two young brothers – is described as 'a bitter domestic civil war': fathers in the novel are for the most part absent, literally or emotionally. 'The private', in Finney's words, 'is linked to the public by the figurative use of the word "war", which calls attention to its polysemantic usage' (Finney 2004: 77) in that both realms are linguistically linked by the same word.

The thematic and perceptual continuities between the first and the central parts of *Atonement* are further hints of the overarching nature of Bryony's narration, continuities otherwise masked by the different styles deployed in the novel's different sections. There are moments, for instance, at which a 'Woolfian' perception seems to enter the war-zone: 'Each successive ridge was paler than the one before. He saw a receding wash of grey and blue fading in a haze towards the setting sun, like something oriental on a dinner plate' (McEwan 2002: 194). This is the language of *The Waves* (1931), anticipated in the first section of the novel, as a prelude to Robbie's reveries: 'In the early evening, high-altitude clouds in the western sky formed a thin yellow wash which became richer over the hour, and then thickened until a filtered orange glow hung above the giant crests of parkland trees' (McEwan 2002: 78).

Some of the comments contained in the letter are, *Horizon*'s editor writes to Bryony, those of 'Mrs Elizabeth Bowen': like Woolf's, Bowen's words, as McEwan suggests, haunt the novel. The imbrications of time and war, in particular, connect *Atonement* to Bowen's World War Two novel *The Heat of the Day* (1949), in which characters seek to preserve the fragments of their shattered worlds. 'The dead were not yet present, the absent were presumed alive', we are told in Part Three of *Atonement*, of the hours before the wounded men arrive at the hospital from France (McEwan 2002: 287). The terms of presence and absence, and their connections to posthumous existence, were at the heart of Bowen's haunted and haunting representations of the city during war-time: 'Most of all the dead, from mortuaries, from under cataracts of rubble, made their anonymous presence – not as today's dead but as yesterday's living – felt through London' (Bowen 1950: 86).

The 'presence' in McEwan's text of these echoes and influences raises two significant, and at points interrelated, issues: the relationship of the contemporary writer to his or her modernist predecessors, and the male writer's negotiations with women's voices and with women writers. McEwan's specific engagement with Virginia Woolf remains ambiguous. As we have seen, Bryony's 'novella', 'Two Figures by a Fountain', so influenced, we are told, by *The Waves* and by Woolf's ideas about fiction, is represented as an evasive text, whose refusal of plot, of 'development', is a denial of human acts and their implications. And yet in *Atonement*, McEwan also turns back to Woolf, and, in particular, to the ways in which she continued to play out the dissolution and the recreation of character in the novel, and the separation between, and interrelationship of, individual consciousnesses.

The novel's epilogue or coda moves into a different form of voicing, as we are presented with Bryony's first-person narration. She describes the ways in which her 'atonement' has taken the form of her writing her novel over and over again. 'Nothing is disguised', Bryony asserts in the closing section, 'London, 1999', but the final version of the novel – the novel we have just read – takes 'a stand against oblivion and despair': 'The problem these fifty-nine years has been this: how can a novelist achieve atonement when, with her absolute power of deciding outcomes, she is also God?' (McEwan 2002: 371).

For some critics, the epilogue to *Atonement* was an unwelcome addition, and the blunt, 'postmodern' ending a betrayal of the novel's earlier subtleties. It could, however, be argued that the epilogue becomes all the more necessary to preserve the balance McEwan seeks between the self-reflective fiction and the illusion of reality. It produces, moreover, a highly ambiguous closure, giving us something of the shifts and alterations in Bryony's understandings of the work of fiction explored at earlier stages in the novel. The 'atonement' achieved – or not achieved – by Bryony's fiction-making remains an uncertain, ill-defined concept. As Dominic Head argues, McEwan seems to be taking some distance from the position, adopted by a number of his literary contemporaries and indeed suggested by a number of his own comments in interview, that 'narrative empathy' is necessarily an 'ethics of fiction' (Head 2007: 174). The novelist's imaginative entry into other minds can never obviate the fact that these minds are, ultimately, his or her own creation. Bryony's conundrum, moreover, uses terms that the novel had earlier seemed to repudiate – 'omniscience', the impersonal God-figure of the author/narrator – pitting these against a word and concept – 'atonement' – whose religious register they would, on the surface, seem to share. The 'belatedness', which reinscribes the structure and closure of *To the Lighthouse*, defines the return to the house and the performance of Bryony's play: the breach in time can in part, but only in part, be bridged by the work and workings of art.

The epilogue is in fact driven not only by the question of the fictive but by the implications of the now elderly Bryony's vascular dementia, which will slowly eradicate first memory and then identity. This context has a very personal resonance for McEwan, who has written of the destruction of his mother's memory through the same neurological disease, the effects of which he also explores in *Saturday*, in his representation of his central protagonist's mother and her loss of the structures of time and temporality: 'Everything belongs in the present' (McEwan 2005: 164). Increased longevity has, in the contemporary Western world, brought with it both more memory and more memory to be lost: McEwan is among a number of contemporary memoirists and novelists writing, shoring up memory, in the face of parental – usually maternal – mental dissolution. This has in turn led to an increased fascination with mental processes, a concern with the nature of 'empathy', and a redefinition of the modernist preoccupation with 'consciousness' in neurological terms. All of these lie at the heart of *Saturday*. The source of the violence which will be directed against Perowne and, later in the day, against his family, is the damaged, defective brain of the character Baxter: 'Here is the signature of so many neurodegenerative diseases – the swift transition from one mood to another, without awareness or memory, or understanding of how it seems to others' (McEwan 2002: 96).

Saturday and the Modernist Novel

Woolf's writing, and specifically *Mrs Dalloway*, also reverberates throughout *Saturday*. Events in Clarissa Dalloway's day are closely matched by those in Henry Perowne's: they include the viewing of a spectacle in the sky; the preparations for an evening party; blockades in the city, on the Saturday of the anti-war protest; the embedding of memories which back the present with the past; the world seen by the sane and the insane, side by side. Time and the city, time in the city, are at the heart of both novels. The structure of the day, the chiming of the hours, and the march of the city appear to propel the protagonists of both *Mrs Dalloway* and *Saturday* ever forward, but spaces of memory and subjectivity – the spheres of 'private time' – are hollowed out from within linear time to produce, in Ann Banfield's phrase, 'arrested moments' (Banfield 2007: 56). Yet there are important differences as well as similarities in the ways in which private and public time, and the relationship between the two, are represented in Woolf's and McEwan's novels.

These differences and similarities have been picked up and developed by Mark Currie, who, in *About Time* (2007), frames his discussion of time in *Saturday* through the philosopher and narrative theorist Paul Ricoeur's account of time and narrative in *Mrs Dalloway*. In Woolf's novel, the passing of the day as it progresses is punctuated by the tolling of Big Ben, whose strokes are, Ricoeur argues, part of the character's experience of time and of its fictive refiguration in the novel. As the numerous events of the day accumulate, pulling the narrative ahead, it is simultaneously pulled backwards by excursions into the past. The striking of Big Ben represents chronological time; what is significant, Ricoeur notes, is the relation that 'the various protagonists establish with these marks of time' (Ricoeur 1985: 105). In Ricoeur's analysis, 'monumental history' secretes a 'monumental time' which has its audible expression in chronological time. Hence the complicity of clock time with the figures and institutions of authority and power in the novel, located at the heart of the imperial city. Septimus Smith, the shell-shocked victim of World War One, is both the hero and the victim of the radical discordance beween personal time and monumental time. The horror of time rises up from the depths of monumental history – the Great War – bringing back from the dead the ghost of Septimus's war comrade Evans. Clarissa, while sharing Septimus's experience of the terror of time, is 'saved' (Woolf 2000: 31) by her ability to plunge 'into the very heart of the moment' (Woolf 2000: 4) and by a relationship with time which is both collusive and subversive: her 'time' is sounded by the church bells of St Margaret's which come in the wake of the great booming voice of Big Ben.

In Currie's reading of the novel, the incident which begins Perowne's day, the burning plane in the sky, is significant for 'the role it performs in transforming clock time into monumental time, since it is through the rolling reports of TV news that this incident passes from the realm of private occurrence into the public domain' (Currie 2007: 130). Currie argues that the 'rolling events of TV and radio news', which function as a form of clock for Perowne, define a 'distinctly modern relation between the present and its representation as retrospect, a relation which seems to define the reality of an event in terms of its representation', and that this 'mastery which is lacking in the experiential present' is valued by Perowne 'over the reinventions of literature' (Currie 2007: 130). He possesses a 'mastery over the present' which produces an alignment between 'his inner life and the public world' (Currie 2007: 131). Whereas *Mrs Dalloway* 'offers a variant of the relation of internal to monumental time in which the anachronicity of the former confronts the relentless forward motion of the latter, *Saturday* corroborates the scientific mind style with its monumental history' (Currie 2007: 131).

This reading to some extent disregards the ways in which remembered events in *Saturday* – a retrospection primarily linked to Perowne's familial relationships rather than to the public domain – pull the present back into the past and create hollowed-out moments or intervals equivalent to those of the modernist novel, in which subjectivity, desire and memory are allowed space and time to burgeon. Currie's arguments do open up, however, the complex terms of McEwan's relationship to his modernist predecessors and the implications of the ways in which he reframes their words. Leaving his house for his day's activities, Henry

Perowne's sensations directly echo those of Clarissa Dalloway at the opening of Woolf's novel. Clarissa, stepping out into the June day, recalls the moments in her youth when 'she had burst open the French windows and plunged at Burton into the open air. How fresh, how calm, stiller than this of course, the air was in the early morning; like the flap of a wave; the kiss of a wave' (Woolf 2000: 3). The 'plunge' is simultaneously into the present of the novel and the past of its central character through the threshold of the window, at which Clarissa is at other junctures in the novel also a watcher. In *Saturday*, McEwan writes:

> As he steps outside and turns from closing the door, he hears the squeal of seagulls come inland for the city's good pickings. The sun is low and only one half of the square – his half – is in full sunlight. He walks away from the square along blinding moist pavement, surprised by the freshness of the day. The air tastes almost clean. He has an impression of striding along a natural surface, along some coastal wilderness, on a smooth slab of basalt causeway he vaguely recalls from a childhood holiday. It must be the cry of the gulls bringing it back. He can remember the taste of spray off a turbulent blue-green sea, and as he reaches Warren Street he reminds himself that he mustn't forget the fishmonger's. (McEwan 2002: 71)

Perowne thus tracks his own thought processes and their paths of association, and the ways in which present impressions bring back sensations from the past. He has no access, however, as Currie observes, to 'the unknowable conditions in which his fiction life is embedded', including 'what he doesn't know of his own intertextual relations to *The Odyssey*, *Ulysses* and *Mrs Dalloway*' (Currie, 2007: 132). For Currie, this unknowing extends beyond Perowne to the novel itself, its commitment to a realistic frame rendering its self-knowledge incomplete, 'in that it cannot show even the most basic awareness of its own fictionality, and so of its own place in the debate between literature and science' (Currie 2007: 132). Yet it could be argued that the novel's intertexuality constitutes precisely its 'awareness of its own fictionality' and that *Saturday* is 'vigilant' less 'in the preservation of its realistic frame' than in its commitment to, in Head's phrase, 'the immediacy of human consciousness' which goes beyond 'mastery' of the present in its attempt to understand and represent the workings of the mind (Head 2007: 192). As in the passage quoted above, with its strong echoes of *Mrs Dalloway*, McEwan is paying a form of homage to modernist representations of consciousness, while, as Head notes, moving in a new direction with his attempt to produce 'a diagnostic "slice-of-mind" novel [. . .] rather than a modernist "slice-of-mind" novel' (Head 2007: 192). McEwan brings to the fore a new interest among writers in neuroscience and the relations between mind and brain: the novel would appear to be committed to a new way of aligning narrative and mental processes, and the forms of knowledge and enquiry associated with both literature and science.

The question of McEwan's engagement with Woolf, and other modernist texts, is thus a highly complex one, and explored in detail by Groes in the next chapter. McEwan's early fictions might have situated him securely as a postmodernist writer. Yet his more recent novels suggest a closer relationship not only with modernism but with the texts that preceded that movement and moment. This is borne out by McEwan's interest in the question of character in fiction. Woolf seems to represent for McEwan a rejection of the centrality of 'plot' and 'character': he returns these to the novel, while extending Woolf's, and the modernists', focus on consciousness and complex temporalities. His fictions ultimately confound absolute distinctions between 'realist', 'modernist' and 'postmodernist' writings, while at the same time revealing the most acute awareness of the particularities of time and of history.

CHAPTER SEVEN

Ian McEwan and the Modernist Consciousness of the City in *Saturday*

SEBASTIAN GROES

Chapter Summary: Ian McEwan's early work presents an archetypal 'Darkest London' of poverty, oppression, squalor and reduced humanity, but *The Child in Time* (1987) introduces a shift in this vision by refracting the city through the lens of modernist texts, ideas and images. *Saturday* (2005) intensifies McEwan's modernist renegotiation of London by bringing the city to life via a complex intertextuality. On the one hand we find canonic modernist works and, on the other, the Victorian cultural critic and poet Matthew Arnold (1822–1888). This chapter uses McEwan's representation of the contemporary city as a means of understanding his complex, uncertain meditation on the state of the world at the beginning of the twenty-first century, the divorce of the private and public realms, the relationship between science and the arts, democracy, and the war in Iraq.

Darkest London

Ian McEwan is one of the foremost explorers of our experience of the modern city, and London in particular has played a central role in this project. His early short stories portray an archetypal version of what Raymond Williams called 'Darkest London', a 'city of darkness, of oppression, of crime and squalor, or reduced humanity' (Williams 1973: 221; 227). These tales align the city with a literary mythology of London as a monstrous and unjust place where young innocents are corrupted, and dragged into abject underworlds of slave labour and prostitution. In 'Disguises' (1975), children are abused by a network of paedophiles in an Islington home. Set in and around Finsbury Park, 'Homemade' (1975) tells the story of a young man who rapes his sister to lose his much resented virginity. 'Butterflies' (1975) also presents a dark city: there 'are no parks in this part of London, only car parks. And there is a canal, the brown canal which goes between factories and past a scrap heap, the canal little Jane drowned in' (McEwan 2006: 72) – she drowns after the narrator sexually assaults her. He also notes that 'a glass of water from a London tap has been drunk five times before', evoking the image of the city as unclean (McEwan 2006: 73). The irony of the imagery, itself recycled, suggests that McEwan acknowledges and challenges traditional treatments of London as a stage for either innocence or experience.

The 'darkest London' tradition tends to feature the 'illegitimate' parts of the city and 'the separated East End' in particular (Williams 1973: 229). McEwan's stories feature Soho, famously associated with pornography, prostitution, adult entertainment and the gay scene. In 'Pornography' (1978), a Soho porn peddler who cheats on two nurses gets his come-uppance in the form of castration. Likewise, the rehearsal of a pornographic Soho musical in 'Cocker at the Theatre' (1975) ironizes the commodification of the body within the urban economy by staging it as adult entertainment. McEwan's city is a spectacle of lust and excess, and a theatre of manipulation and moral decline, crawling with lecherous and violent lowlife. In the dystopian 'Two Fragments: March 199–' (1978), the capital is reduced to post-apocalyptic rubble. When the nameless protagonist walks along 'avenues of rusted, broken down cars', he stops in Soho to warm himself by a fire (McEwan 2006: 53) and is approached by a Chinaman, who takes him home to Chinatown, where a 'few upper-storey windows gleamed dully [and] gave a sense of direction of the street but they shone no light on it' (McEwan 2006: 54). This is a metropolis where culture, technology, civilization and law have vanished, leaving an underworld where society and human thought have been reduced to the basest level of consciousness. *The Child in Time* (1987) is set in an overcrowded, hellish future London, 'a lost time and a lost landscape' (McEwan 1988: 12), in which the protagonist's daughter is kidnapped from a South London supermarket. In the portrayal of London as a desert where restrictions 'on water use had reduced the front gardens of suburban West London to dust' (McEwan 1988: 85), McEwan rehearses a modernist cliché: 'The little squares of lawn were baked earth from which even the dried grass had flaked away. One wag had planted a row of cacti.' The spiritual, cultural and moral depletion evoked by this image overtly echoes T. S. Eliot's London in *The Waste Land* (1922): 'What are the roots that clutch, what branches grow / Out of this stony rubbish?' (Eliot 1969: 61). McEwan's answer is again ambivalent: on the one hand, the sinister publisher Charles Darke becomes a powerful and manipulative politician as anarchy takes hold of a North London suburb; on the other, the protagonist, Stephen Lewis, manages to reclaim his adulthood and sense of social and moral responsibility only after regressing into a childlike state.

The Child in Time complicates the darkest London stereotype by focusing on geographical areas different from the earlier work and, as the echo of Eliot suggests, by offering different images. Paul Edwards has focussed on McEwan's juxtaposition of trains and cars as a symbolic clash between nineteenth- and late-twentieth-century culture and technology under Thatcher (Edwards 1995), but the description of a 1930s housing development in West London intensifies McEwan's play with signs of modernity: 'They were squat, grubbily rendered houses dreaming under their roofs of open seas; there was a porthole by each front door, and the upper windows, cased in metal, attempted to suggest the bridge of an ocean liner' (McEwan 1988: 85). *Enduring Love* (1997) repeats this image in Joe Rose's description of his apartment building: 'In the twenties something resembling the *Queen Mary* ran aground in Maida Vale, and all that remains now is the bridge, our apartment building' (McEwan 1998: 54). The dating and situating of the building, and McEwan's repeated use of the image, are striking. The ocean liner is a stock symbol of modernity: the machinery of the twentieth century connotes international travel, a spirit of progress and optimism about the fate of culture and civilization. This sign of modernity creates the false impression that the stylized and harmonious architecture is actually able to shut out the chaos, madness and violence of darkest London embodied in Joe's stalker, Jed. The shifting representation of London marks an important adjustment to McEwan's earlier portrayal of the city by refracting the representation of the city through the lens of modernity.

A Modernist Consciousness of the City: Three Types of Intertextuality

Saturday (2005) takes Fitzrovia, and a building based upon McEwan's own home, as the setting for a further intensification of this modernist renegotiation of London. The novel narrates 24 hours in the life of neurosurgeon Henry Perowne who, after 'having woken in an unusual state of mind' (McEwan 2005: 17), intends to enjoy his day of leisure, which will also see his family reunited after a period of disharmony. The day's trajectory is thrown off its logical course when the protest march against the impending war in Iraq (15 February 2003) blocks off his intended journey through the city, after which his car collides with that of the criminal, Baxter, who later invades his Regency home (McEwan 2005: 81; 206). The novel openly engages with the post-9/11 state of the world, and the questions raised by the anti-war demonstration. Although Perowne excludes himself from this march, he 'experiences his own ambivalence as a form of vertigo, of dizzy indecision' (McEwan 2005: 141), the book is saturated with debates about the war. At the close of the eventful day, the reader understands that the ambiguity of this 'uncultured and tedious medic' (McEwan 2005: 195) is a reflection of current uncertainties as well as a potent form of resistance to both State dominance and to individual self-righteousness.

At the heart of the novel lies the reinvigoration of a topos as old as storytelling itself – the transformation of the self, which has its forebears in classic writers such as Homer and Ovid. The trajectory of Perowne's growing self-knowledge is tied to his engagement with, and changing perception of, a wide variety of cultural and political debates at the beginning of the twenty-first century. These discussions are shaped by the many competing ideas, voices and literary references to, amongst others, Sophocles (McEwan 2005: 221); Thomas Wyatt (McEwan 2005: 200); Shakespeare (McEwan 2005: 58; 124; 125; 134); John Milton (McEwan 2005: 134); William Blake (McEwan 2005: 27); Mary Shelley (McEwan 2005: 157); Jane Austen (McEwan 2005: 27; 133; 156); Charlotte Brontë; Dickens; Darwin (McEwan 2005: 6; 55; 58); George Eliot (McEwan 2005: 156); Robert Browning (McEwan 2005: 134); Matthew Arnold (McEwan 2005: 231; 269; 279); Tolstoy (McEwan 2005: 66); Flaubert (McEwan 2005: 66); Joseph Conrad (McEwan 2005: 6; 95); Kafka (McEwan 2005: 133); Henry James (McEwan 2005: 58); Saul Bellow (McEwan 2005: epigraph; 122–23); Philip Larkin (McEwan 2005: 56; 138); James Fenton (McEwan 2005: 130; 135); Ted Hughes (McEwan 2005: 130); Craig Raine (McEwan 2005: 130); and Andrew Motion (McEwan 2005: 130; 135). We also find an abundance of references to music, from Wagner (McEwan 2005: 29), Beethoven (McEwan 2005: 68), Schubert (McEwan 2005: 77) and Bach (McEwan 2005: 22) to blues-rock and jazz musicians such as Eric Clapton (McEwan 2005: 26; 132); Branford Marsalis (McEwan 2005: 33); Ry Cooder (McEwan 2005: 33); John Coltrane (McEwan 2005: 68); and John Lee Hooker (McEwan 2005: 131); to painters including Mondrian (McEwan 2005: 78), Cézanne (McEwan 2005: 68) and Howard Hodgkin (McEwan 2005: 181); to artists including Cornelia Parker (McEwan 2005: 142); and to social science writers Fred Halliday (McEwan 2005: 32) and Paul Ekman (McEwan 2005: 141). McEwan utilizes three distinct types of intertextual engagement: first, direct citation and the borrowing of 'voice'; second, the construction of parallels; and, third, echo and allusion.

Alongside the overwhelming extent of intertextual reference, the other distinctive characteristic of *Saturday* is to be found in its representation of the city itself. As a reference to James Joyce's classic short story 'The Dead' (1914) suggests, the explicit site for McEwan's meditations is 'the city, grand achievement of all the living and all the dead who've ever lived here, [which] is fine too, and robust' (McEwan 2005: 77; Joyce 1996: 256). In a television interview with Melvyn Bragg, McEwan stated: 'Inseparable from the idea of having a novel right in the present was to do London again, or to do London properly. To get the taste and flavour of it.' (Bragg 2005). This remark indicates the significance of London within the novel, and hints at McEwan's desire to correct his earlier representation of the city as a site predominantly of darkness and regression, but although *Saturday* restores the traditional image of the city as the seat of civilization and culture, and of light and learning, the city also retains its qualities as a place of darkness. The evolution of McEwan's post-9/11 thought is thus apparent in the recasting of his image of the city, and in the intertextuality which so distinguishes the form of *Saturday*. Rather than adopting the aggressive mode of the highly-politicized work of the 1930s generation of poets, McEwan brings London to life by establishing a dialogue with, on the one hand, modernist works written during the third decade of the twentieth century and, on the other, the Victorian cultural critic and poet Matthew Arnold (1822–1888).

McEwan and the Modernist Hypercanon

Saturday starts with a quiet homage to a writer whose work has been instrumental in shaping McEwan's fiction: Franz Kafka (1883–1924). The opening scene of *Saturday* engages with the classic Ovidian thematics of transformation by creating a parallel with Kafka's classic modernist story 'The Metamorphosis' (1912). Both texts begin with the description of the physical sensation of waking, and Perowne repeats Samsa's initial reaction by moving to the window. However, whereas Gregor's arms and legs have changed into those of an unwieldy insect, Perowne's limbs feel better than usual. Whereas Gregor feels depressed and idiotic, Perowne is euphoric, and presumes that he is entirely rational. Kafka's domestic anti-fairy tale narrates how Gregor is ousted by his family, but *Saturday* is centred on the homecoming of Daisy. McEwan exchanges the magic realist dimension of Kafka's story for realism, and inverts the components of the Kafka story. For Kafka, modernity entails a bestial, alienating experience – Gregor's mechanical, bureaucratic approach to his predicament symbolizes a descent into an animal consciousness that implicitly criticizes the bourgeois conscience. However, rather than fetishizing such alienation, McEwan's novel sets out to investigate homeliness and happiness as a public and political realm.

This subversion of Kafka is affirmed later on in the novel when Perowne recalls John Grammaticus giving 'The Metamorphosis' to Daisy, who in turn makes her father read it:

> Perowne, by nature ill-disposed towards a tale of impossible transformation, conceded that by the end he was intrigued [. . .] He liked the unthinking cruelty of that sister on the final page, riding the tram with her parents to the last stop, stretching her young limbs, ready to begin a sensual life. A transformation he could believe in. (McEwan 2005: 133)

Saturday affirms both the significance of classical mythology and the thematics of transformation by mediating these through modernist parallels, but the text rejects the more radical experiments of modernist and postmodernist literature, including the McEwan of *The Child in Time* (McEwan 2005: 67).

McEwan's opening section also brings to the fore his emulation of modernist representations of consciousness. The distance between Kafka's aloof narrator and the bourgeois consciousness of Samsa foregrounds the latter's unwillingness to voice his regret at submitting his life to the greater good of family and the nation, his passivity in the face of his graceless, pathetic death. The hiatus between narrator and character also implies that language forms an artificial barrier between the self and its narration, that it fragments experience. Perowne is conscious of this gap within the world of *Saturday* (he notes Grete's 'unthinking cruelty', suggesting he is aware of Kafka's third-person narrator), but he is unable to take into account this process when it comes to himself. When looking out on to two figures in the square below, Perowne 'not only watches them, but watches over them, supervising their progress with the remote possessiveness of a god' (McEwan 2005: 13). This process of fragmentation of the self is ironized, however, by Perowne himself being narrated by a fictional authorial presence. It is made clear to the reader that Perowne's experience is at the mercy of the narrator's locutions, which constantly deride him by pointing out the limits of his frame of reference. For instance, 'a reference to Shakespeare's St Crispin's Day speech [. . .] is lost on Perowne' (McEwan 2005: 125), an allusion to *Henry V* which gains additional force when Perowne compares himself to a king (McEwan 2005: 269). Perowne also tries to connect his über-rational mind to the creative members of his family by referring to Blake's poem 'Auguries of Innocence' (1805) and comparing surgery to music, for which the narrator mocks him: 'To see the world in a grain of sand. So it is, *Perowne tries to convince himself*, with clipping and aneurysm: absorbing variation on an unchanging theme.' (McEwan 2005: 27, my emphasis). This disparagement foregrounds the role of the reader, who is forced to collude with the curious voice, based in a complex language and referentiality narrating Perowne's consciousness from the inside while incessantly offering a commentary upon him. It is ironic that many reviewers and critics conflated Perowne with McEwan himself, given that he – the implied author – clearly fashions a critical distance from both his narrator and his protagonist (cf. Sardar 2006; Kowalski Wallace 2007: 470). In fact, the attentive reader should be unsure of how to precisely interpret the relationship between Perowne and his narrator. The loss of narratorial authority undermines any comfortable or simple reading of the novel, while capturing the post-9/11 climate of anxiety.

McEwan's reworking of classical ideas via his modernist interest in consciousness continues with the creation of parallels with two specific hypercanonic texts, namely James Joyce's *Ulysses* (1922) and Virginia Woolf's *Mrs Dalloway* (1925), both of which recount events taking place on a single day. Each captures the minutiae of the quotidian consciousness, and engages in representing the symbolic journeys of their protagonists through a capital city. Reviewers and critics have stressed the similarities between these texts and *Saturday* (Kemp 2005; Tait 2005; Head 2007: 192; Currie 2007: 129, 132, and Marcus in this collection). For Joyce and Woolf, limiting the narration to 24 hours allowed them to focus on the nature of experience in relationship to time. Yet, as a narrated space of time, their meditations on temporality found a reflecting metaphor in the complexities of the modern city, whose perpetual metamorphoses symbolized the modern condition, and drew attention to the workings of human consciousness.

Saturday overtly acknowledges Joyce in the final line of the novel, with Perowne thinking 'faintly, falling: this day's over' (McEwan 2005: 279), which echoes the final line Joyce's story, 'The Dead' (1914), in which Gabriel Conroy 'heard the snow falling faintly through the universe and faintly falling' (Joyce 1996: 256). McEwan's quotation suggests an interest in the formally less radical mode of Joyce's early work rather than the more 'difficult' works such as *Ulysses* (1922) and *Finnegans Wake* (1939). McEwan also refracts Joyce's legacy via Saul Bellow's riposte to *Ulysses*, *Herzog* (1964), which provides the epigraph to *Saturday*. This direct quotation acknowledges that the socio-cultural context is largely defined and shaped by American power – a major concern within *Saturday* – while also recognizing an important formal influence upon the representation. Rather than choosing the stream-of-consciousness technique of Joyce or Woolf, *Saturday* makes use of Bellow's more conventional mode of narration, the restrictive third person discourse combined with the use of free indirect style, which he intensifies by using the present tense mode. Another sign of McEwan's preferred literary company is to be found in Perowne's very name, which is derived from a character in Ford Madox Ford's tetralogy *Parade's End* (1924–28). This is significant because Ford's novels, which sit outside the conventional canon of modernist work, are set partly on the Western Front during the Great War and to a large extent in London: the thematics of war and place further connect *Saturday* with *Parade's End*.

The ideas behind *Ulysses* are, however, important for our reading of *Saturday*. The course and detail of events in *Saturday* echo Joyce's masterpiece: while Perowne makes his morning coffee, he meditates on the technical refinement and aestheticization of the kettle (McEwan 2005: 69), mirroring the scene in which Bloom makes breakfast for Molly, who orders him to 'Scald the teapot' (Joyce 1992: 75). After breakfast, Bloom goes to his outhouse to defecate (Joyce 1992: 83–5), drawing attention to the mundane and profane aspect of life, and in *Saturday* we also follow Perowne's thoughts while he urinates and defecates (McEwan 2005: 57). A subtle but important parallel between *Saturday* and *Ulysses* is to be found in the relationship between the protagonists and their mothers. In Joyce's novel, Stephen Dedalus is ashamed of his refusal to pray at his mother's deathbed and he is subsequently haunted by her ghost (Joyce 1992: 8–11). Perowne's uneasy relationship with his mother, Lilian, is fraught with strikingly similar contradictions. We learn that she was admired as a great swimmer by the young Henry and his friends, having a 'superhuman nature' and showing off her 'demonic speed just for him' (McEwan 2005: 157). However, echoes of Mary Shelley's *Frankenstein* (1818), in which the creature is described by Frankenstein as a 'daemon' having 'superhuman speed' (Shelley 1996: 65), give Lilian a monstrous edge. Like Dedalus, the young Henry patronizes his mother, behaviour he comes to regret:

> There was nothing small-minded about her interests. Jane Austen and George Eliot shared them too. Lilian Perowne wasn't stupid or trivial, her life wasn't unfortunate, and he had no business as a young man being condescending towards her. But it's too late for apologies now. Unlike Daisy's novels, moments of precise reckoning are rare in real life; questions of misinterpretation are not often resolved. (McEwan 2005: 156)

Perowne has no opportunity to be forgiven because his mother suffers from dementia, and his visit to his mother in the nursing home has the quality of a deathbed scene. Yet, when he operates on Baxter, he is both granted and denied his 'moment of precise reckoning': 'By saving his life in the operating theatre, Henry also committed Baxter to his torture' (McEwan 2005: 278). The emphasis on a private realm full of idiosyncrasies and contingencies undercuts any grand political scheme and raises a spirit of anti-authoritarian subversion. In short, both Joyce and McEwan argue for a narrative structure shaped by our private lives that mediates our experience of the world.

Saturday addresses such issues still more explicitly via McEwan's engagement with Virginia Woolf's *Mrs Dalloway* (1925), which also examines an 'ordinary' mind on an ordinary day in order to explore wider social, cultural and political issues. Dalloway's former lover, Peter Walsh, proclaims that it 'was the state of the world that concerned him' (Woolf 1989: 8); Perowne expresses his own concern in precisely these terms: 'it is in fact the state of the world that troubled him most' (McEwan 2005: 80). McEwan's investigation of the relationship between the private experience and the public life is heavily informed by Woolf's novel.

McEwan's handling of Woolf's imagery is striking. In *Mrs Dalloway* a car backfires, causing a 'violent explosion that made Mrs Dalloway jump' (Woolf 1989: 14). An ur-symbol of modernity ruptures Dalloway's experience, drawing attention to the impact of new technology. *Saturday* also foregrounds the car as a symbol of modernity: Perowne's 'silver Mercedes S500 with cream upholstery' is a 'machine [that] breathes an animal warmth of its own' (McEwan 2005: 75). Giving him 'padded privacy' (McEwan 2005: 121), its motor runs in complete silence; 'the car idles without vibration; the rev counter alone confirms the engine is turning' (McEwan 2005: 76). This cocoon is ruptured when Perowne's car collides with Baxter's, unleashing a sequence of violent encounters with darkest London.

McEwan's portrayal of twentieth-century machinery makes it clear that his novel is reclaiming the modernist territory – figuratively and literarily. Perowne does not copy Dalloway's itinerary, but he lives in the square once occupied by Woolf and covers similar territory to Mrs Dalloway, centred on Fitzrovia. Perowne visits a fishmonger (Bond Street in *Mrs Dalloway*; Paddington Street in *Saturday*), leading to a riposte to both Woolf and Joyce. Dalloway finds the window of the fishmonger's empty ('"That is all," she said' [Woolf 1989: 12]), and Joyce evokes an apocalyptic image of the depleted earth ('Vulcanic lake, the dead sea: no fish, weedless, sunk deep in the earth' (Joyce 1992: 73)). However, Perowne finds that everything he needs for his fish stew is present: 'Such an abundance from the emptying seas' (McEwan 2005: 127). McEwan renegotiates the often pessimistic and apocalyptic language of modernist writers, suggesting ironically that although we find ourselves in dark, anxious times they also provide space for culture, leisure and happiness.

The opening episode of *Saturday* involves an archetypal twentieth-century machine, the aeroplane, which also directly parallels *Mrs Dalloway*, where an aeroplane advertises toffee by writing the brand's letters in the London sky (Woolf 1989: 19–21). Like the image of the ocean liner and the car, this passage illustrates how a symbol of progressive modernity and scientific optimism is an ambivalent sign that may be turned against the city as symbol of civilization. Perowne associates the aeroplane with a potential terrorist attack by Al-Qaeda (McEwan 2005: 17), specifying the novel's post-9/11 historical moment while anticipating the terrorist bombings on London on 7 July, 2005: 'The scale of death contemplated is no longer an issue; there'll be more deaths on a similar scale, probably in this city. Is he so frightened that he can't face the fact? The assertions and the questions don't spell themselves out. He experiences them more as a mental shrug followed by an interrogative impulse' (McEwan 2005: 81). The indirect experience of the recent terrorism has shocked Perowne into a paralysing fear that results in an inability to verbalize his anxieties. McEwan's attention to the relationship between the terror of war and linguistic failure is, again, drawn from *Mrs Dalloway*. Septimus's shell-shock expresses itself in linguistic breakdown, which in turn prevents him from constructing the advertisement as a collective narrative and engaging with the world:

> The sound bored ominously into the ears of the crowd. There it was coming over the trees, letting out white smoke from behind, which curled and twisted, actually writing something! making letters in the sky! Every one looked up. [. . .] So, Septimus thought, they are signalling to me. Not indeed in actual words; that is; he could not read the language yet; but it was plain enough, this beauty, this exquisite beauty, and tears filled his eyes as he looked at the smoke words languishing and melting in the sky. (Woolf 1989: 19–21)

Writing, in the form of the skywriting aeroplane, creates a discourse which connects individual minds to a collective narrative – the urban experience itself. Whereas Woolf projects our experience of the world as (linguistically) shared, McEwan's novel argues that our understanding of the contemporary world has become increasingly uncertain because of the post-war disconnection between the private and the public. This divorce can be traced historically in the personal growth of Perowne, who grows up fatherless in west London's Perivale, where each 'near-identical house has an uneasy, provisional look, as if it knows how readily the land would revert to cereal crops and grazing' (McEwan 2005: 158). This external uniformity is contrasted with the compulsive ordering of the family's mental landscape by Lilian: 'Order and cleanliness were the outward expression of an unspoken ideal of love. [. . .] Surely it was because of her that Henry feels at home in an operating theatre.' (McEwan 2005: 155). This suggests that only through his work as a surgeon is Perowne able to connect the private and the public: in the operating theatre '[t]he two were inseparable' (McEwan 2005: 45).

Our Grand Centre of Life is London: McEwan and Matthew Arnold

In the representation of London we nonetheless do find a suggestive means for tracing Perowne's mental and moral trajectory to some form of self-discovery and reconnection to the public realm. *Saturday* begins with an image of the square in which Perowne's Fitzrovia home is situated:

> Standing there, as immune to the cold as a marble statue, gazing towards Charlotte Street, towards a foreshortened jumble of façades, scaffolding and pitched roofs, Henry thinks the city is a success, a brilliant invention, a biological masterpiece – millions teeming around the accumulated and layered achievements of centuries, as though around a coral reef, sleeping, working, entertaining themselves, harmonious for the most part, nearly everyone wanting it to work. And Perowne's own corner, a triumph of congruent proportion; the perfect square laid out by Robert Adam enclosing a perfect circle of garden – an eighteenth century dream bathed and embraced by modernity, by street light from above, and from below by fibre-optic cables, and cool fresh water coursing down pipes, and sewage borne away in an instant of forgetting. (McEwan 2005: 5)

Perowne thinks of the city in classical terms of harmony and aesthetic perfection, successfully merged with (post)modernity. The unclean water that 'has been drunk five times before' (McEwan 2006: 73) has now turned into 'cool fresh water', while any scatological association is expelled by the emphasis on the sewage system. Perowne's city is a clean, light and sanitized Eden, a complete inversion of darkest London.

Perowne's description presents the city, and the world around him, in terms of organic matter ('biological masterpiece'; 'coral reef'), he also diagnoses the city in terms of its pathologies, speaking of '[s]ick buildings, in use for too long, that only demolition can cure. Cities and states beyond repair' (McEwan 2005: 122). Perowne approaches London like a patient etherized upon a table, making it clear that his London is a projection of his own medicalized, curative consciousness, again echoing Peter Walsh: 'It was a splendid morning too. Like the pulse of a perfect heart, life struck straight through the streets. [. . .] A splendid achievement in its own way, after all, London; the season; civilization' (Woolf 1989: 50).

However, the reference to coral reef also alludes to the Victorian cultural critic and poet Matthew Arnold. His poems 'Written in Butler's Sermons' (1849) and 'To Marguerite—Continued' (1852) use the image of coral islands as a metaphor for the idea that although in modernity individuals appear separated from one another, we are in truth all connected 'like sister islands, seen/Linking their coral arms under the sea' (Arnold 1965: 52). The central question posed by *Saturday*, 'And now what days are these? Baffled and fearful, he mostly thinks' (McEwan 2005: 4) also echoes Arnold's early poem 'To a Friend' (1848), which asks: 'Who prop, thou ask'st in these bad days, my mind?' (Arnold 1965: 105). London itself has a central role within Arnold's work. Asked how we justify calling ourselves 'children of God', Arnold answers:

> By the works we do, and the words we speak. And the work which we collective children of God do, our grand centre of life, our *city* which we have builded for us to dwell in, is London! London, with its inutterable external hideousness, and with its internal canker of *publicè egestas, privatum opulentia* [public poverty, private opulence], to use the words which Sallust put in Cato's mouth about Rome, – unequalled in the world! (Arnold 1963: 59)

For Arnold the British capital is the finest expression of culture and civilization, and it is this optimistic vision of the city with which we are presented at the start of *Saturday*. However, beneath the lyricism this passage points out that London is not perfect and harmonious but rather a place where the public and private realms are divorced from one another. Arnold's vision of London is a critical one, above all ironic, self-conscious and ambivalent: the comparison between London and Rome places London within a historical cycle that will eventually lead to decline.

Saturday is saturated with reference to Arnold. His work addressed themes which also recur in McEwan: the changing relationship between science and religion; the importance and challenges of democracy; the growing tensions within the English class system; the nature of culture and of society. His analysis of mid-Victorian England, *Culture and Anarchy* (1869), which contains his definition of the role of culture in society, is particularly resonant within McEwan's novel. Arnold divides culture into two camps. On the one hand, Arnold defines the 'properly' cultured subject as striving after self-conquest and moral perfection, making the will of God prevail while seeking a 'harmonious expansion of *all* the powers which make the beauty and worth of human nature' (Arnold 1963: 48). The key words that capture and promote this desired unity of beauty and intelligence are 'sweetness' and 'light'. The cultured person has a well-developed critical faculty (the refusal to accept ideas simply on authority), openness to classical thought, history, literature and beauty, and is driven by curiosity. On the other hand, Arnold posits the 'Philistines', a category he associates with the middle classes, who define culture as solely a scientific passion that desires 'to see things as they are', and as 'the love of perfection; it is *a study of perfection'* (Arnold 1963: 44–5). This faith is in a predominantly rational and materialist vision of civilization as a machine that can be analysed, dismantled and improved, and this is clearly the category to which Perowne belongs:

> He can't feel his way past the iron weight of the actual to see beyond the boredom of a traffic tailback, or the delay to which he is contributing, or the drab commercial hopes of a parade of shops he's been stuck beside for fifteen minutes. He doesn't have the lyric gift to see beyond it – he's a realist, and can never escape. (McEwan 2005: 168)

Perowne is unable to see beyond the materiality of things, yet the emphasis on the bounds of his imagination acknowledges his regret. His experience of his journey back into London after visiting his mother is particularly striking:

> He tries to see it, or feel it, in historical terms, this moment in the last decades of the petroleum age, when a nineteenth-century device is brought to final perfection in the early years of the twenty-first; when the unprecedented wealth of the masses at serious play in the unforgiving modern city makes for a sight that no previous age can have imagined. Ordinary people! Rivers of light! (McEwan 2005: 168)

Formally, the use of exclamation marks mimics Arnold, and the effect is that Perowne appears to represent the nineteenth-century, modern spirit of progress. However, just as Sallust puts words about Rome in Cato's mouth, McEwan puts Arnold's words into Perowne's without the character's being aware of their origins. Perowne's reference to 'ordinary people' sets up a parallel between the anti-war parade in 2003 and the historical context in which Arnold wrote. Arnold was critical of the Hyde Park riots of July 1866, and he warned against the fact that London's working class was 'beginning to assert and put into practice an Englishman's right to do what he likes' (Arnold 1967: 76). Arnold had a contradictory sense of class, fearing the destabilization of the class system and the

increasing working-class agency over the middle class, while acknowledging that the existing social hierarchies were inadequate for effective
government (Williams 1990: 121). Although 'the class consciousness that
colours Arnold's view no longer applies' (Head 2007: 183–4), Perowne too
is sceptical of the mass of protesters against the war in Iraq. Yet when
Perowne meets Tony Blair (McEwan 2005: 140–44), who mistakes him
for an artist, it is clear that we should be sceptical of state authority too.
McEwan points out the flaw in Arnold's fantasy of the State as the centre
of light and authority by bringing to the fore what Arnold himself calls
'the right reason of the community' (Arnold 1963: 82).

Perowne's exclamation 'Rivers of light!' also aligns him with Arnold.
In his poem 'The Future' (1852), for instance, Arnold notes that '[w]het-
her he first sees light / Where the river in gleaming rings / Sluggishly
winds through the plain [. . .] So is the mind of man' (Arnold 1852:
264). However, as we have seen, Perowne's philistinism is repeatedly
challenged by the narrative, leaving him in a state of uncertainty: 'All
he feels now is fear. He's weak and ignorant, scared of the way consequences of an action leap away from your control and breed new events,
new consequences, until you're led to a place you never dreamed of and
would never chose' (McEwan 2005: 277). Perowne's and Arnold's 'rivers
of light' foreground McEwan's renegotiation of the image of the city.
Raymond Williams reminds us that the city, figuratively and literally, is
indeed a place of light:

> This light was an obvious image for the impressive civilisation of the capital,
> visibly growing in wealth and in conscious public effect. [. . .] As a centre of
> trade and political influence the capital was attracting, also [. . .] every kind
> of talent, from many parts of the world. [. . .] This version of a glittering and
> dominant metropolitan culture had enough reality to support a traditional
> idea of the city, as a centre of light and learning (Williams 1973: 228–9)

McEwan's representation of London in *Saturday* thus corrects his earlier
'darkest London' by supplementing it with the traditional vision of the
city as a place of light and learning, but new uncertainties, a new darkness, are brought to the fore in the post-9/11 metropolis.

The novel challenges Perowne the philistine but it also challenges
Arnold's preferred definition of culture, embodied by his musician son,
Theo, a talented but smug and lazy young man naively seduced by conspiracy theories: his 'world-view accommodates a hunch that somehow everything is connected, interestingly connected, and that certain
authorities, notably the US government, with privileged access to extra-
terrestrial intelligence, is excluding the rest of the world from such won-
drous knowledge' (McEwan 2005: 30). Theo's certainty and conviction
about the Iraq war are mocked as well: 'Naturally, Theo is against the
war in Iraq. His attitude is as strong and pure as his skin and bones. So
strong he doesn't feel much need to go tramping through the streets to

make his point' (McEwan 2005: 151). On the other we find the poets John Grammaticus, a pompous, bohemian 'drinker' (McEwan 2005: 138) who is jealous of his daughter-in-law's success, and Daisy, who is portrayed as priggish, pedantic and right-minded: Perowne 'knows she thinks he's a coarse, irredeemable materialist. She thinks he lacks an imagination. Perhaps it is so, but she hasn't quite given up on him yet' (McEwan 2005: 134). The same irony and knowingness that undermine Perowne therefore undercut Daisy and Theo, whose positions are too certain and self-assured, and in their own ways fall short of Arnold's ideal.

The influence of Matthew Arnold is the most significant factor in the uncertain 'voice' of *Saturday*, a voice which fluctuates from the derisive to the euphoric, from the meditative to the resolute. This voice is, however, adept at making the reader collude with the author, as Baxter's change of mind when hearing Daisy's recital of Arnold's 'Dover Beach' (1867) evidences. In Stefan Collini's words: 'To read Arnold at his best is to find oneself in the company of a mind of such balance and sympathy that we come, without really noticing, to see experience in his terms, and, unusually, to think the better of ourselves for it' (Collini 1988: 1). In contrast, McEwan is highly sceptical of our ability to bridge the gap between the private and public. Perowne's obsession with round-the-clock news broadcasting is an indication of his thwarted desire to connect with the general public in a wider narrative. Mark Currie suggests that there is a 'sense of corroboration between the public narratives of news and private experience. This sense of the gap between public and private [. . .] extends more generally to Perowne's relation to his historical moment, and to his position in the modern city' (Currie 2007: 130–31). Traditionally, it is the city that connects the private with the public, and to a degree it still performs this function for private matters: 'The square's public aspect grants privacy to these intimate dramas' (McEwan 2005: 61). However, at the beginning of the twenty-first century, our capacity to express ourselves directly and authentically has been diminished. Perowne is sceptical about the protest march because it turns into a self-interested televised event organized by what he considers are Saddam's stooges. When he realizes his encounter with Baxter may become violent, he reads the scene via mass media: 'This, as people like to say, is urban drama. A century of movies and half a century of television have rendered the matter insincere. It is pure artifice' (McEwan 2005: 86). McEwan suggests that our contemporary understanding of the self and community is a fantasy about the collective mediated by the narratives and discourses provided by the state, commerce and mass media.

Throughout the novel, reconnections are made between material spaces and spaces of the imagination: on the one hand we find the city, the private home and the operating theatre, and on the other there are music, poetry and the novel. During an epiphany when he watches his son Theo's performance, a passage which recalls the Sirens episode in Homer's *The Odyssey*, Perowne understands that it is the creative imagination that allows a restoration of the private life and the public world. Theo's band performs a song:

> *Baby, you can choose despair,*
> *Or you can be happy if you dare,*
> *[. . .] So let me take you there*
> *City square, city square.* (170–71)

The song returns us to the debates about democracy. Perowne refuses to see the city square, Europe's contribution to the architecture of public space tied to the classical Athenian model of democracy, as a place where the private and public might meet. He does not 'want him [Baxter] hanging around the square' (McEwan 2005: 147). But now he is moved and transformed by the music and the lyrics:

> No longer tired, Henry comes away from the wall where he's been leaning, and walks into the middle of the dark auditorium, towards the great engine of sound. He lets it engulf him. These are moments when musicians together touch something sweeter than they've ever found before in rehearsals or performance, beyond the merely collaborative or technically proficient, when their expression becomes as easy and graceful as friendship or love. This is when they give us a glimpse of what we might be, of our best selves, and of an impossible world in which you give everything you have to others, but lose nothing of yourself. (McEwan 2005: 171)

Perowne, swayed by the musical harmony, is able to forge his connection with the wider public, providing him with a brief glimpse of transcending the bounds of his scientific materialism. The whole passage is couched in an Arnoldian idiom, from terms such as 'sweeter' and 'easy and graceful' to the specific mention of 'our best selves'. Indeed, McEwan is effectively paraphrasing Arnold's own claim for culture:

> But by our *best self* we are united, impersonal, at harmony. We are not in peril from giving authority to this, because it is the truest friend we all of us can have; and when anarchy is a danger to us, to this authority we may turn with sure trust. Well, and this is the very self which culture, or the study of perfection, seeks to develop in us; at the expense of our old untransformed self, taking pleasure in doing what it likes or is used to do, and exposing us to the risk of clashing with every one else who is doing the same! [. . .] We want an authority, and we find nothing but jealous classes, checks, and a deadlock; culture suggests the idea of *the State*. We find no basis for a firm State-power in our ordinary selves; culture suggests one to us in our *best selves*. (Arnold 1963: 95–6)

In conclusion, McEwan brings London to life through an extended attention to the myriad intertexts through which it has been represented.

Saturday works against both overbearing state authoritarianism and individual self-righteousness, and suggests a new era full of uncertainties. Perowne's conscience and belief system are challenged by a series of incidents from which he emerges 'feeling too many things, he's alive to too many contradictory impulses' (McEwan 2005: 262). The novel raises fundamental questions about, on the one hand, the role of the arts and literature in culture and society, and, on the other, the limits of scientific materialism as a means of understanding the world, but it refrains from offering a clear answer. McEwan does, however, give the reader pause with his account of Perowne's changed perception of the square, 24 hours after the start of the novel: 'The air is warmer than last time, but still he shivers. The light is softer too, the features of the square, especially the branches of the plane trees in the garden, are not so etched, and seem to merge with one another' (McEwan 2005: 271). This image unpicks the opposition between darkest London and the London of light as well as the many other oppositions the novel itself contains, and leaves us with a sense of unresolved uncertainty: 'this is a future that's harder to read, a horizon indistinct with possibilities' (McEwan 2005: 276).

CHAPTER EIGHT

On Chesil Beach:
Another 'Overrated' Novella?

DOMINIC HEAD

Chapter Summary: This chapter investigates Ian McEwan's provocative use of the novella form in *Amsterdam* (1998) and *On Chesil Beach* (2007), arguing that he stretches the genre by incorporating discussions of society and history that we conventionally find within the novel. It moves beyond the superficial reception of *On Chesil Beach* as an exploration of the pre-Swinging Sixties thematics and history by pinpointing how the darker subtexts set out to provoke a debate about morality, sexuality, and taboos in contemporary society. Unlike Martin Amis, who connotes pornography with the 'obscenification of everyday life', McEwan's novella emasculates the power of pornography by appropriating its imagery and ridiculing it, and reminds us that repressive morality, idealizations of 'innocence', and a lack of communication can lead to disaster in equal measure.

The publication of *On Chesil Beach* (2007) brought one or two things into focus for observers of McEwan's career, and occasioned a re-evaluation of his *oeuvre* to this point. The publication of another novella – and a book evidently less substantial than his most widely-respected works – confirmed the impression that his books can be divided clearly into 'major' and 'minor' works, following the taxonomy of traditional literary criticism. Following such a schema, the major books would be: *The Child in Time* (1987), *Black Dogs* (1992), *Enduring Love* (1997), *Atonement* (2001), and *Saturday* (2005) (with *The Innocent* (1990), influenced by the Cold War spy novel, and which therefore does not wear its seriousness quite so obviously on its sleeve, a debatable case for inclusion.) These are McEwan's 'ideas' books, engagements with demanding concepts (post-Einsteinian physics, evolutionary psychology, neuroscience), and significant historical and political moments (World War Two, the collapse of communism, the impact of 9/11).

Leaving aside the early short-story volumes, the remaining four works of fiction – all of novella length – would then form the group of minor works: *The Cement Garden* (1987), *The Comfort of Strangers* (1981), *Amsterdam* (1998) and *On Chesil Beach* (2007). While this seems to me a helpful preliminary way of mapping the career, it runs the risk of obscuring some of the significance of the 'minor' works. There is also an underlying truism here: that shorter fiction is determined overtly by structure and device, and that such considerations restrict the experimental treatment of larger issues and themes. This does not mean, however, that larger issues and themes cannot be successfully engaged through a thoughtful application of the novella's formal capacities. This short chapter is designed to identify some of the ways in which McEwan has exploited the novella form.

The fuss about McEwan's shorter books in the literary press has partly to do with the high expectations consequent upon the estimation of his major novels: the novellas pale alongside the weightier books. It has also to do with the assumption that there is some cynical marketing going on; and this is a legacy of the furore caused by *Amsterdam*. I have written elsewhere about this novella in relation to literary prize culture (see Head 2008); so I will merely summarize the essential points here.

Amsterdam, certainly not McEwan's best book, is his only work to have been awarded the Booker Prize, an eventuality that raised the suspicion that McEwan had been awarded the prize for his previous efforts, rather than for the book in question. Yet this is to overlook the point of the project, which was consummated by winning the prize. *Amsterdam* engages with the literary consequences of Thatcherism (extending into the era of John Major's premiership), specifically with the era of entrepreneurial self-promotion and, by extension, the impact that had on the development of literary prize culture. *Amsterdam* may not be McEwan's best book; but it is, technically, a fully realized work within the strict limits McEwan sets himself. Its real significance is how the neatness of its design contributes to its satirical thrust as a book pointedly written *for* the Booker.

Since *Enduring Love* failed to reach the shortlist in 1997 (as had *The Child in Time* a decade earlier), the compelling speculation emerges that McEwan, sensing that his time had come, produced *Amsterdam* in quick time for the 1998 prize. In writing about professional competitiveness, McEwan seems to have mustered his cultural capital in an archly self-conscious gesture: *Amsterdam* was, it seems, a form of 'spoiler' designed to defeat the ambitions of other contenders. There were three other established authors on the 1998 shortlist who had not won the prize, and who had also been short-listed before: Beryl Bainbridge, Julian Barnes and Patrick McCabe. 1998 was the fifth time Bainbridge had been in contention for the prize, and she was considered the favourite by many commentators. McEwan's success was not well received: Will Self, on a live TV broadcast, found occasion 'to do his nut', in the words of Nicholas Lezard (Lezard 1999: 11). *On Chesil Beach,* another novella, was shortlisted in 2007.

The idea of a 'spoiler' is central to the novella and to McEwan's satirical anatomy of the kind of self-contained professionalism that kills off the ethical sense. Each of the two principal characters, Vernon Halliday – editor of a modernizing broadsheet newspaper – and composer Clive Linley, encounters an ethical dilemma that reveals how morality has been displaced by self-interest in the world of the contemporary professional. In the case of Halliday, the moral vacuum is iterated through his decision to publish compromising photographs of the cross-dressing foreign secretary, Julian Garmony, in order to boost sales by cashing in on a mood of moral conservatism. Garmony issues a spoiler, however, and the 'scoop' backfires (McEwan 1998: 124).

Linley's moral test occurs while walking in the Lake District, and finding inspiration for the finale of his 'Millennium Symphony' in the call of a bird. He refuses to attend to a disputing couple who disturb his concentration (a serial rapist and his latest victim, it transpires). When completed, the symphony is deemed to be flawed by its final movement, derivative of Beethoven (McEwan 1998: 176).

This is a satire of the politics of self-interest emerging in the Thatcher–Major era (which Hunter Hayes and Sebastian Groes have earlier explored in McEwan's screenplays, see pp. 26–42). For those readers attuned to the self-consciousness of the work, *Amsterdam*'s satirical portrait of left-intellectual achievement after 1979 will also be deemed to implicate the plight of the writer. In this connection the idea of a spoiler is the lynch-pin of McEwan's gesture. At the end of the novel, when Halliday understands that Linley has killed him in their parallel dastardly acts of murder disguised as euthanasia, he acknowledges 'reverentially' this 'spoiler' (McEwan 1998: 173).

The neatness of the plotting is emblematic of the vacuity of the characters, and this underscores the satirical target: an age in which professional standards invite us to revere the act of spoiling. The full impact of this depended upon the success of *Amsterdam* – perceived as a spoiler itself – in the 1998 Booker Prize: the judging panel dutifully revered McEwan's act of spoiling.

The point of the novella is, then, partly determined by its status as a literary *event*, where the satire bleeds out into the world of literary culture. What is 'spoiled', finally, is any lingering idea that contemporary literary culture is governed by aesthetic values that can be held aloof from the marketplace. That first impression of a consummately realized novella – pandering to the false notion of literary form held in isolation – is a prelude to the invitation to join a broader debate about consumerism and literary prize culture.

The manner in which *Amsterdam*, viewed as a literary event, implicates prize culture in the construction of serious literary fiction demonstrates a point that is familiar with academic critics: that aesthetic effects must have a contextual function. If that function is partly to be understood through the processes of commodification, there is also a more palpable aspect to it. These effects highlight McEwan's ability to engage with contemporaneous issues – a mark of any writer's importance – but in the novellas the effects are exaggerated almost to the point of caricature. The event of *Amsterdam* as a Booker winner may have been a one-off. However, when McEwan's next novella, *On Chesil Beach*, was shortlisted for the Prize in 2007 history did seem to be on the verge of repeating itself. But the true parallel is a formal one: there is a similar breaking of form in *On Chesil Beach*, which means that the discovery of the limits of the novella form is part of its meaning.

In common with the way many short stories and novellas depend upon a single strong symbolic setting or motif, *On Chesil Beach* uses the idea of the seaside as a liminal space to embed, symbolically, its central idea: that one failed wedding night in 1962 can be taken as emblematic of the dividing line between the sexual liberation of the 1960s and the repression that preceded it. Specifically, Chesil Beach, that long stretch of pebbles that separates the English Channel from the Fleet Lagoon, is made to symbolize this epochal change. As the scene of confrontation on the wedding night, after the disastrous sexual encounter of newlyweds Edward and Florence, the beach – immensely difficult to walk on, like all pebble beaches – embodies their separation and failure to communicate.

There is, then, an announced historical ambition to the novella, which seems to rely on the particular strengths of shorter fiction: a focus on one or two characters, an emphasis on interiorized experience, and a plot that hinges on a moment of crisis in which the essential nature of the characters' experience is revealed to themselves and/or to the reader. There is a sense in which the book instructs us to read it in this way. However, what redeems it from this schematic attempt to summarize an epoch is that the principle of representativeness upon which it depends, and which McEwan goes to some lengths to establish, is simultaneously undermined by the idiosyncratic backgrounds of the central characters, backgrounds that reveal them to be curiously *unrepresentative*. For both protagonists, Edward Mayhew and Florence Ponting, there is an element of dysfunctionality in their upbringing – dysfunctional by the standards of 1962 – and this implies a degree of emotional and psychological disorder for both that could be taken as an explanation of their failure to connect, quite as much as can the social mores of the time.

The Mayhew family life is dominated by the mental illness of the mother, brain-damaged after an accident on a railway platform when Edward was small (McEwan 2007: 70). They muddle through, with the father and the children keeping a modicum of domestic order, while also sustaining the 'elaborate fairy tale' that the mother is 'a devoted wife and mother, that the house ran smoothly thanks to all her work'. The fact that the father and the children 'colluded in the make-believe' is crucial

(McEwan 2007: 67). It imposes on the children a form of collective secrecy that suppresses the oddity they know surrounds them: 'the fantasy could be sustained only if it was not discussed. They grew up inside it, neutrally inhabiting its absurdities because they were never defined.' (68)

When, at the age of fourteen, Edward is told of his mother's condition, a mood of instantaneous withdrawal overtakes him. The very term 'brain-damaged', the narrator reports, 'dissolved intimacy', measuring 'his mother by a public standard' (McEwan 2007: 72). Edward experiences 'a sudden space' emerging between himself and his mother, and 'also between himself and his immediate circumstances' so that 'his own being, the buried core of it he had never attended to before, come[s] to sudden, hard-edged existence' (McEwan 2007: 72). The sudden sense of separation from his family makes him realize that 'one day he would leave, and would return only as a visitor' (McEwan 2007: 72).

These realizations – the emergence of a new sense of self, the self-conscious feeling of separation from family – are familiar aspects of adolescent experience. The full impact of this, therefore, is slightly cloaked. Yet Edward's sense of withdrawal, in its suddenness and emotional coldness, reveals a dramatic intensification of routine adolescent development. These can be seen as effects of the dysfunctional family life. It is hard not to conclude that the joint failure of Edward and Florence to commence a family life is partly explained, on Edward's part, by the lack of a domestic model on which to found his expectations, and the absence of an emotionally sustaining upbringing.

A sign of Edward's instability is his predilection for brawling, as a younger man. The culmination of this motif is the recollection of his last street fight, as a student. Edward attacked a man who had gratuitously hit his best friend, perhaps because this friend, Harold Mather, was Jewish, perhaps because he was small and studious and the likely focus of a bully's contempt. This particular incident was, we read, 'unusual in that Edward had some cause, a degree of justice on his side' (McEwan 2007: 92). Catching up with the passing thug, he delivers swift and violent retribution; but, in so doing, he precipitates the end of his friendship with Mather. To begin with, Edward imagines he has hurt Mather's pride, by 'witnessing his humiliation' and 'acting as his champion'. However, he then comes to the conclusion that his behaviour was deemed 'uncool', his crime 'a lapse of taste'. He makes the conscious decision to stay out of fights after this (McEwan 2007: 95).

Neither of these explanations seems satisfactory to explain Mather's withdrawal of his friendship. Edward is unable to formulate a moral explanation for Mather's apparent disgust at the violent propensity of his erstwhile friend. A further moral absence is implied in Edward's decision to give up brawling (to avoid being thought vulgar); and in the apparent instability of this fresh determination. His violent moods are a kind of 'madness' he has kept from Florence, but on his wedding night, we read, 'he did not trust himself' because 'he could not be certain that the tunnel vision and selective deafness would never descend again'. In all of this, there is an implied personal inadequacy. He had preferred to think of his tendency to fight as 'an interesting quirk, a rough virtue'; disabused of this, his 'mortifying reappraisal' focuses on his masculine image, merely (McEwan 2007: 92, 95). Edward's volatility, as well as his moral and emotional lack – whether or not we put it down to his dysfunctional home life – is made to hang over the wedding night in Damoclean fashion.

In the case of Florence there is a series of hints that her father has been abusive, and that her revulsion at the thought of sex may stem from this. The reported memories of Florence about her father, and about the trips the two of them made in his boat from Dover to France, reveal emotional extremes which, although plausible in a pubescent girl in a milder form, suggest an underlying issue when expressed so violently:

> They never talked about those trips. He had never asked her again, and she was glad. But sometimes, in a surge of protective feeling and guilty love, she would come up behind him where he sat and entwine her arms around his neck and kiss the top of his head and nuzzle him, liking his clean scent. She would do all this, then loathe herself for it later. (McEwan 2007: 50)

The physical appeal of the father at such moments, linked to 'guilty love' and self-loathing, contrasts arrestingly with the times when she finds him 'physically repellent' (McEwan 2007: 49).

In similar fashion, the account of Florence's impatience with her parents' political opinions is made to seem typical of a young adult, but then tips over into something more troubling. She is happy to disagree with her mother, but finds it 'harder to contradict' her father because 'she could never shake off a sense of awkward obligation to him'. Among these obligations she numbers 'the journeys: just the two of them, hiking in the Alps, Sierra Nevada and Pyrenees, and the special treats, the one-night business trips to European cities where she and Geoffrey always stayed in the grandest hotels'. (McEwan 2007: 54)

The heavy hint that there is something peculiar about all of these father-and-daughter trips is apparently confirmed in the novella's key scene, when Florence is lying on the marital bed and Edward is undressing. The smell of the sea summons 'the indistinct past', and a memory of 'lying still like this, waiting' in the cabin of her father's boat while he undressed, on a two-day crossing to France when she was 12. In the remembered scene, 'her mind was a blank, she felt she was in disgrace'. However, the memory is indistinct, one occasion merging with another: 'she was usually sick many times on the crossing, and of no use to her father as a sailor, and that surely was the source of her shame' (McEwan 2007: 99–100). Here the writer is evidently asking us to ponder the questions that the character is uncertain about. Is her failure as a sailor the source of her shame? Or is it that her seasickness renders her 'of no use to her father' in another capacity? We cannot help wondering what would possess a father to continue to take a twelve-year-old daughter with no sea legs on a two-day crossing in a tiny vessel with a cramped cabin. Because the memory comes, unbidden, as she is bracing herself for the unwanted sexual encounter with Edward, we cannot help but imagine that this is, for her, the repetition of an earlier horror.

When the sexual scene becomes a debacle, Florence's disgust at the feel of Edward's semen on her skin summons 'memories she had long ago decided were not really hers'. The origin of the repressed sexual memories is surely confirmed by her reaction to this 'alien milkiness, its intimate starchy odour, which dragged with it the stench of a shameful secret locked in musty confinement' (McEwan 2007: 105–6). The echo here of being closeted with her father in the boat's 'cramped cabin' with its 'closed air' is obvious (McEwan 2007: 99–100). When Florence makes her 'brave little joke' in her final conversation with Edward, she summarizes her problem for us: 'perhaps I should be psychoanalysed. Perhaps what I really need to do is kill my mother and marry my father' (McEwan 2007: 154, 153). The attentive reader will already have analysed the character along precisely these lines.

The respective pasts of both Edward and Florence make them entirely unsuited to establishing a domestic life of their own, with a healthy sexual relationship at its heart – not, at least, without prior therapy. Their home lives, from which model experience is absent, have caused both of them to develop in ways that militate against marriage. Neither can these elements of dysfunctionality be taken as exaggerations of broader and more common psychological restrictions or social failings. The central characters are emotional oddities, their marriage doomed to fail.

There is, then, a quite deliberate contradiction at the heart of *On Chesil Beach*, which enriches the work, making it far more than the period piece it announces itself as. That element of public historical analysis remains as the important context of the novella, but the central characters are not ciphers, playing the roles dictated by that historical moment. They are more complex creations than this implies, with private lives that make the novella's crisis an emotional (rather than a historical) inevitability. This leaves us wondering whether or not the apparent central premise is really achieved. If that premise is to anatomize the social mores of a distant social world – and (implicitly) to contract them with the present – we begin to wonder whether or not less dysfunctional characters would have to be presented as experiencing the same fate.

Other readings – or, at least, alternative emphases for reading – *On Chesil Beach* are opened up when the tidy historical drama is seen to unravel. One such emphasis flows from the contrast between past and contemporary sexual mores. Here McEwan would seem to be very much in debate with contemporary culture, and the perceived sense that we live in an increasingly sexualized world. McEwan is also in debate with Martin Amis, whose treatments of pornography may well amount to the depiction of civilization in crisis. In *Yellow Dog* (2003), for example, pornography is conceived as 'the obscenification of everyday life' (Amis 2003: 335). In his musings on pornography, Amis (since *Money* [1983]) has been struck by its repetitive 'codes', one of which is the focus on ejaculation over a woman (e.g. Amis 2003: 289–90). In this context, the pivotal scene of *On Chesil Beach*, in which Florence is traumatized as Edward 'emptied himself over her in gouts' (105), evidently draws on the contemporaneous debate about pornography and 'the obscenification of everyday life', and seems some kind of riposte to Amis. The curious thing, here, is that Amis's moralizing about 'the Money Shot' (Amis 2003: 289), as a travesty of sexuality in its concentration of money, power and hatred, stands in contrast to McEwan's (frankly) comic climactic moment. Of course, the same questions of power do not obtain; but McEwan pointedly conceives of a parallel scene in which ejaculation becomes absurd and disempowering.

Beyond this, there is something arch about the novel, governed by a sexually knowing narrator manipulating his innocent creations. Indeed, the gap between their understanding and experience, and the knowledge of the narrator – and also the author, as the governing intelligence – is discomfiting.

Yet, if this is another way in which the architecture of the novella collapses slightly, it is another instance of McEwan making his focus bleed outwards to provoke debate. As with *Amsterdam*, what could be perceived as an aesthetic limitation, in austere formal terms, becomes the very means by which McEwan makes his identification with his broader context. We are more accustomed to reading novelistic form in relation to society and history than we are the formal attributes of shorter fiction. Perhaps McEwan's novellas help us to redress this balance, though he may be stretching – even exhausting, perhaps? – the limits of the novella in the process.

Journeys without Maps:
An Interview with Ian McEwan

BY JON COOK, SEBASTIAN GROES AND VICTOR SAGE

Sebastian Groes: In recent years, the disappearance of children has increasingly featured in the British media, and also abroad. One may think of the Holly Wells and Jessica Chapman murders, and the disappearance of Madeleine McCann. Belgium saw the Mark Dutroux scandal and in Austria Natascha Kampusch was locked up for eight years. What is striking about the media coverage, and particularly in the Madeleine McCann case of 2007, is the intense, non-stop proliferation of pictures of innocent children in the public realm. One of *Contemporary Critical Perspectives'* contributors calls this a form of 'cultural pornography': children are obsessively equated with innocence and adulthood is perceived as a state of loss, which becomes politicized in a variety of ways. Not only did you write about the effect of a disappeared child on parents in *The Child in Time*, but your entire work is interested in analysing changing cultural and socio-political notions of innocence. How do you read this iconography of innocence as a change in the collective consciousness?

Ian McEwan: We've got to make a distinction between, on the one hand, what we might imagine is public fear or a troubled public consciousness, and, on the other hand, a media environment. The term 'media' is now doubly apt: the media become the mediators of this strange, not entirely trustworthy outpouring of sadness over, for instance, Madeleine McCann. But it's not clear that children are in more danger now than they were in the fifties. It is not for nothing that the disappearing child story has become a staple of the summer holidays: newspapers the world over are suffering from a shrinking readership and therefore the competition is intense. What used to be called the 'silly season' has now taken on a darker meaning.

That said, when I wrote *The Child in Time*, disappearing children were not as often in the news as they are now, and I do think a shift in the collective emotional life in Britain has occurred, right around the death of Diana, which saw an extraordinary outpouring of emotion. The nation woke up from this a year later, as if after a terrible party, wondering at what it had said and done. Since then we've had a number of tragedies, which have given rise to what one writer has called the 'damp teddy syndrome': a person or a child dies, not someone known to you, and yet you take along the teddy bear, the flowers, the poems, the rain comes and finally it's all cleared away by the dustman.

Calling these images of disappeared or murdered children pornographic has a degree of truth. As the influence of Freud in literary and intellectual culture has faded, we have returned to the idea that childhood *is* a form of innocence, that children are *not* consumed by hidden sexual impulses or possessed by the polymorphous perverse. They come into the world not responsible for it, and they are sometimes acted upon by people with terrible intent. This frightens us. The literary imagination is bound to go into dark corners to explore this fear. For most people, the loss of a child is the worst thing that can happen. 'Deep love breeds a fear of loss', I wrote in an oratorio. It troubles us, especially given that we, compared to most other places in the world, lead relatively stable lives here in northwest Europe. The lost child is the ghost that haunts us. As those terrible thoughts run through your mind, your hand tightens on your child's. The imagination flows into unwanted places, and perhaps this is its evolutionary function: to foresee bad outcomes and try to avoid them. Fear may lie at the root of the imagination itself.

S. G.: In the preface to oratorio you just mentioned, *Or Shall we Die?*, you talk about the way imagination operates in the conception of your work. You say that 'the prospect of making shape, a form that is self-sustaining, self-justifying and balanced in terms which you cannot quite define or prescribe [. . .] makes you excited and miserable [. . .] This hypothetical beginning, this particular sweat, is what I take to be imaginative freedom' (McEwan 1983: ix). As your body of works has progressed and you've explored more and more possible storylines, to what extent has 'this particular sweat' changed? Do you feel you need to artificially trigger 'this particular sweat' in order to continue opening up original, exciting narratives that entail a meaningful progression of your authorship?

I. M.: I don't think the creative starting point – the blank page – has changed. Writing continues to involve retreat and silence; often doing nothing at all, creative hesitation, are all-important precursors to starting. I don't have, and never have had, publishers breathing down my neck demanding the next book. A work of art has to be self-generated.

What has changed is the background noise, which is now, with the spread of email, for instance, far greater than it was in the seventies. We live in an age of marvellous machines. I like computers, but it does require conscious effort to close it down, to not go near the email program or the Internet. I liked the old days, a brief window, when the computer was simply a clever form of typewriter.

And what is constant is the element of self-reinvention: in a sense, every new book is the first book, for which a language has to be discovered. Often now, the first few months of writing a novel are not about what's going to happen in it, but about *how* it's going to be told. I come up with an opening of fifteen hundred words, maybe three thousand words, and I stop and spend a lot of time just messing around with it to get the voice, the taste of it. Once I've got the feel of the prose, I feel happier about pushing on.

Victor Sage: This reminds me of when I first met you. You were writing very short pieces and I was impressed by the desire in you to write 'blind': you would do anything to void yourself of all plans. It was in the knowledge that one cannot know oneself. It connected with the kind of strangely ritualized regressions that form a stream in your work. When you first began with those concentrated short stories, sometimes you'd wait five or six weeks for the end of a story to arrive and when it did, it was delivered whole out of your head. Do you still write blind? Are you still interested in testing yourself with the advantage of our not being able to know ourselves in the act of writing?

I. M.: There's always a tension in fiction, and maybe in all arts, between, on the one hand, a sense of the artist in control of his or her material, and, on the other hand, needing to embrace a degree of chance, a degree of luck. To some extent writing a novel has to be a journey without maps. A later draft allows one to smooth the edges and make that tension operate so that it looks as if everything was intended, but in the actual process I feel like I'm only partially in control of the material.

There is a self-organizing quality about a novel: the deeper you get into it, the more your options close down. But *Atonement* certainly began 'blind'. I wrote a paragraph about a girl with some wild flowers stepping into a room looking for a vase, aware of a young man outside. I liked the sentences. I had about seven or eight hundred words and I thought: 'This is the beginning of a novel.'

I picked my way slowly and wrote what became the second chapter of *Atonement*. Even then, I had no clear idea what I was doing; I thought perhaps this was a novel set in the future in which a privileged elite had turned its back, luxuriously, on technological civilization in order to live out a fantasy eighteenth-century Jane Austen-like country house world. Only the lower classes bothered with technology. I'm slightly ashamed of saying this, but in my very first draft Robbie had implants in his brain that permitted him to download directly from the Internet. Cecilia thinks this is terribly lowbrow, like having three ducks flying over your mantelpiece. That's flying blind, I guess.

By the time I started the second chapter, I was already moving in another direction. I needed to give this woman a younger sister and Briony just launched herself on to the page fully-formed, and what is now the first chapter of the novel wrote itself relatively quickly, in two or three weeks. Robbie's implanted electrodes were nonsense – he now was a living character. There was no plan for this novel, but writing it created a plan.

The Child in Time started as a comic novel, and then I stalled for eighteen months before I started again and found another way into it. *Enduring Love* really started as a riposte too. Vic [Sage] once said to me: 'We don't really hear the case for rationality in *Black Dogs*.' I thought I would like to write about a character who is almost pathologically rational but also right in his judgements. But I had no idea how it would begin. There was a lot of floundering before those characters emerged and I discovered *Enduring Love*.

It's an inefficient way of working. It sometimes means sitting days, weeks on end, not filling the page because you can't think how to get out of the corner you've written yourself into. But this kind of writing, if you're prepared to wait, will give it a cohesion you could never get with a back-of-an-envelope plan. It will be cleverer in some important respects. It will be something you never could have elaborated in advance. In *Atonement*, Briony's dying confession is something that she could never have foreseen. When she wrote her first draft, she could not have foreseen her last. It's this element of exploration in the dark, of investigation, and surprise, which lies at the heart of the pleasure of fiction for me.

Jon Cook: I want to ask you about the role of ideas in your fiction. Ideas might be important in two respects. One of them is the way in which your novels are responsive to intellectual or ideological preoccupations in modern culture. Your early work engaged with feminism and the politics of nuclear disarmament, and your subsequent work has been responding to the ways in which we seek to – or perhaps cannot – remember traumatic or catastrophic events such as the Second World War. Ideas also are present in your fiction in the way arguments occur in your fiction. The argument between Joe and Clarissa in *Enduring Love*, for instance, is to do with the troubled affair encountered in their relationship, but they represent two different ideas about what madness signifies: one offers an inter-subjective account of mental disturbance; the other offers a scientific account of mental disturbance. To what degree are you aware of those intellectual preoccupations? And do you write novels to engage with a specific idea in mind?

I. M.: I do have a useful and, I hope, practical sense of what ideas do in the novel. My thoughts on this are also contradictory, and conflicted. They range from Kundera's notion that ideas have *no* place at all because they are the death of the novel, to the notion of the novel as a fundamentally intellectual preoccupation. I like novels, beside emotional and sensual content, to have some muscularity of intellect, and engagement with the world.

In his essay 'Art of Fiction' (1884), Henry James said that one of the prime duties of the novelist is to be 'interesting', which can mean anything you want it to. When I look back, I want to group together four books, *The Child in Time*, *The Innocent*, *Black Dogs* and *Enduring Love*.

During that period, before I actually started work, many of the notes, the messages I sent to myself were about finding dramatic or sensual ways in bringing ideas to life rather than about characters or settings or plots. In other words, I set out to make a novel of ideas – not the true, expository thing that Diderot might write, but rather something which has life and energy at the level of the plot's intricacy and the characters' emotions at the same time as indulging an intellectual preoccupation.

But then I abruptly fell out of love with that notion. When I wrote *Amsterdam*, I had no specific 'ideas' in mind. I had a distinct set of ambitions, but they were not intellectual. *Amsterdam* was a form of farce – I abandoned myself purely to the possibilities of its characters. Although I gave them ideas – Clive Linley, the composer, is introduced with a manifesto about what he thinks music should be – they seemed subsidiary. *Amsterdam* was light-hearted, and it liberated me from abstraction.

Without this novel I could not have begun writing *Atonement*. Once I finished the former, the only notes I made when working towards *Atonement* were character notes. There were no grand organizing ideas for *Atonement* in advance of the writing. In fact, I didn't even think of the title until the end. It developed piecemeal, and it fell into place. I felt that the series of four novels I've mentioned actually had trapped me. I can't say that *Atonement* has no ideas at all, but the ideas contained in it rise like a mist off a swamp of private lives. I hope it is a creative confusion about what kind of position ideas really have inside fiction.

J. C.: During the last decade, you have become interested in science, biology, neuroscience and the like. Does this interest in science have any relationship to this change of ideas you are describing?

I. M.: My interest in science is actually lifelong. It represents for me the only available and credible metaphysics given that I have no religion. The past 20 years biologists have been invading the territory of novelists. I have always thought the defining call of literature is to do with the exploration of human nature, which is also a dominant issue within cognitive and evolutionary psychology. Fundamental notions like consciousness as well as the emotions – surely the novelist's domain – are studied. Emotions like anger, shame and even revenge are studied in beautifully constructed experiments.

Yesterday, I was writing a passage in the novel I'm currently doing [*Saturday*] about my character stopping by a television shop and seeing, multiplied on several screens of different sizes, Tony Blair being interviewed [See McEwan 2005: 140–41]. He can't hear what Blair's saying, but as he's watching, the camera is slowly zooming in on Blair's mouth. We humans are very good at looking at each other's faces, and we have many good evolutionary reasons to be so. Paul Ekman, a psychologist who I've come admire a great deal, talks interestingly about the smile in his work. If you ask someone to fake a smile, there are muscles in the face that are not activated. What Ekman has shown is that the lying smile actually has a real physiological foundation; there are muscles that do not kick in, which do when a smile is honest. As the camera zooms in, I thought, this is the question we want to pose about a politician: is that an honest smile, or not. I could not have had such a speculation without the work of Ekman.

So, science parallels literature as a means by which the world can be understood. There are great, noble and ingenious insights which science has brought us and which literature could never equal. Of course, there are many complex facets of experience for which science has no language and literature does.

Vic Sage reads a passage from *Black Dogs*, in which the main character, Jeremy, gropes his way through his own home, which, in the dark, seems to have changed unrecognizably:

> The shapeless deeper black of the switchboard cupboard was twenty feet or so away and I was guiding myself towards it by trailing my hand along the edge of the kitchen table. Not since childhood had I been so intimidated by the dark. Like a character in a cartoon, I hummed softly, without conviction. No tune came to mind, and my random sequence of notes was foolish. My voice sounded weak. I deserved to be harmed. Once again, the thought came, clearer this time, that all I needed to do was leave. [. . .] I was trapped between my reason, which urged me to move quickly, turn on the power and see by bright artificial light how ordinariness simply continued, as it always did; and my superstitious dread, whose simplicity was even greater than the everyday. (McEwan 1992: 115)

V. S.: That darkness and that superstitious dread are, for me, an important part of the dynamo of your writing. You have a dialectic in this passage that seems very much part of the dialectic of the whole book, which is about rationalism and the regressive aspects of the psyche. It is also about the post-world-war period in which the public life is divorced from the private life, which becomes a kind of regression away from rationalism. Why should there be such darkness in your writing if you're so interested in science?

I. M.: I have no religious faith, but I don't for a moment believe that rationalism, science, some version of positivism, is going to suddenly sweep the religious impulse away. Although I might not subscribe to any supernatural beliefs, I can't count myself free of all of those basic dreads that have impelled religion. Including the fear of dying. The ground can sometimes drop away from you; it is a core feeling. It can steal up in a night of insomnia or when we visit a friend who is dying.

I honestly feel the religious, or the numinous urge in people, is deeply stitched into human nature. Some years ago I wrote a lecture on human nature [the *Van der Leeuw Lezing*, 2002: 'Literature, Science and Human Nature']. Anthropology used to dwell on human variation, attempting to show how vastly different people in contemporary Manhattan were from people in Papua New Guinea. Now, it gives a degree of credence to what is universal in human societies from the social organization of Stone Age cultures to the post-industrial West. Donald Brown's *Human Universals* (1991) demonstrates that one feature strong in all human culture is religion. In religion there is always a core of dread, as well as other elements of delight and transcendence.

J. C.: Another kind of fear which is strong in your fiction is the impossibility of self-knowledge. Although the examined life is the life to be preferred, *Atonement* seems to be about this impossibility of self-knowledge: acts of knowledge turn into forms of rationalization or protection, so that we suddenly become strange to ourselves. One of the compelling moments in your work takes place where this kind of thing arises. In *Black Dogs* for instance, when a father is beating a child in the restaurant, the father himself is slapped across the face. Any impulse to say 'Stop' is suddenly vanquished by the sheer fact of this happening because of this strangeness within human experience.

I. M.: Yes, that's true. But also, what redeems Briony in *Atonement* is precisely the fact that she *has* led an examined life. Her great misdeed pursues her through the years. She will not let herself forget – and this is her atonement.

That episode of *Black Dogs* was drawn from my own experience: I once saw a woman giving a child, a toddler, such a thrashing in a playground that I wondered if she could really be a conscious, sentient human being. I went across I said: 'I don't think you should be doing that.' She told me to fuck off. I was completely ineffectual, but perhaps there was an element of guilt in the vigour of her response.

However, the apparent impossibility of self-knowledge must not allow us to think we exist in a swamp of relative truths. We know more than we once did about ourselves. We know that epilepsy is not caused by possession by the Devil, the plague, or by our wickedness and God's revenge. But it's difficult. We're good at persuading ourselves that things are true when they're not, generally for reasons which are self-serving. The reason I like novels is that they're good at dramatizing the ways in which we fool ourselves. Motivation and belief is a fascinating subject.

S. G.: Vic Sage asked you about darkness and irrationalism in your writing, and in your answer you mention we often forget 'the light we can shine too'. Your dark vision seems supplemented by a vision of love and goodness in people. In the same novel that Sage reads from, the narrator, Jeremy, juxtaposes two distinct visions. On the one hand, there is Bernard, an existentialist who sees no patterns and purpose to life, and his wife June is a semi-religious determinist who sees purpose, God, in everything. Jeremy dismisses both these views and states that 'I would be false to my own experience if I did not declare my belief in the possibility of love transforming and redeeming a life' (McEwan 1998: 20). I was wondering whether you could say something about the way, on the one hand, this tendency towards dark regression, and, on the other hand, this vision of love as a positive force, relate to one another.

I. M.: As far as this word 'darkness' goes, I thought at the time my early short stories were darkly comic. It was only when they were bundled up into a book and reviewed that I saw them described in summary and thought: 'What have I done?!' Clearly, these stories were very odd, and I could hardly complain about the 'Ian Macabre' tag. I can never satisfactorily explain where these stories and the first two novels came from. Ultimately, they led to a loss of faith in fiction, an impasse, in the early eighties.

I suppose it's an easily acceptable premise that love redeems. But when The Beatles sang 'all you need is love', that never seemed enough. The range of problems, large- and small-scale, we face now are not going to be settled by people being nicer to one another, or even loving each other. Yet within the frame of personal lives, love is a great motivating hunger and when it satisfies there is a sense of happiness. The second-order problem is how to hold on to it, once we've found that precious thing. We have built an entire literature around this dual problem: finding happiness, then keeping it.

Saturday was an attempt to describe happiness in a troubled world. Some critics were shocked by the description of a man who wasn't having a divorce, who loved his wife after 20 years, who got on well with his teenage children. To some intellectuals this was an abomination. It shocked people more than any of my child-raping short stories ever did. I think there's bad faith in intellectual culture whereby pessimism has become too easy, too automatic, it's a badge that people wear. There are many terrible, even unsolvable problems we face at present, but I reject the indulgent pessimism of the liberal arts culture. That's why I've come to value the company of scientists. They are not interested only in how things originate or work, but also how problems might be solved. Science is organized curiosity, which is a fundamentally optimistic state: you might not know it now, but you might know it one day. In my work, I'm torn between the truthful description, which is often painful or bleak, and wanting to affirm something about our extraordinary gift of consciousness and the delight of the natural world. As a species, as well as our crudity and vulgarity and cruelty, we have a capacity for courage, kindness, love, and amazing humour. If I ever wrote a science fiction novel, it would involve two or three people on a spaceship speeding away from earth and after 50 years they would feel this intense nostalgia for their imperfect home; they'd miss this wild, inventive, comic imperfection.

S. G.: I would like to discuss this loss of faith in fiction you mentioned earlier in more detail. At the outset of your *oeuvre* there is a great sense of unease about writing as an artistic form. Around the time you were writing *The Comfort of Strangers*, you had a difficult time in allowing fiction to function as a means of communicating ideas about the world. In Margaret Drabble's biography of your mentor at UEA, Angus Wilson, she notes that you were staying at Wilson's house at Felsham Woodside. You were restless and 'walked the woods amidst the wild garlic, brooding on *The Comfort of Strangers* [. . .] Could the contemporary world be rendered in fiction at all, McEwan asked himself?' (Drabble, 1995: 523). To what extent did your early writing emerge from a sense of crisis about novelistic representation that manifested itself in the late sixties and seventies?

I. M.: I'd forgotten about that, wandering about in Angus's woods, wondering what kind of fiction could please me, or excite me. I had lost faith in writing. I had been tied to a restricted aesthetic of the novel that I now find quite puzzling. It was the existential trap, the novel cleansed of all reference to place or recognizable public spaces, with no connection to time or historical context. This mode of writing didn't permit itself the luxury of describing inner states; it was all down to what someone said or did. This was my home-grown version of Kafka. Kafka doesn't tell you exactly where Gregor Samsa [in the short story 'Metamorphosis'] is when he wakes up, or what year it is. So, by the early eighties I was feeling deeply dissatisfied and I decided to write screenplays. Maybe the depressing, dark quality of my writing at the time reflected my sense of the limits of fiction itself. Working with the director Richard Eyre in the early eighties loosened me up: I returned to the novel with more appetite, more pleasure.

S. G.: In the light of this remark on existentialist writers, I was wondering whether Alain Robbe-Grillet, the writer and literary critic who defined the *roman nouveau*, was part of the influence on this crisis of representation?

I. M.: I read *Jealousy* (1957), and one or two others, but they didn't have much impact. His writing seemed as much of a *cul-de-sac* as my own. When I was researching *The Innocent* in the mid-eighties, I spent a lot of time wandering along the Wall and the perimeter of West Berlin, thinking: 'What a great subject.' The Wall ran right through people's lives, right through their houses, a huge political fact, the frontier of a war, divider of families: a perfect subject for a novelist. I remember asking friends in West Germany who had written well about the Wall, and everyone mentioned the same novel, Peter Schneider's *Der Mauerspringer* (1982). But nothing else. My friends explained that the general view was that the Wall was a subject for journalists, not for novelists. Novelists wrote about higher things. I felt a twinge of guilt, because only three years before I could have lived in a city with a wall down the middle and not written about it, for those same lofty existential reasons. If Chicago had a Wall, the Chicago Wall, could you imagine Saul Bellow ignoring it? If it ran through New Jersey, would Philip Roth ignore it? If it ran across New England, would Updike ignore it? No. Nor would Mailer, nor would Pynchon. And here in Europe, some of us had written ourselves into a corner. Martin Amis and I once decided on the archetypal existential plot: a guy without a name arrives in a nameless town on an unnamed mission and waits in a nameless hotel for a nameless guy to phone him . . . and of course, he never does. No wonder I was unhappy in Angus Wilson's woods.

S. G.: However, it seems to me that the early influence of Kafka on your work can also be retraced in the Surrealism that is part of the aesthetics of your work. In particular a strong sense of nausea brought about by vertigo is present throughout your work. There is a great example of this in *The Child in Time*, when Stephen, lying in bed looking at his wife, imagines having an out-of-body experience of sorts: 'He was looking down at her from an immense distance now, from several hundred feet. He could see the bedroom, the Edwardian apartment block [. . .] the mess of South London, the hazy curvature of the earth [. . .] He was rising still higher, faster. At least, he thought, from up here where the air was thin and the city below was taking on geometric design, his feelings would not show, he could retain some composure' (McEwan 1987: 22). In your latest novel, *On Chesil Beach*, Florence associates her love for Edward 'with a definable physical sensation, as irrefutable as vertigo' (McEwan 2007: 97). The difference between these examples is that in the first the vertigo is shown, mimetic, and in the second it is told, diegetic. In what ways have your attempts at creating nausea and vertigo changed as you've grown older?

I. M.: I think you are referring to certain states of mind when the world appears super-real, either because you are in an emotional state, or because you haven't looked before and now you *do* need to look. Sometimes you can only impart the nature of the physical world, especially its particular visual quality, by trying to convey that strong, dizzying sense of how amazing it is that anything exists at all, and that there are conscious beings like ourselves to notice it. Put simply, this is the sweat for writers, to find a persuasive language for things and events in the world.

This is a commonplace example: you return to the room you left hours or days before. No one has been in it, all items are exactly as you left them, everything is exactly the same. But the sameness can be highly charged; the exact arrangement of the objects in the room might be the product of the intentions you have forgotten – that discarded shirt, that shoe on its side. Perhaps you even prefer to forget. The objects seem to hold a memory, perhaps they even accuse you. But of course, they hold nothing at all. They are merely themselves.

This dual aspect can be dizzying. We are visual creatures. Forty per cent of our brains are involved in visual processing. Our language is saturated with visual references, far more than any other sense. The key to emotions, feelings and the swirl of human exchange is best fixed if you can capture the visual essence correctly. In his famous preface to *The Nigger of Narcissus* (1897), Conrad wrote: 'My task which I am trying to achieve is, by the power of the written word to make you hear, to make you feel – it is, before all, to make you *see*.'

But I don't know what's changed. I'm sure I could find plenty of 'mimetic' moments in my recent work, particularly *Saturday* and *On Chesil Beach*. But yes, there is always a danger that the world is not so keenly observed or felt as you age. The senses dim somewhat and there is the danger that you simply become desensitized to the miracle of being alive. I hope not, but this goes back to the earlier question about loss of faith in the nature of fiction. Capturing a single detail can revive my pleasure in writing: if it's vertiginous, I'd be very pleased.

S. G.: This surrealism and sense of vertigo in your work is tied into questions about narrative authority, and more generally about how your poetics have changed over the course of more than 30 years of writing. While in your early novels we often encounter first-person narrators, your later novels have a clear authorial presence in the form of a third-person narrator, which may suggest a growing occupation of realist territory as a basis for your narratives?

I. M.: I've lost all interest in first-person narrative. I could hurl a book across the room when I feel that the writer is hiding slack writing and clichés behind his characterization – writing badly because this is how a character speaks. I want narrative authority. I want Saul Bellow, I want John Updike, I want Chekhov, I want Nabokov and Jane Austen. I want the authorial presence taking full responsibility for everything. Although the narrator of *On Chesil Beach* is not a character you could describe, or has any past or future, it is a presence which assumes the aesthetic task of describing the inside of two people's minds. Then the reader can make a judgement. Of course there is a way of loading a first-person narrative voice with authorial insight, or brilliant turns of phrase, but most writers don't try for this – it's difficult.

S. G.: To conclude, you've mentioned walking in Felsham Woods and West Berlin. You are a keen walker, and a particular fan of the Chilterns, where the heart-stopping opening scene of *Enduring Love* is set. In *Black Dogs*, Jeremy states that he feels 'purged after [his] five hour walk' (McEwan 1992: 123). In *Amsterdam*, the narrator states: 'Everyone he knew seemed perfectly happy to get by without wilderness – a country restaurant, Hyde Park in Spring, was all the open space they ever needed. Surely they could not claim to be fully alive' (McEwan 1998: 80).

I was wondering what walking, besides getting away from London and work, means to you?

I. M.: Walking returns me to the essentials: we live on a giant rock hanging in sterile space. If you walk for several days, it's surprising how quickly everything else in your life drops away. And how quickly a long walk translates itself into metaphor – life's journey, if you like. To stand in some high, beautiful place and reflect how easily you might not have existed at all – that's benign vertigo. I don't know how people can live without it.

This interview is a compilation of two separate conversations with Ian McEwan. The first took place with Jon Cook and Victor Sage at the University of East Anglia, Norwich, on 15 November 2003. The second interview was conducted by Sebastian Groes at McEwan's house in London, on 4 December 2007.

References

Works Cited by Contributors

Foreword: Ian McEwan and the Rational Mind, Matt Ridley

Connolly, C. (1997), *Literary Review*, 19 September, 3–4.

Introduction: A Cartography of the Contemporary: Mapping Newness in the Work of Ian McEwan, Sebastian Groes

Bragg, M. (2005), *South Bank Show*. Season 28, Number 638. First broadcast 20 February, 2005.

Colebrook, C. (2006), *Gilles Deleuze*. Oxford: Routledge. First published in 2002.

Dawkins, R. (1976), *The Selfish Gene*. Oxford: Oxford University Press.

Drabble, M. (1995), *Angus Wilson*. London: Secker & Warburg.

Groes, S. and Amis, M. (2004), 'A Hatred of Reason', in *The London Magazine*, June/July, 44–51.

Haffenden, J. (1885), *Novelists in Interview*. London: Methuen.

Leith, W. (1998), 'Form and Dysfunction', *The Observer*, 'Life', 20 September, 4–5; 7–8.

Lloyd, J. (2002), 'George W. Bush's Unlikely Bedfellows, *New Statesman*, 11 March, http://www.newstatesman.com/200203110006 [Accessed 4 July 2005].

Malcolm, D. (2002), *Understanding Ian McEwan*. Columbia: University of South Carolina Press.

Mars-Jones, A. (1990), 'Venus Envy'. *Chatto Counterblasts No 41*. London: Chatto & Windus.

Martin, Nicole (2008), 'Ian McEwan: I Despise Militant Islam', *The Telegraph*, 22 June, 2008, http://www.telegraph.co.uk/news/2174813/Ian-McEwan-I-despise-militant-Islam.html [Accessed 17 August, 2008].

McEwan, I. (1981), *The Comfort of Strangers*. London: Jonathan Cape.

—(1985), *Rose Blanche*. London: Jonathan Cape.

—(1986), 'Schoolboys', in Carey, J. (ed.), *William Golding: The Man and his Books*. London: Faber.

—(1988), *The Child in Time*. London: Picador. First published by Jonathan Cape, 1987.

—(1989), *A Move Abroad*: 'Or Shall We Die' and *The Ploughman's Lunch*. London: Picador.

—(1990), *The Innocent*. London: Jonathan Cape.

—(1994), *The Daydreamer*. London: Jonathan Cape.

—(1997), *Enduring Love*. London: Jonathan Cape.

—(1998a), *Black Dogs*. London: Vintage.

McEwan, I. (1998b), *Amsterdam*. London: Jonathan Cape.

—(2001a), *Atonement*. London: Jonathan Cape.

—(2001b), 'Beyond Belief', *The Guardian*, 12 September, http://www.ianmcewan.com/bib/articles/9-11-02.html [Accessed 12 May, 2008].

—(2002a), 'Literature, Science and Human Nature', lecture delivered 7 November, in Groningen, http://www.vanderleeuwlezing.nl/mcewan_eng.htm [Accessed 8 January, 2006].

—(2002b), 'Mother Tongue', in Leader, Z., ed., *On Modern Fiction*. Oxford: Oxford University Press.

—(2005a), *Saturday*. London: Jonathan Cape.

—(2005b), 'Save the Bootroom, Save the Earth', March 19, *The Guardian*, http://www.guardian.co.uk/artanddesign/2005/mar/19/art1 [Accessed 8 July 2008].

—(2005c), 'How Could we have Forgotten That This was Always Going to Happen?', *The Guardian*, 8 July, http://www.guardian.co.uk/world/2005/jul/08/terrorism.july74 [Accessed 16 July, 2008].

—(2005d), 'The Master', *The Guardian*, 'Review', April 7, http://www.guardian.co.uk/books/2005/apr/07/fiction.saulbellow

—(2006), *First Love, Last Rites*. London: Vintage.

—(2006), *In Between the Sheets*. London: Vintage.

—(2006), 'A Parallel Tradition', *The Guardian*, April 1, http://www.guardian.co.uk/books/2006/apr/01/scienceandnature.richarddawkins [Accessed 18 June, 2008].

—(2007a), *On Chesil Beach*. London: Jonathan Cape.

—(2007b), 'End of the World Blues', the Royal Society of Arts/New Writing Worlds Lecture 2007, first delivered at the University of East Anglia, 27 June 2007, first published in *The Guardian*, Review, 31 May 2008, http://www.guardian.co.uk/books/2008/may/31/fiction.philosophy [Accessed 7 August, 2008].

—(2008a), *For You*. London: Vintage.

—(2008b), 'McEwan Addresses Recent Statement on Islamism', 26 June, http://www.ian-mcewan.blogspot.com [Accessed 18 August, 2008].

—(2008c), 'The Child in Time', *The Guardian*, Review, 12 July, http://www.guardian.co.uk/lifeandstyle/2008/jul/12/familyandrelationships.elementsoffiction [Accessed 3 August, 2008].

Sage, L. (1992), *Women in the House of Fiction*. Houndmills and London: Macmillan.

Sardar, Z. (2006) 'The Blitcon Supremacists', *The Guardian*, 9 December, http://www.guardian.co.uk/commentisfree/story/0,,1968091,00.html [Accessed 15 May, 2007].

Soal, J. (2008), 'McEwan Sees Funny Side of Climate Change in Novel Reading', *The Guardian*, 2 June, http://www.guardian.co.uk/books/2008/jun/02/hay-festival2008.hayfestival [Accessed 17 July, 2008].

Chapter One: Surrealist Encounters in Ian McEwan's Early Work, Jeannette Baxter

Barthes, R. (1990), *The Pleasure of the Text*, trans. R. Miller. Oxford: Blackwell (1973).

Bataille, G. (2001), *Eroticism*, trans. M. Dalwood. London: Penguin (1957).

Bataille, G. (ed.) (1995), 'Formless', in 'Critical Dictionary', *Encyclopaedia Acephalica*. London: Atlas Press (1929).

Bradbury, M. (1993), *The Modern British Novel*. London: Penguin.

Breton, A. (1972), 'Second Manifesto of Surrealism' in *Manifestoes of Surrealism*, trans. R. Seaver and H. R. Lane. Ann Arbor: University of Michigan Press (1929).

Broughton, L. (1991), 'Portrait of the Subject as a Young Man: the Construction of Masculinity Ironized in "Male" Fiction', in P. Shaw and P. Stockwell (eds), *Subjectivity and Literature from the Romantics to the Present Day*. London: Pinter, pp. 135–45.

Foster, H. (1993), *Compulsive Beauty*. Cambridge, Massachusetts: MIT Press.

Freud, S. (1920), *Three Contributions to the Theory of Sex*, trans. A. A. Brill. New York: Plain Label Books.

Haffenden, J. (1985), *Novelists in Interview*. London: Methuen, 168–90.

Krauss, R. (1986), 'Corpus Delecti' in Rosalind Krauss and Jane Livingstone (eds), *L'Amour Fou: Photography and Surrealism*. Hayward Gallery, London, July–September, 1986. London: Arts Council.

Lomas, D. (2007), 'V is for Vertigo', *Papers of Surrealism*, D. Ades, D. Lomas, J. Mundy (eds) (December 2007), ISSN 17501954, http://www.surrealismcentre.ac.uk/papersofsurrealism/journal7/index.htm

Martin, J-H. (2005), *Andy Warhol: The Late Work*. New York: Prestel Publishing.

McEwan, I. (1997a), *First Love, Last Rites*. London: Vintage (1975).

—(1997b), *In Between the Sheets*. London: Vintage (1978).

—(2006), *The Cement Garden*. London: Vintage (1978).

Moore-Gilbert, B. (1994), *Art in the 1970s*. London: Routledge.

Nairn, T. (1977), *The Break-Up of Britain: Crisis and Neo-Nationalism*. London: New Left Books.

Ricks, C. (1979), 'Adolescence and After: An Interview with Ian McEwan' in *The Listener*, 101, 12 April, pp. 526–7.

Ryan, K. (1994), *Ian McEwan*. Plymouth: Northcote House.

Sontag, S. (2001), 'The Pornographic Imagination' in George Bataille, *Story of the Eye*, trans. J. Neugroschal. London: Penguin (1967).

Chapter Two: 'Profoundly dislocating and infinite in possibility' – Ian McEwan's Screenwriting, M. Hunter Hayes and Sebastian Groes

Edemariam, Aida (2008), 'Enduring Fame', *The Guardian*, August 18, http://www.guardian.co.uk/uk/2007/aug/18/film.aidaedemariam [Accessed 4 August 2008].

Hamilton, I. (1978), 'Points of Departure', *New Review*, 5 (2), 9–12.

Hutcheon, L. (2006), *A Theory of Adaptation*. New York: Routledge.

McEwan, I. (1979), *In Between the Sheets and Other Stories*. New York: Simon and Schuster.

—(1981), *The Imitation Game: Three Plays for Television*. London: Jonathan Cape.

McEwan, I. (1983b), 'Writers and the Cinema – A Symposium'. *Times Literary Supplement*, 18 November, 1287–8.

—(1985), *The Ploughman's Lunch*. London: Methuen.

—(1988), *Soursweet*. London: Faber and Faber.

—(1989), *A Move Abroad*. London: Picador. [Contains *Or Shall We Die?* and *The Ploughman's Lunch*, and an illuminating preface on fiction writing.]

—(2002), 'Mother Tongue', in Z. Leader (ed.), On Modern British Fiction. Oxford: Oxford University Press, pp. 34–44.

—(2006), 'A Parallel Tradition'. *The Guardian*, 1 April.

Mo, T. (1990), *Sour Sweet*. London: Abacus. First published by André Deutsch in 1982.

Ryan, K. (1999), 'Sex, Violence and Complicity: Martin Amis and Ian McEwan', in *An Introduction to Contemporary Fiction*. Cambridge: Polity, pp. 203–18.

—(2007), *Ian McEwan*. London: Northcote House. First published in 1994.

Chapter Three: *The Innocent* as Anti-Oedipal Critique of Cultural Pornography, Claire Colebrook

Deleuze, G. and Guattari, F. (2004), *Anti-Oedipus*, trans. Robert Hurley, Mark Seem, and Helen R. Lane. London and New York: Continuum. First published by the Athlone Press, 1984. Originally published as *L'Anti Oedipe* (1972) by Les Editions de Minuit, Paris.

Freud, S. (1950), *Beyond the Pleasure Principle*, trans. J. Strachey. London: Hogarth.

Freud, S. (1959), 'On Narcissism' in Riviere, J. and Strache, J. (eds), *Collected Papers*, Vol. 4. New York: Basic Books.

Laplanche, J. (1999), in Fletcher, J. (ed.), *Essays on Otherness*. London: Routledge.

McEwan, I. (1988), *The Child in Time*. London: Picador. First published in 1987 by Jonathan Cape.

—(1990), *The Innocent, or The Special Relationship*. London: Jonathan Cape.

—(2005), *Saturday*. London: Jonathan Cape.

—(2007), *On Chesil Beach*. London: Jonathan Cape.

Wicke, J. (1991), 'Through a Gaze Darkly: Pornography's Academic Market', *Transition*, 54, 68–9.

Chapter Four: Words of War, War of Words – *Atonement* and the Question of Plagiarism, Natasha Alden

Andrews, L. (1977), *No Time For Romance*. London: Harrap.

—(2005), Personal communication. 11 December.

Broughton, L. (1991), 'Portrait of the Subject as a Young Man: the Construction of Masculinity Ironized in "Male" Fiction', in Philip Shaw and Peter Stockwell (eds), *Subjectivity and Literature from the Romantics to the Present Day*. London: Pinter.

Elias, A. J. (2001), *Sublime Desire: History and Post-1960s Fiction*. Baltimore: The Johns Hopkins University Press.

Hutcheon, L. (1995), *A Poetics of Postmodernism: History, Theory, Fiction*. London: Routledge.

Langdon, J. (2006), 'Revealed: How Booker Prize Writer Copied Work of the Queen of the Hospital Romance', *The Mail on Sunday*, 27 November, 36–7.

Lee, H. (2001), 'If your Memory Serves you Well . . .', *The Observer*, 'Review', 23 September, 16.

Lyall, S. (2006), 'Novelists Defend One of Their Own', *New York Times*, 7 December, late edn, E1.

McCrumb, R. (2006), 'Warning: the Words you are About to Read may be Stolen', *The Observer*, 'Review', 3 December 2006, 13.

McEwan, I. (2006), 'An Inspiration, Yes. Did I Copy from Another Author? No', *The Guardian*, 27 November, 1–2.

Radloff, A. (unpub.), 'The Memoir of Mrs. A. Radloff', in possession of Department of Documents, Imperial War Museum, London.

Radloff, A. (2005), Interview with Natasha Alden on 11 November 2005.

Radloff, A. (2005), Personal communication.

Roberts, G. (2006), 'Plagiarism (or Why I Need Atonement) by Ian McEwan', *The Daily Mail*, 4 December, Sect. ED IRE.

Sutherland, J. (2002), 'Life Was Clearly Too Interesting in the War: An Interview with Ian McEwan', *The Guardian*, 3 January, http://books/guardian.co.uk/departments/generalfiction/story/0,6000,627239,00.html [Accessed 17 June 2007].

Talk of the Nation (2006), radio broadcast, National Public Radio, Washington DC, 13 December.

Wagner, E. (2006), 'Plagiarism? No – It's Called Research', *The Times*, 27 November, 3.

Chapter Five: Postmodernism and the Ethics of Fiction in *Atonement*, Alistair Cormack

Belsey, C. (1980), *Critical Practice*. London: Methuen.

Butler, M. (1997), *Jane Austen and the War of Ideas*. Oxford: Oxford University Press. First published in 1975.

Finney, B. (2002), 'Briony's Stand Against Oblivion: Ian McEwan's *Atonement*', *Journal of Modern Literature*, 27 (3), 68–82.

Head, D. (2007), *Ian McEwan*. Manchester: Manchester University Press.

Kermode, F. (2001), 'Point of View', *London Review of Books*, 23 (19), 4 October, 8.

Leavis, F. R. (1982), *The Great Tradition*. Harmondsworth: Penguin. First published in London by Chatto & Windus, 1948.

Lee, H. (2001), 'If your Memory Serves you Well . . .'. *The Observer*, 'Review', 23 September, 16.

MacCabe, C. (1979), *James Joyce and the Revolution of the Word*. London and Basingstoke: Macmillan.

McEwan, I. (2001), *Atonement*. London: Jonathan Cape.

Reynolds, M. and Noakes J. (2002), *Ian McEwan: The Essential Guide*. London: Vintage.

Wood, J. (2002), 'The Trick of the Truth'. *The New Republic Online*, http://www. powells.com/review/2002_03_21.html (21 March 2002).

Woolf, V. (1992), *Mrs Dalloway*, with notes by E. Showalter. Harmondsworth: Penguin. First published in 1925.

Chapter Six: Ian McEwan's Modernist Time – *Atonement* and *Saturday*, Laura Marcus

Banfield, A. (2007), 'Remembrance and Tense Past', in *The Cambridge Companion to the Modernist Novel*, M. Shiach (ed.). Cambridge: Cambridge University Press, 48–64.

Bowen, E. (1949), *The Heat of the Day*. London: Jonathan Cape/The Reprint Society, 1950.

Currie, M. (2007), *About Time: Narrative, Fiction and the Philosophy of Time*. Edinburgh: Edinburgh University Press.

Finney, B. (2002), 'Briony's Stand Against Oblivion: Ian McEwan's *Atonement*', *Journal of Modern Literature*, 27 (3), 68–82.

Head, D. (2002), *The Cambridge Introduction to Modern British Fiction, 1950–2000*. Cambridge: Cambridge University Press.

Head, D. (2007), *Ian McEwan*. Manchester: Manchester University Press.

James, H. (2003), Preface to *A Portrait of a Lady*. London: Penguin. Preface originally published in the 1908 New York edition of the novel.

McEwan, Ian (1987), *The Child in Time*. London: Jonathan Cape.

—(1998), *Black Dogs*. London: Vintage.

—(2002), *Atonement*. London: Vintage.

—(2005), *Saturday*. London: Jonathan Cape.

Middleton, P. and Woods, T. (2000), *Literatures of Memory: History, Time and Space in Postwar Writing*. Manchester: Manchester University Press.

Noakes, J. and Reynolds, M. (2002), *Ian McEwan: the Essential Guide*. London: Vintage.

Ricouer, P. (1985), *Time and Narrative*, Volume 2, trans. McLoughlin, K. and Pellauer, D. Chicago: University of Chicago Press.

Royle, N. (2003), *The Uncanny*. Manchester: Manchester University Press.

Woolf, V. (2000), 'Character in Fiction', in *Selected Essays*, D. Bradshaw (ed.). Oxford: Oxford University Press. First published in 1924.

—(2008), *Mrs Dalloway*. Oxford: Oxford University Press. First published in 1925.

—(1992a), *To the Lighthouse*. London: Penguin. First published in 1927.

—(1992b), *Orlando*. Oxford: Oxford University Press. First published in 1928.

—(1931), *The Waves*. London. Leonard and Virginia Woolf.

Chapter Seven: Ian McEwan and the Modernist Consciousness of the City in *Saturday*, Sebastian Groes

Arnold, M. (1965), *The Poems of Matthew Arnold*, ed. K. Allott. London: Longmans, Green and Co.

Bragg, M. (2005), *The South Bank Show: Ian McEwan*. Produced for ITV. Season 28, Episode 13. First broadcast 20 February.

Collini, S. (1988), *Arnold*. Oxford and New York: Oxford University Press.

Currie, M. (2007), *About Time*. Edinburgh: Edinburgh University Press.

Dickens, C. (1986), *Our Mutual Friend*. London: Penguin. First published 1864–5.

Edwards, P. (1995), 'Time, Romanticism, Modernism and Modernity in Ian McEwan's *The Child in Time*.' *English*, 44, 178, 48–51.

Eliot, T. S. (1969), 'The Waste Land', in *T. S. Eliot: The Complete Poems and Plays*. London: Faber and Faber, 59–80.

Ford, F. M. (2002), *Parade's End*. London: Penguin. First published 1924–8.

Head, D. (2007), *Ian McEwan*. Manchester: Manchester UP.

Joyce, J. (1992), *Ulysses*. London: Penguin. First published in Paris by Shakespeare and Co. in 1922.

—(1996), 'The Dead', in *Dubliners*. London: Penguin. First published in 1914.

Kemp, P. (2005), 'Master of the Mind Game'. *The Sunday Times*, 'Culture', 30 January, 41–2.

Kowalski, E. W. (2007), 'Postcolonial Melancholia in Ian McEwan's *Saturday*', in *Studies in the Novel*, 39 (4), 465–80.

McEwan, I. (1988), *The Child in Time*. London: Picador. First published by Jonathan Cape, 1987.

—(1998), *Enduring Love*. London: Jonathan Cape.

—(2001), *Atonement*. London: Jonathan Cape.

—(2005), *Saturday*. London: Jonathan Cape.

—(2006), 'Cocker at the Theatre', in *First Love, Last Rites*. London: Vintage.

—(2006), 'Disguises', in *First Love, Last Rites*. London: Vintage.

—(2006), 'Homemade', in *First Love, Last Rites*. London: Vintage.

—(2006), 'Pornography', in *In Between the Sheets*. London: Vintage.

—(2006), 'Two Fragments: Saturday and Sunday, March 199–', in *In Between the Sheets*. London: Vintage.

Sardar, Z. (2006), 'The Blitcon Supremacists', The *Guardian*, 9 December, http://www.guardian.co.uk/commentisfree/story/0,,1968091,00.html [Accessed 15 May 2007].

Shelley, M. (1996), *Frankenstein*, ed. P. Hunter. London and New York: Norton.

Tait, T. (2005), 'A Rational Diagnosis'. *Times Literary Supplement*, 3515, 11 February, 21–2.

Williams, R. (1973), *The Country and the City*. London: Chatto & Windus.

Williams, R. (1992), *Culture and Society: Coleridge to Orwell*. London: Hogarth. First published in Great Britain by Chatto & Windus, 1956.

Woolf, V. (1989), *Mrs Dalloway*. London: Grafton. First published by the Hogarth Press, 1925.

Chapter Eight: *On Chesil Beach* – Another 'Overrated' Novella?, Dominic Head

Amis, M. (1983), *Money*. London: Jonathan Cape.

—(2003), *Yellow Dog*. London: Jonathan Cape.

Head, D. (2008), *The State of the Novel: Britain and Beyond*. Oxford: Blackwell.

Lezard, N. (1999), 'Morality Bites', *The Guardian*, 'Saturday Review', 24 April, 11.

McEwan, I. (1998), *Amsterdam*. London: Jonathan Cape.

—(2007), *On Chesil Beach*. London: Jonathan Cape.

Further Reading

The most rigorous and up-to-date bibliography of McEwan's work can be found on the official Ian McEwan website: www.ianmcewan.com/bib/. The details of McEwan's work below are of the first edition published in the United Kingdom, followed by the first US edition. Editorial annotations are enclosed in brackets where suitable.

I Works by Ian McEwan

Short story collections
(1975). *First Love, Last Rites*. London: Cape; New York: Random House.
(1978). *In Between the Sheets*. London: Cape; New York: Simon and Schuster.

Uncollected stories
(1975). 'Intersection'. *Tri-Quarterly*, Fall, 63–86.
(1975). 'Untitled'. *Tri-Quarterly*, Winter, 62–63.
(1977). 'Deep Sleep, Light Sleeper'. *Harpers and Queen*, August, 82–85.
(1984). 'Disguises'. Utrecht: De Roos. [A limited edition of the short story with illustrations by Tom Eyzenbach.]

Novels
(1978). *The Cement Garden*. London: Jonathan Cape; New York: Simon and Schuster.
(1981). *The Comfort of Strangers*. London: Jonathan Cape; New York: Simon and Schuster.
(1987). *The Child in Time*. London: Jonathan Cape; Boston: Houghton Mifflin.
(1990). *The Innocent*. London: Jonathan Cape; New York: Doubleday.
(1992). *Black Dogs*. London: Jonathan Cape; New York: Nan A. Talese.
(1997). *Enduring Love*. London: Jonathan Cape; New York: Anchor Books.
(1998). *Amsterdam*. London: Jonathan Cape; New York: Nan A. Talese, 1999.
(2001). *Atonement*. London: Jonathan Cape; New York: Nan A. Talese, 2002.
(2005). *Saturday*. London: Jonathan Cape; New York: Nan A. Talese.
(2007). *On Chesil Beach*. London: Jonathan Cape; New York: Nan A. Talese.

Children's fiction
(1985). *Rose Blanche*. London: Jonathan Cape. [Picture book about a young girl who discovers a concentration camp in her Nazi-occupied hometown. With illustrations by Roberto Innocenti.]
(1994). *The Daydreamer*. London: Jonathan Cape.

Screenplays
(1985). *The Ploughman's Lunch*. London: Methuen.
(1988). *Soursweet*. London: Faber.
(1993). *The Good Son*. [Unpublished.]

Oratorio/Libretti
(1983). *Or Shall We Die?* London: Jonathan Cape.
(2008). *For You*. London: Vintage.

Collections
(1981). *The Imitation Game: Three Plays for Television*. London: Cape; Boston: Houghton Mifflin, 1982. [Contains three plays for television: 'Jack Flea's Birthday Celebration', 'Solid Geometry' and 'The Imitation Game', originally published in *Quarto*, April 1980.]
(1989). *A Move Abroad*. London: Picador. [Contains *Or Shall We Die?* and *The Ploughman's Lunch*, and an illuminating preface on fiction writing.]

Key articles, essays, interviews and lectures by McEwan
(1978). 'The State of Fiction – A Symposium', *The New Review*, 5:1, Summer, 50–51.
(1982). 'An Only Childhood', *The Observer*, 31 January, p. 41. [On McEwan's upbringing.]
(1986). 'Schoolboys', in J. Carey (ed.), *William Golding: The Man and His Books*. London/New York: Faber/Farrar, Straus & Giroux, 157–60.
(1990). 'An Interview with Milan Kundera', in Malcolm Bradbury (ed.), *The Novel Today*. London: Fontana, pp. 205–22.
(2001). 'Beyond Belief', *The Guardian*, 'G2', 12 September, p. 2. [Reaction to the terrorist attacks on America on 11 September 2001.]
(2001). 'Only Love and Then Oblivion', *The Guardian*, 15 September, p. 1. [Reaction to the terrorist attacks on America on 11 September 2001.]
(2001). 'Let's Talk about Climate Change', *openDemocracy.net*, 21 April, http://www.opendemocracy.net/debates/article-2-114-882.jsp [Accessed 22 November, 2007.]
(2002). 'Mother Tongue – a Memoir', in Leader, Z. (ed.), *On Modern British Fiction*. Oxford: Oxford University Press. [On the death, and his memories, of his mother]
(2003). 'Strong Cases For and Against War – But we Don't Hear Them', *The Daily Telegraph*, 10 February. [On the war in Iraq.]
(2005). 'Faith v Fact', *The Guardian*, 7 January, p. 6.
(2005). 'How Could we have Forgotten That This was Always Going to Happen?', *The Guardian*, 8 July. [On the terrorist attacks on London, 7 July 2005.]
(2006). 'Literature, Science and Human Nature', in *Human Nature, Fact and Fiction: Literature, Science and Human Nature*, Robin Headlam-Wells and Johnjoe McFadden (eds). London and New York: Continuum. [This is a reprint of the *Van der Leeuw Lezing*, a lecture given by McEwan in 2002.]
(2006). 'A Parallel Tradition', *The Guardian*, 1 April. [On the 30th anniversary of Richard Dawkins's *The Selfish Gene*.]

(2008). 'The Day of Judgement', *The Guardian Review*, 31 May. [McEwan's analysis of end-time thinking in relationship to the rise in religious fundamentalism.]

(2008). 'The Child in Time', *The Guardian Review*, 12 July. [McEwan's foreword to his newfound brother Dave Sharpe's memoir *Complete Surrender.*]

II Critical Material

Book-length studies

Byrnes, C. (2002), *The Work of Ian McEwan: A Psychodynamic Approach.* Nottingham: Paupers' Press.

Childs, P. (ed.) (2006), *The Fiction of Ian McEwan: A Reader's Guide to Essential Criticism.* Houndmills, Basingstoke: Palgrave.

Childs, P. (ed.) (2006), *Ian McEwan's* Enduring Love. *Routledge Guides to Literature.* London: Routledge.

Clarke, R. and Gordon, A. (2003), *Ian McEwan's* Enduring Love: *A Reader's Guide.* London and New York: Continuum.

Grant, D. (1989), *Contemporary Writers: Ian McEwan.* London: Book Trust and the British Council.

Head, D. (2007), *Contemporary British Novelists: Ian McEwan.* Manchester: Manchester University Press.

Malcolm, D. (2002), *Understanding Ian McEwan.* Columbia: South Carolina Press.

Reynolds, M. and Noakes, J. (2002), *Ian McEwan: the Essential Guide.* London: Vintage. [Discusses *The Child in Time, Enduring Love* and *Atonement.*]

Rooney, A. (2006), *York Notes on* Atonement. London: Longman.

Ryan, K. (1994), *Ian McEwan. Writers and their Work.* Plymouth: Northcote House.

Schemberg, C. (2004), *Achieving At-one-ment.* Frankfurt and Oxford: Peter Lang.

Slay, Jack (1996), *Ian McEwan. Twayne's English Authors Series.* Boston, MA: Twayne.

Book chapters

Adams, M. (1986), 'Ian McEwan', in L. McCaffery (ed.), *Postmodern Fiction: A Bio-Bibliographic Guide.* New York: Greenwood Press, pp. 459–62.

Blakey, V. (2004), 'God Novels', in A. Richardson and E. Spolsky (eds), *The Work of Fiction: Cognition, Culture and Complexity.* Aldershot: Ashgate, pp. 147–65.

Broughton, L. (1991), 'Portrait of the Subject as a Young Man: the Construction of Masculinity Ironized in "Male Fiction"', in P. Shaw and P. Stockwell (eds), *Subjectivity and Literature from the Romantics to the Present Day.* London: Pinter, pp. 135–45.

Brown, R. (1994), 'Postmodern Americas in the Fiction of Angela Carter, Martin Amis and Ian McEwan', in A. Massa and A. Stead (eds), *Forked Tongues? Comparing Twentieth-Century British and American Literature.* London: Longman, pp. 92–110.

Childs, P. (2005), ' "Fascinating violation": Ian McEwan's children', in N. Bentley (ed.), *British Fiction of the 1990s*. London and New York: Routledge, pp. 123–34.

Childs, P. (2005), 'Ian McEwan: The Child in All of Us', in P. Childs (ed.), *Contemporary Novelists: British Fiction since 1970*. Houndmills: Palgrave-Macmillan, pp. 160–79.

Civelekoglu, F. (2007), 'Gothic Literature from a Cultural Ecological Perspective: Ian McEwan's *The Comfort of Strangers*', in I. van Elferen (ed.), *Nostalgia or Perversion? Gothic Rewriting from the Eighteenth Century until the Present Day*. Newcastle: Cambridge Scholars Publishing, pp. 86–94.

Currie, M. (2007), 'Fictional Knowledge', in M. Currie, *About Time*. London: Edinburgh University Press, pp. 107–37.

Davies, R. (2003), 'Enduring McEwan', in D. Lea and B. Schoene (eds), *Posting the Male: Masculinities in Post-War and Contemporary British Literature*. Amsterdam: Rodopi, pp. 105–23.

Docherty, T. (1999), 'Now, Here, This', in R. Luckhurst and P. Marks (eds), *Literature and the Contemporary*. Harlow: Longman, pp. 50–62.

Johnstone, S. (1985), 'Charioteers and Ploughmen', in A. Martin and N. Roddick (eds), *British Cinema Now*. London: BFI Publishing, pp. 99–110.

Ledbetter, M. (1996), 'The Games Body-politics Plays: a Rhetoric of Secrecy in Ian McEwan's *The Innocent*', in M. Ledbetter, *Victims and the Postmodern Narrative, or Doing Violence to the Body: an Ethic of Reading and Writing*. Basingstoke and London: Macmillan, pp. 88–103.

Lewis, P. (1991), 'McEwan, Ian (Russell)', in L. Henderson (ed.), *Contemporary Novelists*. London: St James Press, pp. 621–23.

Mars-Jones, A. (1990), 'Venus Envy', in *Chatto Counterblasts*, 14. London: Chatto and Windus.

Massie, A. (1990), *The Novel Today: A Critical Guide to the British Novel 1970–1989*. London: Longman, pp. 49–52.

Matthews, S. (2006), 'Seven Types of Unreliability', in Childs, P. (ed.), *Ian McEwan's* Enduring Love: *Routledge Guides to Literature*. London: Routledge.

Morrison, J. (2003), 'Unravelling Time in Ian McEwan's Fiction', in J. Morrison, *Contemporary Fiction*. London and New York: Routledge, pp. 67–79.

Moseley, M. (1998), 'Ian McEwan', in M. Moseley (ed.), *British Novelists Since 1960, Second Series, The Dictionary of the Literary Biography*, Vol. 194. Detroit: Gale.

Pifer, E. (2000), 'Ian McEwan's *The Child in Time*', in E. Pifer, *Demon or Doll: Images of the Child in Contemporary Writing and Culture*. Charlottesville and London: University of Virginia Press, pp. 19–21.

Richter, V. (1999), 'Tourists Lost in Venice: Daphne Du Maurier's *Don't Look Now* and Ian McEwan's *The Comfort of Strangers*', in M. Pfister and B. Schaff (eds), *Venetian Views, Venetian Blinds: English Fantasies of Venice*. Amsterdam: Rodopi, pp. 181–94.

Ryan, K. (1999), 'Sex, Violence and Complicity: Martin Amis and Ian McEwan', in R. Mengham (ed.), *An Introduction to Contemporary Fiction*. Cambridge: Polity, pp. 203–18.

Seaboyer, J. (2005), 'Ian McEwan: Contemporary Realism and the Novel of Ideas', in J. Acheson and S. C. E. Ross (eds), *The Contemporary British Novel Since 1980*. Edinburgh: Edinburgh University Press, pp. 23–34.

Taylor, D. J. (1989), 'Ian McEwan: Standing Up for the Sisters', in *A Vain Conceit: British Fiction in the 1980s*. London: Bloomsbury, pp. 55–9.

Walkowitz, R. L. (2005), 'Ian McEwan', in Brian W. Shaffer (ed.), *A Companion to the British and Irish Novel 1945–2000*. Oxford: Blackwell, pp. 504–14.

Wells, L. (2006), 'The Ethical Otherworld: Ian McEwan's Fiction', in P. Tew and R. Mengham (eds), *British Fiction Today*. London and New York: Continuum, pp. 117–27.

Wood, J. (1996), 'England', in J. Sturruck (ed.), *The Oxford Guide to Contemporary Writing*. Oxford: Oxford University Press, pp. 134–7.

Journal articles

Banks, J. R. (1982), 'A Gondola Named Desire', in *Critical Quarterly*, 24 (2), 27–31.

Benyei, T. (1997), 'Places in Between: The Subversion of Initiation Narrative in Ian McEwan's *The Innocent*', in *British and American Studies*, 4 (2), 66–73.

Crosthwaite, P. (2007), 'Speed, War, and Traumatic Affect: Reading Ian McEwan's *Atonement*', in *Cultural Politics*, 3, 51–70.

Delrez, M. (1995), 'Escape into Innocence: Ian McEwan and the Nightmare of History', in *Ariel: A Review of International English Literature*, 26 (2), 7–23.

Delville, M. (1996), 'Marsilio Ficino and Political Syncretism in Ian McEwan's *Black Dogs*', in *Notes on Contemporary Literature*, 26 (3), 11–12.

D'Hoker, E. (2006), 'Confession and Atonement in Contemporary Fiction: J. M. Coetzee, John Banville, and Ian McEwan', in *Critique: Studies in Contemporary Fiction*, 48 (1), Fall, 31–43.

Edwards, P. (1995), 'Time, Romanticism, Modernism and Modernity in *The Child in Time*', in *English*, 44 (178), 41–55.

Finney, B. (2004), 'Briony's Stand against Oblivion: The Making of Fiction in Ian McEwan's *Atonement*', in *Journal of Modern Literature*, 27 (3), 68–82.

Forceville, C. (2002), 'The Conspiracy in *The Comfort of Strangers*: Narration in the Novel and Film', in *Language and Literature*, 11 (2), 119–52.

Hidalgo, P. (2005), 'Memory and Storytelling in Ian McEwan's *Atonement*'. *Critique: Studies in Contemporary Fiction*, 46 (2), 82–91.

Ingersoll, E. G. (2004), 'Intertextuality in L. P. Hartley's *The Go-Between* and Ian McEwan's *Atonement*', in *Forum for Modern Language Studies*, 40 (3), 241–258.

——(2005), 'City of endings: Ian McEwan's Amsterdam', in *Midwest Quarterly: A Journal of Contemporary Thought*, 46 (2), 123–38.

James, D. (2003), ' "A Boy Stepped Out": Migrancy, Visuality, and the Mapping of Masculinity in Later Fiction of Ian McEwan', in *Textual Practice*, 17 (1), 81–100.

Johnstone, R. (1985), 'Television Drama and the People's War: David Hare's *Licking Hitler*, Ian McEwan's *The Imitation Game*, and Trevor Griffiths's *Country*'. *Modern Drama*, 28 (2), 189–97.

Kohn, R. E. (2004), 'The Fivesquare *Amsterdam* of Ian McEwan', in *Critical Survey*, 16 (1), 59–76.

MacCabe, C. (2007), *Critical Quarterly*, 49 (2). [Edition devoted to the plagiarism case surrounding *Atonement*.]

Matthews, P. (2006), 'The Deeper Impression of Darkness: Ian McEwan's *Atonement*'. *ESC*, 32 (1), 147–60.

Moriarty, M. (1984), 'A Pint of Barthes and a Ploughman's Lunch'. *LTP: Journal of Literature Teaching Politics*, 3, 79–90.

Müller-Wood, A. and Carter Wood, J. (2007), 'Bringing the Past to Heel: History, Identity and Violence in Ian McEwan's *Black Dogs*', *Literature and History*, 16 (2), 43–56.

Reynier, C. (1994), 'Psychic Journey into Artistic Creation: a Reading of Ian McEwan's Reflections of a Kept Ape', in *Journal of the Short Story in English*, 22, 115–25.

Roger, A. (1996), 'Ian McEwan's Portrayal of Women', in *Forum for Modern Language Studies*, 32 (1), 11–26.

Sampson, D. (1984), 'McEwan/Barthes'. *Southern Review*, 17 (1), 68–80.

Seaboyer, J. (1999), 'Sadism Demands a Story: Ian McEwan's "The Child in Time" '. *MFS: Modern Fiction Studies*, 45 (4), 957–86.

Stan, S. (2004), '*Rose Blanche* in Translation', in *Children's Literature in Education*, 35 (1), 21–34.

Wallace Kowalski, E. (2007), 'Postcolonial Melancholia in Ian McEwan's *Saturday*', in *Studies in the Novel*, 39 (4), 465–80.

III Interviews

Appleyard, B. (2007), 'The Ghost in My Family'. *The Sunday Times*, Review, 25 March, p. 1.

Begley, A. (2002), 'The Art of Fiction CLXXIII: Ian McEwan'. *The Paris Review*, 44 (162), Summer, pp. 30–60.

Billen, A. (1992), 'A Goodbye to Gore'. *The Observer*, 14 June, p. 29.

Casademont, R. G. (1992), 'The Pleasure of Prose Writing vs. Pornographic Violence: an Interview with Ian McEwan'. *The European English Messenger*, 1 (3), Autumn, pp. 40–5.

Cowley, J. (1997), 'The Prince of Darkest Imaginings'. *The Times*, 6 September, p. 9.

Danziger, D. (1987), 'In Search of Two Characters'. *The Times*, 27 June, 13.

Daoust, P. (1997), 'Post-shock Traumatic: Profile of Ian McEwan'. *The Guardian*, 4 August, p. 6.

Franks, A. (1992), 'McEwan's Best Bitterness'. *The Times*, 27 June, p. 4.

Gerard, J. (2005), 'The Conversion of Mr Macabre'. *The Sunday Times*, Review, 23 January, 5.

Gormley, A. (2005), 'The Consolation of the Elemental'. *The Independent*, 1 July, pp. 20–22.

Grimes, W. (1992), 'Rustic Calm Inspires McEwan Tale of Evil'. *The New York Times*, 18 November, p. 25.

Haffenden, J. (1985), *Novelists in Interview*. London: Methuen, pp. 168–90.

Hamilton, I. (1978), 'Points of Departure'. *New Review*, 5 (2), pp. 9–21.

Hunt, A. (1996), 'Ian McEwan'. *New Fiction*, 21, Winter, pp. 47–50.

Johnson, D. (1990), 'The Timeless and Timely Child'. *The Times*, 8 September, pp. 16–17.

Kemp, P. (1992), 'Hounding the Innocent'. *The Sunday Times*, 14 June, pp. 6–11.

Lawley, S. (2000), 'Desert Island Discs'. *BBC Radio 4*, 16 January.

Leith, W. (1998) 'Form and Dysfunction'. *The Observer*, 20 September, pp. 4–8.

Pilkington, E. (1992), 'Berlin mon Amour'. *The Guardian*, 13 June, p. 29.

Smith, A. (1987), 'Ian McEwan'. *Publisher's Weekly*, 232, 11 September, pp. 68–9.

Tonkin, B. (2005), 'The Difference a Day Makes'. *The Independent*, 28 January, pp. 24–5.

Walter, N. (1997), 'Looks Like a Teacher: Writes Like a Demon'. *The Observer*, 24 August, p. 2.

IV Filmography

'Jack Flea's Birthday Celebration' (1976), written by I. McEwan, directed by M. Newell and produced by T. Prem for the BBC. UK.

'Solid Geometry' (1979), adapted by I. McEwan from his own story, directed by M. Newell and produced by S. Gilbert for the BBC. (Production halted 1979.) UK.

The Imitation Game (1980), written by I. McEwan, produced and directed by R. Eyre. Script first published in *Quarto*, 1980. UK.

The Ploughman's Lunch (1983), written by I. McEwan, directed by R. Eyre and produced by S. Relph and A. Scott for Greenpoint Films Limited. UK.

'The Last Day of Summer' (1984), adapted by I. McEwan from his short story, directed by Derek Banham for the BBC. UK.

Soursweet (1988), adapted by I. McEwan, directed by Mike Newell for British Screen Productions. UK.

The Comfort of Strangers (1990), adapted by H. Pinter, directed by P. Schrader for Erre Produzione. Italy.

The Cement Garden (1993), adapted and directed by A. Birkin for Laurentic Film Productions. UK.

The Good Son (1993), written by I. McEwan, directed by J. Ruben.

The Innocent (1993), written by I. McEwan, directed by John Schlesinger and produced by N. Heyman for Island World. USA.

First Love, Last Rites (1997), adapted by D. Ryan, directed by J. Peretz for Forensic Films. USA.

'Solid Geometry' (2002), adapted and directed by D. Lawson for Grampian Television. UK.

Enduring Love (2004), adapted by J. Penhall and directed by R. Michell for Pathé Pictures International. UK.

'Butterflies' (2005), adapted and directed by M. Jacoby for Samsa Film. Luxembourg.

Atonement (2007), adapted by C. Hampton and directed by J. Wright for Working Title Films. UK.

V Websites

http://en.wikipedia.org/wiki/Ian_McEwan [Provides useful links and a bibliography.]

http://en.wikipedia.org/wiki/Ian_McEwan

http://www.contemporarywriters.com/authors/?=auth70 [Chronology and Critical Perspective by Sean Matthews.]

http://www.ianmcewan.com [McEwan's official website edited by Ryan Roberts.]

http://www.litencyc.com/php/speople.php?rec=true&UID=3041   [Critical Overview by Peter Childs. Requires subscription.]

Index